THE DECOLONIAL IMAGINARY

THEORIES OF REPRESENTATION AND DIFFERENCE

General Editor, Teresa de Lauretis

THE DECOLONIAL IMAGINARY

WRITING CHICANAS INTO HISTORY

EMMA PÉREZ

INDIANA
UNIVERSITY
PRESS

Bloomington & Indianapolis

This book is a publication of

Indiana University Press
601 North Morton Street
Bloomington, IN 47404-3797 USA

http://www.indiana.edu/~iupress

Telephone orders 800-842-6796
Fax orders 812-855-7931
Orders by e-mail iuporder@indiana.edu

Library of Congress Cataloging-in-Publication Data

Pérez, Emma, date
The decolonial imaginary : writing Chicanas into history / Emma Pérez.
p. cm. — (Theories of representation and difference)
Includes bibliographical references and index.
ISBN 978-0-253-33504-3 (cl : alk. paper). — ISBN 978-0-253-21283-2
(pbk : alk. paper)
1. Mexican American women—History. 2. Feminism—United States.
I. Title. II. Series.
E184.M5P418   1999
305.4'886872073—dc21   98-51190

5   6   7   8   12   11   10   09

para mi amá
EMMA ZEPEDA PÉREZ

y para mi papí
JOSÉ CAMPOSANO PÉREZ
August 24, 1924–May 4, 1996

C O N T E N T S

ACKNOWLEDGMENTS

I have incurred debts through the years: intellectual, emotional, and psychic. To begin, I must name my advisers at the University of California, Los Angeles, where I completed my Ph.D. in history. Juan Gómez-Quiñones patiently advised and inspired me, while Kathryn Kish Sklar sparked my interest in women's history. Later, when I joined the Department of History at the University of Texas at El Paso, I was fortunate to inherit colleagues who graciously encouraged me. Students in my Chicano/a history course (3309) indulged me as I grappled with the ideas in this book. I feel fortunate to have had such unique, engaging students at UTEP. They have taught me well. I have also had excellent teaching assistants. Elia Pérez and John Marquez were much more than TA's. Both offered friendship and intellectual engagement.

In 1995, I taught graduate courses in the History of Consciousness Program at the University of California, Santa Cruz. The graduate students volunteered discerning insights and propelled me to move in new directions. They were Maylei Blackwell, Luz Calvo, Catriona Rueda Esquibel, Margaret Derosia, Kehaulani Kauanui, Wendy Minkoff, Keta Miranda, Charla Ogaz, Phil Rodriquez, and Isabel Velez. The faculty at History of Consciousness—James Clifford, Angela Davis, Donna Haraway, Hayden White, and especially Teresa de Lauretis—were generous and forthcoming. That same year I taught creative writing in the Chicano/a Studies Department at the University of California, Santa Barbara. I continued revising the manuscript in Santa Barbara, where I spent two summers mulling over ideas with Chéla Sandoval, a stimulating thinker and theorist. Those summers, Elizabeth Marchant and Rafael Pérez-Torres opened their sanctuary to me. I'm also grateful to scholar-activist Yolanda Broyles-González.

Postdoctoral fellowships from Mexican American Studies at the University of Houston, the Ford Foundation, and the Center for Studies on Ethnicity and Race in America at the University of Colorado in Boulder through the Rockefeller Foundation supported me while I conducted research or wrote different sections of this book. At the University of Houston, Tatcho Mindiola and Nicolás Kanellos gave me the opportunity to pursue research on Houston women. I owe thanks to my assistant, Elva Macias, and also to Omar Valerio for his computer skills. At the Houston Metropolitan Research Center, archivist and historian Thomas Kreneck dedicated hours to helping me with oral interviews and sharing his own insights. At CSERA, Evelyn Hu-Dehart was remarkably dynamic and reassuring. Elisa Facio took the time to familiarize me with Denver. Other financial support came from the Southwest Institute for Research on Women at the University of Arizona in Tucson. My colleague Charles Ambler alerted me to a Faculty Development Grant from UTEP, which allowed me to travel to archives in Houston and Mexico City.

At the School of Criticism and Theory held at Dartmouth College in the summer of 1993, I outlined the foundational premises for this book. The seminar on "The Postcolonial" with Homi K. Bhabha prompted me to envision my notion of the Decolonial Imaginary. I am grateful to Homi for his generosity and charm, but particularly for his postcolonial perspective, in which I found hope for survival.

Many friends read chapters of this manuscript and offered invaluable insights: Norma Alarcón, Caren Kaplan, Antonia Castañeda, Ernesto Chávez, Lisbeth Haas, Raquel Rubio-Goldsmith, and Chéla Sandoval. The readers for Indiana University Press, Vicki Ruiz and Deena González, made suggestions that improved the book. Vicki asked instructive questions, and Deena went through the manuscript meticulously, in the way that only she can. I am perpetually grateful to her for years of friendship. Teresa de Lauretis, series editor, compelled me to clarify my concepts and to illuminate the theory that I propose on the Decolonial Imaginary. Teresa's friendship, warmth, and incisive critique continue to captivate me. I must mention that watching films with Teresa is a solemn and majestic experience. To all my readers, thank you, and forgive my oversights. The staff at Indiana University Press has been efficient and generous. Senior sponsoring editor Joan Catapano and copy editor Jane Lyle were consistently patient and kind.

There are friends whose scholarship guided me, as well as friends who listened willingly while I tossed around concepts. The list is long, but I will name a few: Gloria Anzaldúa, Jennifer Brody, Norma Cantú, Angie Chabram Dernersesian, Teresa Córdova, Rosa Linda Fregoso, Camille Guerin-González, Thomas Kinney, Patricia Limerick, Arturo Madrid, Cynthia Orozco, Elizabeth Salas, Rosalia Solórzano, Sandy Soto, Shirlene Soto, tatiana de la tierra, Deborah Vargas, Yvonne Yarbro-Bejarano, and finally Alicia Gaspar de Alba (aka "B.C."), with whom I share a "writing life."

My family was loving and forgiving while I stayed home to write this book. My sisters Yolanda and Cristelia Pérez and my brother, José Roberto Pérez, offer consistent love. My sisters' partners, Nicolás Kanellos and

John Causek, are always supportive. Rhonda Hatch Rivera is warm and welcoming. John Michael Rivera, my nephew, cultural critic in his own right, has been an inspiration. Sonja Pérez, my "baby" sister, came into this world to teach me the meaning of unconditional love. A feminist cultural critic, Sonja has always listened intently and offered insights. I'm also unduly indebted to my partner, Scarlett Bowen, for compiling the index to this book. Her many talents, along with her passion, continue to enchant me.

Finally, my mother, Emma Pérez, and my father, José Pérez, deserve gratitude for their love—unconditional and encouraging. I dedicate this study to them. My mother's family, in Texas for generations, urged me to unravel the history of tejanas. My father's family, who emigrated from Coahuila and Nuevo León to Texas during the Mexican Revolution, incited me to seek answers about revolutionists. Conversations with my father are my cherished memories. I miss you, Dad.

INTRODUCTION

Let us question the past and it will teach what we
must once more remember.
—Antonio Mediz Bolio, *The Land of the Pheasant and
the Deer* (1983)

Historical truth is the least of our concerns.
—Sigmund Freud, *Screen Memories* (1900)

Truth is what *man* silences through the very practice
of language.
—Michel de Certeau, *The Writing of History* (1975)

This project is an archaeology of discursive fields of knowledge that
write Chicanas into histories. Each chapter following the first, historiographic chapter is a case study, or genealogy, in which a specific discursive field is produced and analyzed as "things said" come into existence
to imprint the historical body of Chicanas. Deconstructing systems of
thought and the manner in which they frame Chicana stories—whether
linearly, which is the sanctioned European and Euroamerican historical
method; or vertically, which is Foucauldian; or cyclically, which is pre-
Colombian—is my task.

History monographs pose particular historiographic questions to advance the accepted official arguments. There is a complicit and implicit
understanding about what is privileged in current debates. Studies that
reiterate the discussion most successfully set the norm for upcoming
works. A historian must remain within the boundaries, the borders, the
confines of the debate as it has been conceptualized if she/he is to be a
legitimate heir to the field. Breaking out of the borders is like choosing to
go outside, into the margins, to argue or expose that which no one will risk.
Going outside the accredited realm of historiography means daring to be
dubbed a-historical. It means traversing new territories and disciplines,
mapping fresh terrains such as cultural studies, women's studies, ethnic
studies, and of course, Chicana/o studies.

This work attempts to go beyond the sanctioned historiographic debates to probe the discursive fields that shape Chicana stories. Only in this
way, by going outside in order to come back in with different kinds of
inquiries, can I confront the systems of thought that produce Chicana

history. I take a postmodern approach for a number of reasons. Postmodernism is often infuriating for precisely the same reasons that postmodern claims are useful. Nothing is taken for granted. Nothing is accepted at face value. Nothing is real. All is imagined and therefore disputable. The systems of thought which have patterned our social and political institutions, our universities, our archives, and our homes predispose us to a predictable beginning, middle, and end to untold stories. History books become copies of each other, mimicking style, organization, and content. That which is different, fragmented, imagined, non-linear, non-teleological, has no place in the stories we construct about Chicanas. But as members of a discipline with the proper papers in order—whether doctorates, publications, or honorary titles—we must sustain an "order of things" to please the tradition, to prove we are the authorized heirs who may or may not decide what is and what is not a contribution to the field of history. In this spirit, with these "laws" in mind which beg interrogation, I agree with Michel Foucault, who advocated that we "leave it to our bureaucrats and our police to see that our papers are in order. At least spare us their morality when we write."[1]

The "tradition" and "discipline" of *his*tory is infused with morality, with how the documents "should" be interpreted and written, with ponderings over what is and what is not the definitive story. I have no intention of offering conclusive stories about Chicanas and our past, a past that crosses geographic terrains and political borders. I am more concerned with taking the "his" out of the "story," the story that often becomes the universalist narrative in which women's experience is negated. Women's history began the project of refuting male experience as the norm. Joan Wallach Scott, for example, has been instrumental in contesting how women have been conceptualized in a field that unwittingly universalizes the male experience.[2] To begin in that way is to begin with a fundamental interrogation. How much have women been a part of the stories? Is it possible to recover much, given that the archives have been preserved for the "great men" who have made contributions, in one way or another, whether presidents, generals, or imagined forefathers? The documents on or by women that have been preserved in libraries are often the papers of the wives, daughters, or family members of "great men."

In the United States, locating documents about Mary Austin Holley, cousin to Stephen F. Austin, the colonizer of Texas in the early nineteenth century, was a simple process. She was literate in English, kept a journal, and wrote letters throughout her life. All were gathered and deposited in an archive at the University of Texas at Austin, and fittingly so.[3] The names match the institutions. But at the other end of the spectrum we have Malintzin Tenepal, La Malinche, La India, whom Chicanas idealize as the mother of a hybrid race. Although she was probably literate and polylingual, she had the misfortune of belonging to the race that would be conquered and colonized. Her words were not transcribed by anyone who may have listened at a time when orality was the method of passing tales to the next generation. History, after all, is the story of the conquerors, those who have won. The vanquished disappear. Even when Bernardino de Sahagún and Diego de Landa pursued the "real" story from the Aztecas or Mayas in the sixteenth century, the information became diffused as the Spaniards wrote what they thought they heard from their native informants.[4] Bartolomé de las Casas and Bernal Díaz, both chroniclers for the Spanish Crown, exalted La Malinche as a heroine because she stood beside Cortés.[5] Later, as Mexico became increasingly nationalist after the Mexican Revolution, she became La Chingada to the Mexicanos, the men who damned her for *"chingando" con Cortés.*[6] Where, then, is the space for the story about women such as La Malinche? How has her legend been imagined, by whom and for whom? Our written Chicana history is often infected with judgments and moralizing.

As I attempt to take the *his* out of the Chicana story, I am also aware that I too am marked with the *his*tory I have inherited. There is no pure, authentic, original history. There are only stories—many stories. The ones that intrigue me are the tales by or about women, whether told by men or women; both interest me as I reconstruct the past. This is not to say that the stories are not real and are only imagined in a postmodern sense. That is neither my belief nor my purpose. That which is real for someone is the imaginary for another, especially if the wish is to rectify that reality decades later. For us today, the lines between the real and the imaginary are blurred. Many of us try with our passions to reconstruct the epics, dramas, comedies, and tragedies in a narrative that will echo "truth." We want so much to unearth the documents and organize the "facts" that will disclose the "real truth." And what we know, what we discover as we venture into other worlds, is that we can only repeat the voices previously unheard, rebuffed, or underestimated as we attempt to redeem that which has been disregarded in our history. Voices of women from the past, voices of Chicanas, Mexicanas, and Indias, are utterances which are still minimized, spurned, even scorned. And time, in all its dialectical invention and promise, its so-called inherent progress, has not granted Chicanas, Mexicanas, Indias much of a voice at all. We are spoken about, spoken for, and ultimately encoded as whining, hysterical, irrational, or passive women who cannot know what is good for us, who cannot know how to express or authorize our own narratives. But we will. And we do.

While this study appears to be a provocation to the discipline of history, it is instead an exposition which emerges from my love of history. Historian Joan Scott has guided the shift in my own thinking about the origins and meanings of historical events and their causes. In *Gender and the Politics of History*, Scott suggests that emphasizing "how" something occurred will shift the focus to "the study of processes, not of origins, of multiple rather than single causes, of rhetoric or discourse rather than ideology of consciousness."[7] The politics of meaning, then, becomes the aim of a history that interrogates the construction of knowledges accepted and condoned in society, thus granting power to those who make knowledge. By employing Foucault's archaeology as a foundational methodological tool toward what he calls genealogy, both of which are imprinted with the power/knowledge paradigm, I am challenging the written story and its myth. Archaeology asks that disciplines, their categories, their grids and cells be exploded, opened up, confronted, inverted, and subverted; genealogy recognizes how *his*tory has been written upon the body.

Part one of this book will reconstruct "things said" through archaeology; parts two and three will utilize both archaeology and genealogy while acknowledging that "things said" are always an inscription upon the body. In *The Archaeology of Knowledge*, Foucault had not fully developed his thesis regarding power/knowledge, except to point to its basic relationship to discourse. For the historian, discourse is "where power and knowledge are joined."[8] Referring to this book as "the lost text," Homi Bhabha pointed to the interstitial spaces in Foucault's method of archaeology as the space where the gaps unfold the unspoken and unseen.[9] I also argue that for historians, revitalizing Foucault's archaeology, the precursor to his genealogical method, can help us examine where in discourse the gaps, the interstitial moments of history, reappear to be seen or heard as that third space. Thus, Chéla Sandoval's notion of differential consciousness is also useful to my uncovering of women's history.[10] Sandoval theorizes that differential consciousness allows for mobility of identities between and among varying power bases—for example, the move from liberal to socialist to feminist ideologies as forms of tactical intervention, or practice.[11] I argue that the differential mode of consciousness to which Sandoval refers is precisely third space feminist practice, and that practice can occur only within the decolonial imaginary. In other words, Sandoval employs differential consciousness to critique hegemonic feminists who appropriate and assimilate third world women's feminism into hegemonic feminist theories, and therefore third world feminist voices disappear into an interstitial space that third world women occupy.[12] Like differential consciousness, the decolonial imaginary in Chicana/o history is a theoretical tool for uncovering the hidden voices of Chicanas that have been relegated to silences, to passivity, to that third space where agency is enacted through third space feminism.

Finally, Foucault's methodology is useful to historians because archaeology seeks to uncover discursive practices by unmasking them. It is self-reflexive in intent, and it is in that self-reflection where coloniality is exposed. Through his own self-reflection, Foucault was undoing European history. When he declared, "Taking a relatively short chronological sample within a restricted geographical area—European culture since the sixteenth century—one can be certain that man is a recent invention within it," Foucault admittedly restricted himself to Europe without engaging coloniality. Yet he was critical of the "knowledge of things and their order" that made possible coloniality and the construction of the Other. He concluded in *The Order of Things*, "man is an invention of recent date. And one perhaps nearing its end." In essence, he claimed that European white man would no longer be central to history and its interpretations.[13] Stories of the past would begin to focus on the margins and the marginal, hence the colonized. My contention is that Chicana history has been a conscious effort to retool, to shift meanings and read against the grain, to negotiate Eurocentricity whether within European historical models or within the paradigms of United States historiography. Foucault's methods help to undo the very nature of a Chicano/a historiography that can potentially descend into the pitfalls of coloniality when systems of thought remain unchallenged.

I also draw on Hayden White's *Metahistory* to probe the Chicano/a historical imagination of the twentieth century in chapter 1. But beyond White's metahistory is his analysis of the "content of the form."[14] How do we write history without narrativizing? Why is literature reduced to or expanded by the "imaginary" while history can only be "real"?[15] "What are the 'artistic' elements of a 'realistic' historiography?" is, for me, the question that plagues historians seeking truths and narrativizing facts, facts that are only fragments waiting for the historian who will interlace data and episodes into a persuasive story that others of the craft may believe in.[16]

Let me track this book to illustrate why it has moved in this archaeological, metahistorical direction. This work began as a doctoral dissertation. It sought to investigate Chicana social movements on both sides of the Mexico–U.S. border during a volatile era in Chicano/a history—the Mexican Revolution. The project was initially intended as a comparative analysis of social movements among women in Mexico and women in the southwestern United States, but I ended up studying Yucatecan women in and of themselves, perhaps naively arguing that Chicana feminist origins lie south in Mexico. Generally, I asked, did the revolution transform race, class, and gender relations? Later, as I began revisions to hone the dissertation into a monograph, I found myself returning to my original questions regarding the formation of Chicana nationalist identities beyond the geographic and political border of the United States. Chronologies and origins, however, no longer concerned me as much as an enunciative moment. Foucault's premise that "discourse must be treated as it occurs, and not in the distant presence of the origin" allowed me to think again about seeking origins that serve only to impose false continuities.[17] I found it necessary to traverse centuries and borders to unravel contemporary Chicana feminisms rooted in a past which may be understood as an enunciation in the present. Deconstructing systems of thought that frame Chicana history is my task. In other words, I experiment with a consciousness of Chicana knowledge. In the case studies, a specific discursive field emerges from the "things said," thereby mapping identities and feminisms.

Chicanas are marked by a unique diasporic configuration. The Mexican Revolution was a historical moment that introduced a population to a region formerly Spanish and Mexican. Thousands of Mexicanas migrated to the United States as a diaspora. New types of Chicana identities formed out of new mergings: Chicanas born in the United States, many with generations in the region, merged with Mexicanas from Mexico. As a historian trained in U.S. history, I chose to research Mexican women on both sides of the border, recognizing differences; yet language, culture, race, class, and gender evoked parallels rooted in centuries of common history. Despite geo-political borders, those of us who study Chicanas and Chicanos face historiographic dilemmas regarding the placement of people who, although Mexican or mixed Native American by birth, entered a unique double bind as a diasporic yet colonized race in the nineteenth-century United States. From the earliest historiographic essays to more current ones, scholars have consistently argued for a conceptual framework that addresses transgressive Chicano and Mexicano experiences in which culture is understood globally. For me, such a paradigm would analyze systems of thought that construct cultural identities carved by a complex history.

In part one, I highlight archaeology. It is through Foucault's method of excavating words and their inherited meanings that I begin my own digging for words that have shaped Chicano/a historiography. The first chapter interrogates historiography as a colonialist project which has engineered Chicano history in the last decades. At the same time, and more importantly, Chicano historiography has been framed in resistance to the colonialist project. Borrowing from theorists and philosophers of history as well as cultural feminist critics, and building upon the pioneering studies of Chicana feminist historians, I argue that traditionalist historiography produces a fictive past, and that fiction becomes the knowledge manipulated to negate the "other" culture's differences.[18] I also argue for the emergence of a Chicano/a historical imagination that constructs a specific consciousness as reflected in published works since the 1970s, when Chicano/a history began to be conceptualized and theorized, particularly by historian Juan Gómez-Quiñones. His historiographic essays have made a lasting impression on the "poetics," or the making, of Chicano/a history.

In part two, "From Archaeology to Genealogy," I feature Foucault's method of honoring silences, the gaps, the unthought; his archaeology privileges the words of theory over its practice. But at the same time, as I uncover case studies of Chicana feminist thought, I begin to use his genealogical method, in which social practice takes precedence over theory—the imprint of the word upon the physical, psychic, historical body is his genealogy. The three chapters of part two are case studies of specific Chicana feminist thought and practice. Chapter 2 places Yucatán and the Mexican Revolution at center stage, explaining how feminism was articulated and woven into a rigid nationalist model. Chapter 3 traces the movement of the Mexican Revolution into the United States by way of Mexican intellectuals and revolutionaries, specifically through the Partido Liberal Mexicano. I propose that in many ways the script written by the ideologues of the Mexican Revolution was appropriated by Chicano nationalists in the movement of the 1970s and again in the recent 1990s. Chapter 4 illustrates how Mexicanas, as members of a diaspora, expressed their agency in Texas during the early decades of the twentieth century. I put forth my own notion of diasporic subjectivities to augment immigrant identities. I believe that to settle upon Chicano/a experiences as only immigrant erases a whole other history, the history of a diaspora, of a people whose land also shifted beneath them. Finally, in part three I discuss a genealogy of Chicana identities and sexualities as counter-hegemonic responses to dominant cultures. I do so by meditating upon desire: desire as a medium for social change, desire as revolution, desire as love and hope for a different kind of future—a postcolonial one. I extrapolate from Sigmund Freud's theory of the psyche to argue how the Oedipus complex has left its colonial imprints upon other cultures, in this case Chicana/o culture.

I want to warn you that I do not believe in a beginning, a middle, and an end of history. I do not ascribe to a linear temporality as the only means for speaking and writing history. I do know that fragments coexist, and I want to assign some order to these things, these fragments. The chronology outlined from parts one to three is the tool imposing meaning upon the suggested order. Historians are trapped by the pitfalls of chronology—the imposed meanings of linearity; yet I believe that a conscious, self-reflexive order at the very least acknowledges that meanings are as subjective as the events chosen to be told chronologically. I am also eager to trace transformations through centuries or decades, while change, the historian's project, will not be so apparent. My imagination has proposed an order so that we may have a dialogue as you read. Whether we agree or disagree does not concern me as much as the dialogue and its potential to stimulate critique. I also want to warn that if you seek categorical, definitive answers, you will not find them. I will submit more questions, more interventions, as I continue to speak from the margins, as I continue to experiment with my own "sitio y lengua," never forgetting that I am simulating voices that lived and thrived long before me, before you, before any of us.[19]

Part One

ARCHAEOLOGY:

COLONIALIST HISTORIOGRAPHY, WRITING THE NATION INTO HISTORY

Chapter 1

SEXING THE COLONIAL IMAGINARY

(EN)GENDERING CHICANO HISTORY, THEORY, AND CONSCIOUSNESS

Historiography is, by its very nature, the representa-
tional practice best suited to the production of the
"law-abiding" citizen.... [I]t is especially well suited
to the production of notions of continuity, whole-
ness, closure, and individuality that every "civilized" society wishes to see itself as incarnating.

—Hayden White, *The Content of the Form* (1987)

... neither of these two "national histories" [Mexico
and the United States] have provided the space in
which to tell the story of this population.

—Juan Gómez-Quiñones, *Roots of Chicano Politics,
1600–1940* (1994)

In the case of historiography, fiction can be found at
the end of the process, in the product of the manipu-
lation and the analysis. Its story is given as a staging
of the past.

—Michel de Certeau, *The Writing of History* (1975)

THE DECOLONIAL IMAGINARY

Political borders, geographic boundaries, and discursive categories
have shaped late-twentieth-century historical knowledge. We cannot escape the boundaries that our Chicana/o minds have inherited as we take
imaginary journeys beyond the Río Bravo into Mexico and Latin America
or across the Atlantic Ocean to Asia, Africa, and Europe, traversing borders and centuries to link time and space. To learn history, we categorize
time linearly and map regions geographically. Historians assign names to

epochs and regions that reflect spatio-temporal characteristics: the Trans-Mississippi West, the frontier, the Renaissance, the Progressive Era, the Great Depression, the sixties. Within these categoric spaces, we continue to conceptualize history without challenging how such discursive sites have been assigned and by whom. One fundamental result of such traditional approaches to history is that these spatio-temporal models enforce a type of colonialist historiography. In the 1960s, a new discipline of Chicano studies was developed, transforming U.S. history, which had not included those on the margins. Now American studies, cultural studies, women's studies, and even postcolonial studies are reinscribing how U.S. history will be formulated. Chicano/a history has become recognized in history departments and in some academic circles. Restricted to the boundaries of arguments that came before, Chicano/a historians have tended to build a discipline that mimics the making of the frontier, or "American West," while at the same time opposing the ideological making of the "West." In this chapter, I outline the spatio-temporal categories of traditional histori-ography and examine how these categories influence and direct even the most radical Chicano/a history that longs for resistance. Secondly, I will offer my notion of the decolonial imaginary as a political project for recon-ceptualizing histories. And finally, I want to provide another paradigm, an alternative model for conceptualizing a subaltern and self-consciously oppositional Chicano/a historiography that can account for issues of the modern and the postmodern, immigrations and diasporas, and genders and sexuality. I call it a theory of Chicano/a historical consciousness. I will spend most of my time breaking that down.

In these efforts, I do not turn away from history to dismiss or negate the historian's purpose. In her explanation of postmodernism as it relates to history, Linda Hutcheon states that the contradictory nature of post-modernism "installs and then subverts the very concepts it challenges."[1] For her, postmodernism "questions from within"[2] as it "returns to confront the problematic nature of the past as an object of knowledge for us in the present."[3] I, too, turn away from history to confront it in a different way, to challenge, as Spivak would say, "from within but against the grain"[4] by asking, How have we come to study history, especially Chicana/o history? Where do we start as Chicano/a historians? What methods do our monographs engage? Which structures bind us in our studies? "To challenge history or its writing is not to deny either."[5] It is to ask questions such as, How is Chicano/a history being written? By whom is Chicana/o history written? For whom is the history written? What space is created for Chicana/o history? Do subjugated histories only replicate, copy, and duplicate dominant first world methods and tools, or is Chicana/o history written as something new coming into being, or both at once? How do we know? How do we identify a decolonizing, postcolonial, or opposi-tional method?

Here I will address the question, What are the discursive formations that pattern the twentieth-century Chicana/o historical imagination defined as our self-conscious recognition of who we are now and how we arrived here? All history is constituted by discursive formations. Foucault would say that "discursive formations produce the object about which they speak";[6] moreover, it is discourse itself that "unifies the whole system of practices."[7] My argument is that Chicana/o history, like any other subaltern history, will tend to follow traditional history's impulse to cover "with a thick layer of events," as Foucault writes, "the great silent, motionless bases"[8] that constitute the interstitial gaps, the unheard, the unthought, the unspoken. These interstitial gaps interrupt the linear model of time, and it is in such locations that oppositional, subaltern histories can be found. Foucault's redefinition of archaeology, understood as a method, disrupts linear continuity to locate silences within the interstices. Bhabha finds in Foucault's archaeology the gaps where a possible postcolonial imperative exists.[9] I argue that these silences, when heard, become the negotiating spaces for the decolonizing subject. It is in a sense where third space agency is articulated. Bhahba also points out that the "Third Space of enunciations" is "the precondition for the articulation of cultural difference."[10] "[I]t is the 'inter'—the cutting edge of translation and negotiation, the in-between space—that carries the burden of the meaning of culture."[11] In the same manner, Chéla Sandoval's theory of differential consciousness, the "activity of weaving 'between and among' oppositional ideologies," is also that third space where I find the decolonizing subject negotiating new histories.[12]

Like Edward Said's *Orientalism* and Tzvetan Todorov's *Conquest of America*, which led us to acknowledge the significance of signs when the Spanish and Aztecas met, this book proposes a new category.[13] This new category, the decolonial imaginary, can help us rethink history in a way that makes Chicana/o agency transformative. To think of the past as a colonial imaginary opens up traditional categories such as the "West" or the "frontier." Traditional historiographical categories, questioned only from within for revision, have been built upon that which came before, and therefore have contributed to the colonial. The categories themselves are exclusive, in that they already deny and negate the voice of the other. Conceptualized in certain ways, they already leave something out, leave something unsaid, the silences and gaps that Foucault's discursivity could help uncover. Chicana/o historiography has been circumscribed by the traditional historical imagination. This means that even the most radical Chicano/a historiographies are influenced by the very colonial imaginary against which they rebel. The colonial imaginary still determines many of our efforts to write history in the United States. Historians who are more traditional in their approach often claim that history is an objective science. When writing the history of the Southwest, the historian who accepts the notion of objectivity can often ignore the colonial relations that are already in place and write a study replete with a coloniality that has not been disputed, but rather has been accepted as the norm.[14]

The subjectivity introduced by, for example, Chicanas/os and Native Americans of the Southwest is a subjectivity that has challenged histories of the region at least since the 1960s, and in many cases since the early twentieth century. These challenges have pushed the detached observer, writer, historian to examine the ways in which the colonial imaginary is structuring the very form of their/our objectivity by compelling authors to situate themselves in the making of the "frontier" or the "United States of America."[15] Ironically, in the early 1970s, Rodolfo Acuña, Tomás Almaguer, Mario Barrera, and others proposed that Chicanos/as constituted a population of internally colonized people. Many Chicana/o academicians since then have resisted with knee-jerk reactions any mention of coloniality,[16] and Chicano/a social scientists have subsequently criticized the model because it does not offer empiricists an answer with solid evidence.[17] Others are eager to cross over to postcoloniality. I believe that the time lag between the colonial and postcolonial can be conceptualized as the decolonial imaginary. Bhabha names that interstitial gap between the modern and postmodern, the colonial and postcolonial, a time lag.[18] This is precisely where Chicano/a history finds itself today, in a time lag between the colonial and the postcolonial.

If we are dividing history into these categories—colonial relations, postcolonial relations, and so on—then I would like to propose a decolonial imaginary as a rupturing space, the alternative to that which is written in history. I think that the decolonial imaginary is that time lag between the colonial and postcolonial, that interstitial space where differential politics and social dilemmas are negotiated.[19] The decolonial imaginary is intangible to many because it acts much like a shadow in the dark. It survives as a faint outline gliding against a wall or an object. The shadow is the figure between the subject and the object on which it is cast, moving and breathing through an in-between space. Bhabha writes, "It is not the colonialist self or the colonized Other, but the disturbing distance in-between that constitutes the figure of colonial otherness."[20] I would change his colonial otherness to *decolonizing* otherness. The historian's political project, then, is to write a history that decolonizes otherness.

By fusing the words "decolonial" and "imaginary," each term riddled with meaning, I locate the decolonial within that which is intangible. Here the imaginary conjures fragmented identities, fragmented realities, that are "real," but a real that is in question. In the Lacanian sense, the imaginary is linked to the mirror stage, at which a child identifies the "I" of the self in a mirror, an image is reflected back, and the subject becomes object.[21] For my purpose, the imaginary is the mirrored identity where coloniality overshadows the image in the mirror. Ever-present, it is that which is between the subject and the object being reflected, splintering the object in a shattered mirror, where kaleidoscopic identities are burst open and where the colonial self and the colonized other both become elements of multiple, mobile categoric identities. The oppressed as colonial other becomes the liminal identity, partially seen yet unspoken, vibrant and in motion, overshadowed by the construction of coloniality, where the decolonial imaginary moves and lives. One is not simply oppressed or victimized; nor is one only oppressor or victimizer. Rather, one negotiates within the imaginary to a decolonizing otherness where all identities are at work in one way or another.

Similarly, the decolonial imaginary is located in Chicano/a historiography in between that which is colonialist and that which is colonized. I believe that when written from an interstitial space, Chicana/o history happens oppositionally. The (en)gendering of Chicano history—that is, the writing of women into the field—occurs in a similar way. Where women are conceptualized as merely a backdrop to men's social and political activities, they are in fact intervening interstitially while sexing the colonial imaginary. In other words, women's activities are unseen, unthought, merely a shadow in the background of the colonial mind. Yet Chicana, Mexicana, India, mestiza actions, words spoken and unspoken, survive and persist whether acknowledged or not. Women's voices and actions intervene to do what I call sexing the colonial imaginary, historically tracking women's agency on the colonial landscape. The historiographic essays from which I will cite either cast women aside, where they are veiled in Chicano historical writings; or integrate gender with race and class formations; or, finally, foreground gender as the inaugural category of analysis.

My commitment to history also moves me to see it with another "I/eye": the "I" which was often denied in the writing of history, where subjectivity was once unacceptable, yet inevitable.

METAHISTORY

If history is the way in which people understand themselves through a collective, common past where events are chronicled and heroes are constructed, then historical consciousness is the system of thought that leads to a normative understanding of past events. Historical knowledge is the production of normative history through discursive practice. Metahistory, then, does not record or re-create that accepted past; rather, it is the study of thought in which an intrinsic philosophy of history arises. Hayden White postulates in *Metahistory* that all historical interpretation can be identified within four tropes; moreover, the historical imaginations of nineteenth-century philosophers of history cultivate their thoughts and meanings within these tropes.[22] For White, "the theory of tropes provides a way of characterizing the dominant modes of historical thinking" in which the "deep structure of the historical imagination" can be identified.[23]

Adopting White's method, I argue that the "deep structure of the historical imagination" of contemporary Chicano historians has constructed a distinct knowledge of Chicano history in the twentieth century, a knowledge that manifests four periods and four dominant modes of thinking. As I reviewed the development of Chicano/a historical consciousness since the 1970s, I was intrigued with White's tropes and their usefulness to history's categories, for I believe that Chicano/a historians are also "captives of tropological interpretation"[24] expressed through these dominant modes of thinking and writing Chicano/a histories. The modes of thinking, I believe, are those which frame a Chicano historical consciousness in the twentieth century, a consciousness born from a need to explicate finally a community's struggle to survive.[25] In other words, in studying any text in Chicano history, one inevitably follows the time frame laid out by the "Great Events" of Chicano history and practices one or more of the four modes of interpretation.[26] Chicano history has unfolded in four general thematic areas, which are in themselves modes of thinking as well as interpretation: (1) ideological/intellectual—"Chicanos are heroes/intellectuals"; (2) immigrant/labor—"Chicanos are immigrant laborers/colonized workers"; (3) social history—"Chicanos are also social beings, not only workers"; and (4) gendered history—"Chicanos are also women." The Great Events are periodized as (1) the Spanish Conquest of 1521; (2) the U.S.–Mexican War of 1846–48; (3) the Mexican Revolution of 1910 (leading to post-revolution migrations); and (4) the Chicano/a movements of the 1960s and 1970s.[27]

Historical studies echo one or more of these periods or modes of interpretation whether authors invoke them or not.[28] The imprints of the Spanish Conquest in the sixteenth century must be referenced by anyone probing the Spanish colonial Southwest from 1521 to 1821—perhaps the era least studied by Chicana/o historians. One must cross boundaries from the United States to Latin America and then to Europe to peruse the Spanish colonial Southwest. Studies on the native populations before 1521 are fewer and are held suspect by the tradition of history, because written documents are not plentiful. Oral tradition, codices, and archaeological remnants are only a few of the tools for studying pre-Colombian history in the Americas, and these methods are often considered illegitimate by traditional historians. Unfortunately, many pre-Colombian studies, seen through the lens of the Spanish Conquest, echo the period's imprints.[29]

Chicano historical periodization is also structurally problematic. Trained under the rubric of a U.S. history in which the Southwest does not exist before 1848, Chicanos/as become historians under spatio-temporal bounds dependent upon a colonial moment. In this temporal scheme, the Mexican period from 1821 to 1836 is conflated with the coming of the U.S.–

Mexican War of 1846–48 and the annexation of northern Mexico to the United States as a colony. Hence, post-1848 Chicana/o history is readily confirmed as "real" Chicano history, the rupture where Chicanas/os become U.S. citizens. Often, the documents must be U.S.-born in order to qualify as Chicano/a history, or they must be linked by kinship to those left behind in Mexico. Without the familial link, then, Chicano/a origins cannot be determined.[30] The monographs that reflect the period after the Mexican Revolution emphasize Chicanas/os as incoming immigrants whose realities were profoundly defined by their experience in the United States. In this case, the historical imagination of Chicanas/os of the post-revolution period excises pre-twentieth-century conditions, and the colonial periods of the sixteenth and nineteenth centuries assume another kind of reading. A colonial past is occluded to emphasize a shared immigrant experience with, for example, European immigrants in the United States. A subcategory under the Mexican Revolution of 1910 is World War II. Immigration retains a certain character through the first four decades of the twentieth century, and World War II as an event may have directly affected Chicanos/as, but it was not a war precisely of, for, or against Mexicans.[31] Finally, the historical studies of the Chicano movements of the 1960s and 1970s curiously emulate ideological stances prominent during the Mexican Revolution. The social movements of the sixties and seventies wanted to cultivate revolutionary motive and ideology, looking backward to leaders who had helped foment revolution. What appears is a cyclical tracking of the past's intellectuals to re-create the present. Many invoked Emiliano Zapata, Pancho Villa, Ricardo Flores Magón, and las Adelitas as the heros and heroines who could provide guidance for the Chicano/a movements.[32] Their writings reflect a conscious hero-heroine construction. I will address this again in chapter 3.

Historiography is the writing and the study of history, yet in that writing theories are constructed, albeit unwittingly. The writing of history, I would argue, is the space in which historians build upon what has been written, thereby constructing theories that will become the prominent ideologies of any given area of study. Historians theorize arguments in relation to studies, discursively formed, to agree or disagree with the specific field under scrutiny and its intellectual direction. Historiography has a brief life span for Chicano history, and an even briefer one for Chicana history. A handful of Chicano historians envisioned "Chicano" history just as they were being trained in the 1970s. Before the seventies, Mexican and Mexican American scholars, along with a few Euroamericans, published monographs that would classify areas in Chicano/a studies, but for the most part the field of study had not yet been named "Chicano." Manuel Gamio, Paul Taylor, Ernesto Galarza, and Carey McWilliams made inroads in immigrant/labor studies.[33] Carlos Castañeda, on the other hand, wrote volumes utilizing ecclesiastical records.[34] George

I. Sánchez investigated education and the overall discriminatory practices against Mexicans in the United States, while Jovita González and Américo Paredes theorized culture and folklore.[35] These scholars, most of whom wrote during the early and middle twentieth century, laid the groundwork for an emerging Chicano/a consciousness, which may have seemed "mainstream" but was in fact oppositional. As David Gutiérrez notes, these "pioneering intellectuals" produced scholarship with a "quietly political nature."[36] Moreover, while seemingly advancing "objectivity," Sánchez also had a "self-consciously political agenda."[37] By combing through Sánchez's monographs, as well as through the works of these early intellectuals, Gutiérrez probed the interstitial third space where a middle voice quietly articulates a position that remains unheard unless one excavates deeply. Oppositional history was being articulated by these early scholars, whose work exhibited a significant intervention. Another consciousness was already emerging.

In the 1970s, when the first group of self-identified Chicano historians reflected on the past, two historiographic essays reviewed published works up to that point, few as they were. I resurrect the essays, dated as they might be, to trace what historians asked of themselves and the questions they posed for upcoming scholars of Chicano/a history. How women fared—that is, the sexing of the colonial imaginary—distinctly concerns me. Historians Juan Gómez-Quiñones and Luis Arroyo canvassed future historians to create a conceptual paradigm that unraveled the complex relationships between Chicanos and their society. Culture, its kinship to race and class, would be a crucial element in a diagram that illustrated economic exploitation of and racial discrimination against Mexican American laborers. Culture was interrogated, pre-dating the intent of current cultural critics. Although the historians failed to raise gender, much less sexuality, as a category of analysis, the trend in early academic studies was to deliberate about women only when they were being depicted as exploited workers alongside men.

The historiographic essays predisposed a flourishing discipline toward a class analysis in which race was explicated through the culture of the worker, thereby privileging historical materialism.[38] Such an analysis would reinterpret history by highlighting human activity as the prime mover of society. As people construct their era's events, they also inherit historical circumstances that either inhibit or enhance personal or collective consciousness. With gender infused into the framework, for example, social relations between women and men would have been configured differently, perhaps prompting the recognition that low wages were not the only problem at hand. But none of the initial studies seriously considered gender or sex beyond an economic explanation.

In the last decade, have historians developed a paradigm that reflects cultural and social changes where gender, too, is scrutinized? Although historians who research a topic do not necessarily intend to develop a model that reflects change, as historians we nevertheless apprehend change as a continuous movement over the years, decades, and centuries. The intellectuals and ideologues of the 1960s and 1970s asked us to reclaim the writing of Chicano history by adopting a unified strategy or approach. How would our work reflect a mobilizing strategy? How has change been employed to create the historian's imaginary? How much has change—that "empty category," according to Foucault—devised imagined or real histories?[39] Can an emphasis on discourse liberate and revise history? When and how does power/knowledge intervene to bear upon discourse? At this juncture, I believe, the writings of Chicano history have focused on social change, but the discourse has been shaped so that gender/sex does not have to be part of the paradigm.[40]

In this way, I believe that postmodern questions provide a fresh look at Chicana/o history and the manner in which gender/sex is contemplated and negated. Paradigms that take into account only the cultural condition of the worker have been useful, but constricting. While I would not abandon historical materialism, I would build upon a model with Sandoval's differential consciousness, with the interstitial space where Bhabha locates culture, and with Foucault's dream of "a history that would be both an act of long, uninterrupted patience and the vivacity of a movement, which, in the end, breaks all bounds"—in essence, an archaeology in which movement does not rely on a teleological history.[41] It is the "living openness of history,"[42] where discontinuity is witnessed without the pervasive desire to synchronize or to totalize that which is in the historian's imaginary, to which Foucault refers.

> I did not deny history, but held in suspense the general, empty category of change in order to reveal *transformations* at different levels.[43]

That is not to say that social change is not also Foucault's project, but that for Foucault, archaeology focuses on the transformation of discursive fields, while social change becomes the project of the genealogist. Transformation simply means that social change is possible without the dialectical promise of a teleological history. The archaeologist also has a task to "describe in theoretical terms the rules governing discursive practices."[44] Historiography, on the other hand, is subject to rules established by the field's specialists where change is conceptualized linearly. Archaeology "as a method isolates those discursive objects in the field to ask what role do these discourses play in society?"[45] In my mind, this question can move historiography toward a conscious self-reflexive method.

The possibility of a self-reflexive, yet structural, method for Chicano history may have been what Gómez-Quiñones and Arroyo had in mind; however, their method was, for the most part, dismissed by historiographers, who, ironically, built upon similar structures. Alex Saragoza assessed Gómez-Quiñones and Arroyo, but his select historiography resisted categorization by periods, topics, or subfields, and instead attended to more recently published works in Chicano history.[46] His major premise was that Chicano history in the 1980s moved beyond the binarism of "them versus us." For Saragoza, the flaws in Acuña's internal colonial model consisted in victimizing Chicanos by reducing their history to a binary opposition in which they were doomed to be victims and Anglos their oppressors. He claims early in the essay that his is not a thorough historiography. Interestingly, he identified three themes in contemporary Chicano history as the structure emerging from the writings: (1) ideology and culture, (2) changes in the U.S. economy, and (3) immigration from Mexico. He observed women as family members, but gender itself was inconsequential. His approach hurls women against the backdrop of Chicana/o historical writings.

Addressing gender/sex, embracing it as part of the whole, is not the work of Saragoza and many Chicano historians before the 1990s. Instead, an apparent concern with women, with gendered categories, with Chicanas, is contained, rather than explored, in themes such as intermarriage and family history, in which women become appendages to men's history, the interstitial "and" tacked on as an afterthought. Adapting stereotypes— for example, women as wives and mothers—reveals more about what is unsaid and unthought than about gender itself. The stereotypes serve to produce particular systems of thought. These studies marginalized women as the mothers or wives of men and denied them any contribution to a community. When community studies introduce women, they do so mostly to show women in relation to eminent men.[47] Historians are more likely to resurrect Emma Tenayuca or Louisa Moreno as labor leaders in the 1930s and 1940s.[48] This is not to argue that these women do not deserve attention; however, in early Chicano history, unless Mexican American women were married to visible community men or unless they were as highly profiled as Tenayuca or Moreno, their lives remained invisible, enduring between the spaces of a colonial imaginary, obscured in the sex-gender systems that fade in and out of the historical imagination.

In his historiographic article published in 1993 on Mexican Americans and the history of the American West, Gutiérrez unwittingly replies to Saragoza.[49] While Saragoza adjudicates upon "The Significance of Recent Chicano-Related Historical Writings," Gutiérrez cleverly dares to ask, "Significant to Whom?" Unlike Saragoza, Gutiérrez locates Chicana scholars who published as early as the 1970s and champions Chicana historians, along with Euroamerican women historians, who coerce their male counterparts to address gender.[50] His integrative approach to gender is refreshing. He also foregrounds the leading areas of the history of the West as (1) social history, (2) cultural criticism, and (3) feminist studies, a significant overlap with the modes of interpretation I find appearing repeatedly.[51] Social history for Gutiérrez is the umbrella under which immigration/labor would be found.

Cynthia Orozco, Vicki Ruiz, and Antonia Castañeda have written essays highlighting gender at the same time that they review literature. Orozco targets Chicano male historians who deliberately, or unconsciously, omit women's agency in labor history. She insists upon male consciousness as the culprit who cannot recognize or acknowledge women in history.[52] To her credit, Orozco pinpoints consciousness, its appeal, and its power as the conservative force that inhibits male thinkers.

Ruiz also makes a plea for the consolidation of gender in Chicano male writings.[53] In her otherwise favorable review, she points out how gender is stereotyped, unexplored, and decentered in five separate studies published in 1982 and 1984. Only one study "incorporates women's experiences throughout the text."[54] For Ruiz, both John Chávez and Mauricio Mazón neglect women in their histories, while Mazón reduces "pachuquitas'" agency by fixating on their "tight" clothes. Francisco Balderrama also leaves women's activities unexplored, and Richard Griswold del Castillo mentions women, but only peripherally.[55] In Ruiz's opinion, Albert Camarillo's is the only monograph that integrates a gendered history.

Castañeda critiques the traditionalist Spanish Borderlands school in her essay "Gender, Race, and Culture: Spanish-Mexican Women in the Historiography of Frontier California."[56] In a thorough explication, she ferrets out women in the writings of late-nineteenth-century historians such as Hubert Howe Bancroft, where an "implicit gender ideology influences their discussions of race, national character, and culture."[57] She exposes how "Anglo, middle-class norms of women's proper behavior" were and are imposed upon Mexican women.[58] In my view, Castañeda traces the colonial imaginary as a sexualizing imperative in frontier California. Here she points out how incoming Euroamericans sexualized Mexican women in their diaries and travel logs. In another incisive essay, revealing the intimate bond between sexual violence and colonization, she theorizes the impact of sex on the colonial imaginary, thereby providing a method for tracking sex on the frontier's landscape in eighteenth-century California.[59]

Having summarized a few of the historiographic articles pertinent to Chicano history, I turn now to the initial intent of this chapter.[60] My essay avoids and criticizes the notion of a comprehensive approach to Chicano historiography. Instead, I would like to explore texts which have chiseled the features of Chicana/o history, texts which have been studied, read, cited, and noted since the inception of Chicano history in the 1970s, texts which, to my mind, best exemplify a deep Chicano/a historical imagination in the twentieth century. I will place the books into four thematic categories, each of which is a method of interpretation. (See the list on the left in table 1.) Of course, the categories overlap, and each book conforms to more than one of the four, just as the texts may reflect one or more of the Great Events of Chicano history. Please note: This is not a recommended paradigm; nor is it an appeal for a structuralist model. It is merely a diagram illustrating a Chicano/a historical imagination and its practice, both linearly and schematically—a practice which created dominant Chicano discourses that excluded voices unfitting to the structures laid out, whether consciously or unconsciously.

The right column of the table represents a shift in the consciousness of the Chicano/a historical imagination. While works may not necessarily represent this shift, they are instead somewhere in between, in an interstitial space, as movement occurs from the first to the second column. As the decolonial imaginary disrupts the Chicano/a historical imagination, a new consciousness is born in which "Chicano/a" identity is forced beyond its borders by new cultural critiques; in which the Mexican immigrant experience can parallel transnational, third world diasporas; in which social history derives its appeal from its multicultural imperative; in which gender as a category of analysis explodes as technologies remap the category to reinvent fresh ways of interpreting sexualities and social/political desires. My main focus will be on the texts that correspond to the four thematic categories in the left column, with a brief mention of those texts that represent the shift into the right column. It is also important to stress that the categories on the right, although schematically drawn, overlap and overstep each other to explode out of the scheme, always transforming and branching into new categories. Therefore, they are not fully developed—nor could they be.

In the left column, categories 1 and 2 overlap, just as 2 and 3 entwine, and finally elements of 4 are found inside 1, 2, and 3. The right column has arrows indicating that movement into different modes is always occurring. While the arrows appear linear, the movement is not.

TABLE 1

A THEORY OF CHICANO/A HISTORICAL CONSCIOUSNESS

1970s/80s/90s	*Decolonial Time Lag*
1. Ideological/Intellectual ⟶	New Cultural Critique ⟶
2. Immigrant/Labor ⟶	Colonized Diaspora ⟶
3. Social History of the Other ⟶	History of the Other as the Same (Multiculturalism) ⟶
4. Gendered History ⟶	Technologies of Sexualities/ Desire/Gender ⟶

Ideological/Intellectual

"Chicanos are heroes/intellectuals."

Under this category, most authors/historians want to point out similarities between two objects in the face of differences. Much of the literature published in the 1960s and 1970s signaled Mexicans as the forgotten
heroes and heroines of the frontier. This move toward oppositional history
denounced works by Walter Prescott Webb, for example, who valorized
the Texas Rangers. Américo Paredes's *With His Pistol in His Hand* and
Julian Samora's *Gunpowder Justice* vehemently disparaged the Texas Rangers' anti-Mexican, racist practices.[61] As these Chicano scholars condemned
historical injustices, they also constructed the heroes, such as Paredes's
Gregorio Cortez, whose arrest and conviction for allegedly murdering an
Anglo sheriff represented a cultural collision with Euroamerican settlers.
Cortez was for Chicanos a wrongfully accused hero who killed in self-
defense and managed to elude the Texas Rangers for days before he was
caught and tried by an all-white jury in early-twentieth-century Texas.
Cortez is probably one of the better-known Chicano heroes in Texas, while
Joaquín Murrieta claimed fame in California.[62]

Published works that focused on women as heroines were not as
numerous as those that focused on men, but they were decidedly significant. Marta Cotera's pamphlet *Diosa y Hembra: The History and Heritage
of Chicanas in the U.S.*, Adelaida Del Castillo's article on Malintzin Tenepal, and Alfredo Mirandé and Evangelina Enríquez's book *La Chicana*
idealized specific women as the forgotten idols of Chicano history.[63] The
most cited of these works is Del Castillo's interpretation of La Malinche,
who became, instead of the betrayer of the people, the new Chicana
heroine.

Heroes and heroines, then, became the subject of third world writers,
the intellectuals of communities. The emergence of the third world into
writing shifted the sites of discursive territories. Imprinted with the leg-
acies of imperialism, colonization, race wars, and gender and class hier-
archies, early works by third world writers addressed imperialism and
coloniality as they affected race, class, gender, and even sexuality. Franz
Fanon, Albert Memmi, and Paolo Freire especially impressed Chicano/a
writers. Highly influenced by these global writers, the third world intellectuals of the 1960s and 1970s linked the social and political struggles of people of color in the United States with those of Africa, Latin America, and
Asia. Karl Marx, followed by Louis Althusser, also informed Chicano/a
intellectual works in the 1970s and 1980s, a departure from the scholars of
the early and mid-twentieth century.[64] Historians were no exception. A
Marxist—that is, historical materialist—analysis streamlines early studies
by Chicanos/as. A more popular text is Acuña's *Occupied America*, which
collapses both the ideological/intellectual space and the immigrant/labor

category. Gómez-Quiñones's works, however, gravitate toward the ideological/intellectual category. His early essays, even when topically favoring labor studies, are punctuated by Chicano "intellectual precursors" whom he locates during the Mexican Revolution. His dissertation, for example, pinpoints influential Mexican intellectuals, while his biography of Ricardo Flores Magón fuses the hero with the intellectual.[65] In 1977, Gómez-Quiñones theorized "On Culture" long before cultural critics began interrogating the meaning of Chicana/o identities.[66] Identity became class-bound, and culture was dictated by class and region. In his latest book, *Roots of Chicano Politics, 1600–1940*, Gómez-Quiñones begins with a chapter called "Political Culture of the North," in which, for the most part, a historical materialist analysis supersedes all others.[67]

Marxist historians, such as Gómez-Quiñones and Acuña, infused the narrative with theory, convinced that certain truths had been uncovered finally. Like Memmi, who spells out that "the colonialist likes neither theory nor theorists," Chicano/a historians refuted history narratives in which Chicanos/as were neither seen nor heard.[68] Like colonialists, traditional and non-Marxist historians suspiciously eye theory, reasoning that one must remain "true" to the documents. Peter Novick, in *That Noble Dream*, introduced to the field what had been on the minds of many: the idea that objectivity was both fallacy and illusion. He traced the field of United States history and its move into professionalism, marking the American Historical Association as the site where Euroamerican men conferred to lay the bedrock of the discipline.[69] But the voices of "others," the marginalized, were not even imagined to exist at the AHA. Not until the 1930s, with the wellspring of Spanish Borderland scholars, did historians concede that the Anglo-Saxon East was not the Spanish-Mexican West. No longer restricted to Anglo-Saxon colonialist historiography, a modern brand of colonialist historiography named the social-racial dynamics in the Southwest in the name of the Spanish.

The historical study of Chicanas/os, however, was no longer restricted to studies conducted by Euroamerican researchers who once bolstered stereotypes about Mexican Americans in the United States. Before Acuña popularized the internal colonial model in his first edition of *Occupied America*, published in 1972, Chicano historiography had only quietly subverted colonialist historiography. The studies by George I. Sánchez and Carlos Castañeda, published in and around the 1940s, did not overtly question colonialist minds in the Southwest, yet their work pioneered the inception of the internal colonial model.[70] Once control of northern Mexico's land had been won in 1848, the next stage was to enforce a colonialist knowledge in order "to erect the past as a pedestal on which the triumphs and glories of the colonizers and their instrument, the colonial state, could be displayed."[71] Building monuments and naming battlefields after those who had "won the West," the colonialists eulogized their victories. In Texas, the Alamo Mission and San Jacinto battlefield continue to occupy firm spaces as they contribute to the production of colonial knowledge. In these spaces statues and photographs of Anglo-Texan, or Texian, heroes such as Sam Houston and Stephen F. Austin comfort the hearts and minds of Texian nationalists, who still celebrate the former republic's history with a fervor. Chicano historians responded and envisioned heroes on the frontier as an oppositional retort to Anglo heroes such as these.[72]

Acuña's text marked a historical moment, one that was mimicked by oppositional scholars, in which the legacy of the frontier was impugned, then vindicated, in a double movement. Ranajit Guha illustrates the double move in the following passage:

> [T]he appropriated past came to serve as the sign of the Other not only for the colonizers, but ironically for the colonized as well. The latter, in their turn, reconstructed their past for purposes opposed to those of their rulers and made it the ground for marking out their differences in cultural and political terms. History became thus a game for two to play as the alien colonialist project of appropriation was matched by an indigenous nationalist project of counter-appropriation.[73]

For many, *Occupied America* signifies a Chicano/a nationalist project of counter-appropriation.[74]

Immigrant/Labor

"Chicanos/as are immigrant laborers"
and/or "Chicanos are colonized workers."

In this category, all is reduced to "work." While the dicta are similar in that they both highlight laborers/workers, they are also each other's opposites. To be an "immigrant" and to be "colonized" are conditions that are in tension, yet complementary. In other words, to be an immigrant and to emerge from a history of colonization in the United States are predicaments that are opposite sides of the same coin. Both operate at once. This is precisely why the history of Chicanos/as is unique in comparison with the histories of other immigrants in the U.S.

Euroamerican studies such as Carey McWilliams's *North from Mexico*, published in 1949, set the stage for a singular understanding of migrant workers, a diaspora traveling from Mexico to the United States.[75] The assumption, of course, was that Mexicans were/are immigrants. Distinctions between European and Mexican immigrants were superficial, if they were made at all. Not until Acuña's controversial *Occupied America* did a

Chicano historian theorize a conceptual framework that implicitly disputed the historiography of immigration.[76] Acuña's was not a popular treatise among traditionalists, but for many Chicanos/as, he and other scholars opened a site for a different discourse privileging "colonized" over "immigrant." Chicano historians debated coloniality in the Southwest after 1848, many agreed, and many found discrepancies with the internal colonial model. Regardless of the debates, however, the idea of an America "occupied" made a lasting imprint in the formation of Chicano history by naming a new discursive field. Monographs by Chicanos embellished upon embedded colonial social relations in the Southwest, including one of the most regularly cited, Mario Barrera's *Race and Class in the Southwest*, in which he applied the paradigm to the Southwest labor market to argue how a two-tier wage system sustained "internal," regional, colonization.[77]

As a racial group, Chicanos/as have been constructed by a "legacy of conquest"[78] in a homeland where a political border divided a community accustomed to crossing the Río Bravo going north and then south again as easily as easterners found themselves crossing the Mississippi River, yet able to retain their rights, their language, and their culture. But after the political boundary divided northern Mexico from the south, moving back and forth was not so simple anymore. Sixty years after annexation, Mexicans south of the Río Bravo found themselves crossing again to escape the carnage of the Mexican Revolution.

As immigrants became laborers, "work" became the privileged site for scholars who wrote "labor history." Mexicans and Chicanos/as became laborers, with little mention of their lives beyond the fields or factories. In an anthology edited by Rosaura Sánchez, published in 1976, Chicanas were workers who suffered under a capitalist economy precisely because they were workers. These early immigrant/labor studies accentuated the worker's condition, a genderless, sexless, social condition. Mark Reisler, Laura Arroyo, Anna Nieto-Gómez, Rosaura Sánchez, Lawrence Cardoso, David Montejano, and Emilio Zamora, for example, cultivated the immigrant labor/colonized worker paradigm more closely; but at this juncture, women were mostly perceived as exploited workers, along with men, in the labor market.[79] Perhaps the only work that hinted at women's exploitation beyond the labor market is Anna Nieto-Gómez's.[80] Overall, however, gender exploitation beyond "surplus value" was not addressed. Monographs by historian Vicki Ruiz and Camille Guerin-González contest gender ideology, perhaps even "sexing" the labor market, by sifting through family labor dynamics to locate women's exploitation in the labor market and within the family.[81]

While immigration is clearly an issue with which to contend for the Mexican community in the Southwest, does the literature express difference? Is European immigration conflated with Mexican immigration to blur differences? Is similarity assumed precisely because the category "immigrant" is not interrogated? While similarities may be exposed when groups are compared, if one invokes a decolonial imaginary, how would the similarities change for different immigrant groups in the U.S.? Moreover, wouldn't different types of questions be posed? Would a new paradigm in which racialized diasporas were examined bring new insights to Mexicans as immigrants? Would diaspora studies transform the locus of immigration studies, and would we find within diaspora studies the racialization of immigrants, thereby distinguishing "ethnic white" from "ethnic people of color" migrations and dispersions?[82] Perhaps the use of "ethnic" is its own political intervention. These questions, perhaps naive ones, could be tested only by scholars who engage in studies of migrations and dispersions.[83] My question, however, is, Does the signifying term "immigrant" remain static where gender is concerned? I am inclined to believe that gender as a category of analysis remains constricted when it is examined under the condition of "immigrant." There is nowhere to go, there are no new questions to ask, and perhaps the most problematic issue is that gender is erased except in the anecdotal stories about women's lives, with no analysis of their concerns. In chapter 4, I attempt an interrogation of "immigrant" women and put forth "diaspora" as a transformative and oppositional subjectivity for women specifically.

Social History of the Other (as History of the Same)

**"Chicanos/as are also social beings,
not just workers."**

When we employ social history methodology, we eagerly trace social change from the bottom up, seeking common people by digging through census manuscripts, city directories, tax records, deeds, wills, police and criminal records, and other primary sources that reconstruct communities. For many, social history is the grand design, the essence around which we catalogue history. The scheme integrates all other schemes. Family history, labor history, immigration history, women's history, intellectual history, urban history—all harmonize, conjoin, and synthesize under the rubric of the "new" social history. Social historian Albert M. Camarillo, in his essay "The 'New' Chicano History: Historiography of Chicanos of the 1970s," prophetically identifies the coming of a method around which all others will coalesce.[84]

Social history of the other as history of the same is the only category with respect to which a movement from column one to column two can be witnessed in published works.[85] Since the work of social historians in the late seventies and early eighties, a history of the other has magically been conflated with a history of the other as the same. Conclusions in the studies lead to the erasure of differences so that the "other" becomes not unlike the majority "same." In an effort to document racism, as well as economic and gender inequalities, the social historian theorizes that tangible means such as quantification—for example, comparing numbers and tables—will cause people to become alarmed at social injustices, and to decide that everyone deserves equal treatment. Reforms will remedy injustices. The racial, social, gendered group being oppressed will receive equal treatment under the law because they are the same as the dominant group in their difference.

With the ascent of social history's quantifying orderliness, Chicano historiography entered the reformist malady of "sameness." Those who opposed its assimilationist imperative infused conflict and contradiction into the narrative, but the move toward "sameness" seemed like a teleological inevitability with an inherently liberal, reformist thrust. Can we salvage history from sameness, from an assimilationist course, when the argument for the other as the same is what allows for necessary social reforms? Can we adapt social history methods to reconstruct communities that are "not predicated on transcendental becoming"?[86] It is within this Hegelian notion of becoming that Mexicans in the United States have been placed to achieve "equality," hence sameness with white ethnic groups. But Chicano/a history is caught in a time lag between the colonial and the postcolonial, the modern and the postmodern, the national and the postnational. What remains is the ontological wish to become that which would allow a liberatory future promised by the postcolonial, postmodern, and postnational. The historical inheritance, discursive and nondiscursive, of the colonial imaginary in the United States has not permitted that ontological wish to come true. It is almost as if we are doomed to repeat the past, to move, not ahead, and certainly not dialectically, but in circles, over and over, as our communities "become" another kind of colonized/colonizer with the colonial imaginary overshadowing movements. Perhaps our only hope is to move in many directions and knowingly "occupy" an interstitial space where we practice third space feminism to write a history that decolonizes the imaginary. But where will the grand scheme of social history lead Chicano history? What began as liberating, revolutionary history from the bottom up, a history of the masses, the common folk, has reduced all that is examined to a sameness in its difference.

Fernand Braudel and the Annales school in France mapped out a unique language in which to write history, where "great human events are studied only in the larger context of long enduring material and economic structures."[87] The school's thinkers were not necessarily predicting the future of social history as a history of the same, but rather extrapolating how humans are engineered by their material conditions.[88] Once the history of neglected social, racial, gendered groups was dug up through quantitative methods, however, all would be equal in the "becoming" of the same. In other words, historians must create order from chaos, and quantitative method organizes and classifies people and their lives to reconstruct communities in a manner that reduces differences into sameness. Differences are quantified and tabulated into a grid to showcase, for example, inequities between women and men, brown and white, poor and rich. By comparing grids and tables, a social historian unveils how societies are unequal. Equality, however, must be secured for all people; hence, equality—a sameness in difference—becomes the privileged signifier in social history.

Stephen Thernstrom, employing the Annales methods, opened up another world for U.S. historians when he excavated the lives of common men who could be found only in city directories and the like. In *The Other Bostonians* (already the other is claimed as the history that will be told), Thernstrom sifted through the names of blue-collar and white-collar workers who did not figure prominently in Boston's elite society. The common citizen, the other, is finally valued, but only men received attention in the study.[89] Thernstrom's work was tailored by Chicano/a historians to fit the Chicano/a population. In *Chicanos in a Changing Society*, Albert Camarillo clarified the pertinence of Thernstrom's methods, and even borrowed from him the occupational categories under which to list Chicano workers.[90] Other prominent social histories by Mario Garcia, Richard Griswold del Castillo, Ricardo Romo, Pedro Castillo, Arnoldo De León, and others utilized quantitative methods to uncover the history of the other as more than just workers. Life at home, in churches, with community clubs and organizations filled social and cultural gaps in knowledge about a population whose lives had been discerned only in fields and factories.

When conflict and contradiction are reassessed within social history, they seem to impugn a binarism which categorically unifies all Euroamericans as oppressors and all Mexican Americans as their victims. David Montejano reflects upon the racial tension and class conflict that shaped Texas in the nineteenth and twentieth centuries without privileging the binaries of "us versus them."[91] Ramon Gutiérrez elucidates how gender differences and conflicts designed a unique native society in precolonial and colonial New Mexico. Lisbeth Haas traces colonial California's history from the eighteenth to the twentieth centuries to locate the impression of space upon identities. George J. Sánchez probes the cultural complexities of Mexican immigrants as they "became" Mexican American in Los Angeles during the first four decades of the twentieth century. Forthcoming monographs by Antonia Castañeda and Deena González identify multiple conflicts in eighteenth- and nineteenth-century California and New Mexico, where women lived persistent contradictions. Finally, Vicki Ruiz's text provides a comprehensive history of Chicanas.[92]

Historically, Chicano/a communities have been split by class, by generational differences, by gender. Multiple conflicts between and among racial, ethnic, and gendered categories have been an important element of a method which began as the history of the other.[93]

Gendered History

"Chicanos are also women, Chicanas."

Gendered history appeared to be an irony, a universal joke on a tradition that had negated half its population. A reversal of methods, theories, narratives was to be the new order. All would have to be rethought, revised, rewritten. The negation of woman paralleled Marx's dialectics as a contrast to Hegel's; that is, feminists writing history had found that which would turn everything on its head by (en)gendering history.

Chicana history, or Chicana studies, constructed, theorized, enunciated, and redirected the questions asked by Chicano/a historians in the 1970s and 1980s. Inside each of the overlapping categories I have listed—intellectual/ideological, immigrant/labor, and social history—women have been relegated to silences, which are measured differently by Chicanas/os (en)gendering history. The historiographic questions challenged an implicitly phallocentric field. Feminism, as a methodological tool, would unleash systems of thought from restrictive categories, the categories of modernity in which Chicana history had been trapped. However, although historians of women questioned traditional history that excluded women, excluded the way gender carved history, women of color historians questioned how feminism, too, had its flaws; hence the early studies in my first three categories feared that feminism would neglect race. The gendered history that many women of color contemplated, however, claimed that one could not study women of color without reflecting upon the intersections of race and class with gender.

Gendered history transpired with a distinct intent in the 1980s. The anthologies *Mexican Women in the U.S.* and *Between Borders,* both edited by Adelaida del Castillo, still displayed a Marxist analysis in which class underscored women's exploitation, but gender was brought to the forefront and the patriarchy became a category to debate.[94] *Chicana Voices,* first published in 1986 and reprinted in 1990, is a compilation of the proceedings to the conference for the National Association for Chicano Studies held in Austin in 1984.[95] The anthology characterizes an interstitial move from an orthodox Marxist critique to a firm feminist position unafraid to earmark feminism as a paradigm that could locate the "intersections of class, race, and gender."[96] The collection *Building with Our Hands*, published in 1993, further enunciates feminist visions.[97] In the introduction and conclusion, Chicana scholars articulate cultural feminisms patterned by racial and social questions.

Essays that track feminisms through the 1970s, 1980s, and 1990s were written by Chicana feminists who berated the "madness" in Chicano studies for negating mostly heterosexual Chicana voices.[98] Anna Nieto-Gómez was often the lone feminist voice in the early Chicano male-centered nationalism of the 1970s.[99] Teresa Córdova's comprehensive, thorough thought-piece on Chicana feminism from the 1970s to the 1990s is one of the few essays from a consciously heterosexual perspective that do not relegate Chicana lesbians to the margins, but rather integrate and acknowledge the contributions by Chicana lesbians to a more radical feminism.[100] Gloria Anzaldúa, Alicia Gaspar de Alba, Deena González, Cherríe Moraga, Carla Trujillo, and Yvonne Yarbro-Bejarano, however, were the first to dare to broach the topic of Chicana lesbians within Chicana/o studies.[101]

Alma García, in "Studying Chicanas: Bringing Women into the Frame of Chicano Studies," argues that integration of Chicanas into Chicano studies requires more than merely a topical addition of "woman."[102] This "tacked-on" approach does not integrate gender with race and class, but rather leaves women outside of the main topic. García schematically traces how works in Chicana studies have fit the following three categories: "Chicanas as Great Women," "Chicanas as Workers," and "Chicanas as Women." She pleads for a leap into her fourth category, "Toward an Incorporation of Women into Chicano Studies." Interestingly, García and I have charted similar rules of formation, but our conclusions do not coincide. She conflates studies on women as workers with studies on women as social beings. Many of the social history texts, for example, which I place in category 3, she classes as studies on work. Her category "Toward an Incorporation of Women into Chicano Studies" is similar to what I classify as "Gendered History." However, I contend that this category is also limited, and a leap toward technologies of desire/sexualities/gender may be the point of departure for new studies on Chicanas/women of color/queers. Her fourth category is her liberatory signifier for Chicano/a studies, but I would contend that it is another of modernity's entrapments, while a jump toward technologies of desire/sexualities/gender would allow for a third space feminist analysis implementing the decolonial imaginary to move beyond woman as an essentialist category.

CHICANA HISTORY: MYTHS AND METAPHORS

I have discussed within each of my taxonomies how Chicanas have been assigned secondary status, either as heroines who are idealized, as workers who are exploited along with men, or, as in social history, as women who are only members of a family. But how has Chicana history fared within the gendered history of Euroamerican women historians? The apparent historiographic literature would be that of the American West and how Chicanas have been written about within that scope. Works by Vicki Ruiz, Antonia Castañeda, Deena González, and Sarah Deutsch, to name a few, have scrutinized traditional writings in the American West to engender its history.[103]

I turn, however, to historian Joan Kelly, who asked, "Did women have a Renaissance?" as an example of Euroamerican women's historiography to probe how Chicana history has been marked and pushed aside within European constructs.[104] Kelly inverted meanings, inviting us to place at the center those on the margins, in this case European women in history. For a consideration of the question "Did women have a Renaissance?" for Chicanas, certain claims within that historical construct were possible. But the system of thought had to be disputed. That is not to say that I dismiss the topic simply because it is a European construct. The question can be shifted and redesigned to address Chicana history. Kelly's question intrigued me, but I was similarly intrigued with Mexicanist Anna Macías, who did not ask, but pointedly stated, "The Mexican Revolution was No Revolution for Women."[105] Macías and Kelly reached identical conclusions about male-centralist paradigms that did not include women's voices. Both confronted and inverted traditional systems of thought.

If I remained within the temporal and spatial epoch historically unified and defined as the Renaissance, then I would be restricted to the fifteenth and sixteenth centuries of Spain's own Renaissance. These centuries of Spanish history are pertinent to Chicana history. The Spanish Renaissance explorers/discovers were also the conquerors/colonizers who invaded the Americas searching for wealth, only to stumble upon the "other," the indigenous population. Historians of Spain's empire have argued that *el siglo de oro*, the Golden Age, was possible precisely because the Americas provided the wealth from gold and silver mines in Mexico and Peru. Joan Kelly's question opened the historiographic space to scrutinize the Renaissance as a historical moment that further privileged those already privileged. European men who were writers, artists, and intellectuals embraced the conquests and invasions, which brought them gold and silver. Some elite women benefited from the empire's wealth, but not in the same way as men. If I shift the question, as a historian of Chicanas/Mexicanas, and replace "Renaissance" with "Revolution" to follow Kelly's example of inverting traditionalist historiographic questions, then the space of the "other" is relocated. Chicana history, then, *is* the history of the other within Euroamerican women's historiography.

Perhaps one of the most astute renderings of Chicanas as the other to appear as an intervention in Chicano studies and women's studies was

Anzaldúa's *Borderlands/La Frontera*.[106] Fifteen years after the publication of Acuña's *Occupied America*, Anzaldúa published a book which would influence not only the developing transdisciplinary area of cultural studies, but also historiography. Anzaldúa's book was to be the progression toward postmodern, postnational identities for Chicanas/mestizas. *Borderlands/La Frontera* became the keywords, the cohesive metaphoric linchpins for many late-twentieth-century writings. The Chicana feminist theoretician intervened with a treatise that presented history as only another literary genre. Debates circulated about the book's historical errors, but many historians simply missed the metaphor and read too literally. Anzaldúa's conscious myth-making, like José Vasconcelos's "raza cósmica," opened a site for gendered discourse about *la nueva mestiza*.[107]

Both Acuña and Anzaldúa wrote the "other" without making the "other" the same or placing the "other" within the same. Both texts "marked out a new domain of inquiry"; both were "a new conceptualization of consciousness's relation to the world."[108] Both texts brought an untried, cutting-edge perspective to Chicana/o studies, and both have been held suspect by the academy because they venture beyond the confines of the academy's authorized debates. They move into unexpected territory, daring to risk a distinct line of inquiry. Both interrogate existing discursive fields. Acuña's, as I have mentioned, belongs in the first column, where the Chicano/a historical imagination has been construed by a form of opposition to the colonial imaginary since the 1970s. Unlike Anzaldúa's feminist approach, he places woman, the concept-metaphor, as laborer and commodity subsumed under a nationalist domain. While Acuña offers a counter-appropriation of a nationalist project, Anzaldúa writes oppositionally to Acuña, issuing a "new" postnationalist project in which *la nueva mestiza*, the mixed-race woman, is the privileged subject of an interstitial space that was formerly a nation, and is now without borders, without boundaries. The concept-metaphor woman, formerly known as "worker" in Chicano nationalist discourse, is challenged by Anzaldúa, who critiques that discursive "nation" as a space that negates, dismisses, and occludes feminists, queers (*jotas y jotos*), and anyone who is not of "pure" Chicano blood and lineage. Mestizaje, for Anzaldúa, is redefined and remixed into an open consciousness: "it is a consciousness of the Borderlands" where a "hybrid progeny" conflates "racial, ideological, cultural and biological cross-pollinization."[109]

> The work of mestiza consciousness is to break down the subject-object duality that keeps her a prisoner and to show in the flesh and through the images in her work how duality is transcended.[110]

In the same paragraph, Anzaldúa attempts to reconcile the dualities male–female and white–people of color by introducing a postcolonial consciousness, a consciousness of hope in which "queerness" is in the forefront. For me, the borderlands are also the interstices where the decolonial imaginary glides to introduce the possibility of a postcolonial, postnational consciousness.

To juxtapose these two texts, *Occupied America* and *Borderlands/La Frontera*, at the end of this essay is to take a diachronic leap from categories 1 to 4, where the theoretical conditions of both texts coexist. In other words, a specific Chicano nationalist discourse that negates "woman" still lives and breathes, at the same time that a wave of Chicana/o consciousness ruptures old models to build upon new technologies in which identities are not bound to a rigid, schematic past.

The postmodern imperative has already configured Chicana/o cultural studies. Some cultural and literary critics dabble in historicism, prodding Chicano/a history in fresh directions beyond restricted borders toward transdisciplinarity.[111] But I can already hear "purists" denouncing theory, denouncing a move away from "objective science." In the following abridged quote, familiar to many, Foucault asserts how a history that defies order, privileging ideas and knowledge, is still repudiated by traditionalists who cannot acknowledge their own ideological trappings.

> The cry goes up that one is murdering history whenever, in a historical analysis—and especially if it is concerned with thought, ideas, or knowledge—one is seen to be using in too obvious a way the categories of discontinuity and difference, the notions of threshold, rupture, and transformation, the description of series and limits. One will be denounced for attacking the inalienable rights of history. . . . But one must not be deceived. . . . What is being bewailed, is that ideological use of history by which one tries to restore to man everything that has unceasingly eluded him for over a hundred years.[112]

That which has eluded "man" for centuries is the ideological use and abuse of history.[113] In the nineteenth century, government discourse was constructed by the state historian, who could rationalize a narrative that would uplift the government in power. A patriotic story would be told and passed down to new generations to advance a nationalist cause.[114]

Has Chicano/a history mimicked a patriotic story so much that a nationalist cause, in the name of decoloniality, has become the privileged history project? Or has Chicano/a history become the history of the other as the same to guarantee equal political and social rights to those historically excluded from the center's privileges? Or perhaps history is moving too far away from "science" and empiricism, onto the threshold of postmodernity and postcoloniality. Ashis Nandy, writing about coloniality in *The Intimate Enemy: Loss and Recovery of Self under Colonialism*, may offer Chicana/o historians insight when he says, "If the past does not bind social consciousness and the future begins here, the present is the 'historical' moment, the permanent yet shifting point of crisis and time for choice."[115]

How will we choose to describe our past, now, at this moment, as an enunciation in the present? If "history shows that everything that has been thought will be thought again by a thought that does not yet exist,"[116] then what will we choose to think again as our history, the history that we want to survive as we decolonize a historical imaginary that veils our thoughts, our words, our languages?

In part two, I will discuss the shaping of Chicano/a consciousness by the discourse of the Mexican Revolution. I believe that Chicano/a historical consciousness has been constructed by the choices we historians have made, political choices that often occluded a gendered history, but I will do my best to pull that history into the forefront as part of the consciousness of a historical moment. Part two of this book offers case studies situated in and around the Mexican Revolution. I am, in a sense, exposing how historians have participated in a politics of historical writing in which erasure—the erasure of race, gender, sexualities, and especially differences—was not intentional, but rather a symptom of the type of narrative emplotment unconsciously chosen by historians.[117] I am wondering what will happen if emplotment becomes a conscious act as we write the events that become our official stories. In the following section, I will submit case studies, but I, too, am emplotting by choosing specific narrative techniques. I arrange the events and make arguments that suit me, arguments that I am pleased to excavate from the text of the documents as I create a Chicana history in which I can believe.[118]

Part Two

FROM ARCHAEOLOGY TO GENEALOGY:

DISCURSIVE EVENTS AND THEIR CASE STUDIES

Chapter 2

FEMINISM-IN-NATIONALISM

THIRD SPACE FEMINISM IN YUCATÁN'S SOCIALIST REVOLUTION

Feminism causes divorce, feminine associations
against marriage, and the vice of Lesbianism, which,
by an immense misfortune assumes large propor-
tions in the cities.
—Ignacio Gamboa, *La Mujer Moderna* (Yucatán,
1906)[1]

Mexican essayist Ignacio Gamboa wrote *La Mujer Moderna* to publicize convictions profoundly critical of feminism. Pamphlets such as his circulated in middle- and upper-class homes, where women like those who attended Yucatán's feminist congresses, the pedagogic congresses, or any political or social event during Yucatán's socialist era may have praised Gamboa, criticized him, or just ignored him.

Tracking "things said" about feminism by the intellectuals and leaders of a historical event—in this instance, the Mexican Revolution—can make clear the production of discursive formations. Often, what is recovered in such a Foucauldian "archaeology" of "things said" is not "genesis, continuity, or totalization,"[2] but instead repetition. "Things said" are repeated without any kind of evolutionary or revolutionary transformation. It is as if the dialectic has failed women's voices. But has it? If indeed we consider rhetoric about feminism within nationalist movements, we seem doomed to repetition over the centuries. How often have feminists been accused of lesbianism and anti-marriage sentiments (as if either is an insult) because they claim feminist identities? Almost a century later, Gamboa's accusations are still hurled at feminists; however, social and political movements through the decades have opened up spaces for feminists who no longer fear being silenced or censured by ideologues who essentialize women's voices.

While the repetition of "things said" is engaging, the modicum of social change that can be traced—if, that is, we want to trace change—is also fundamental. Change can always be unveiled across the centuries, just as continuity can be hailed. Both are inherent tools for the historian; both are differential by degrees. My interest remains social change, but my focus is to probe change as it is formed discursively, in the past, by the present.

As a historian, I have been trained to locate origins, to trace continuities and changes, and to unify that which seems out of synchronicity, to categorize facts and words which seem to be "lost in space," lingering alone, anxious for a historian who will assign categories to these "things said." On the other hand, if one studies history only from a Foucauldian stance, to rupture totalities and dispute origins, one can become disillusioned; yet disillusion may be essential in order to interrogate differences and subjectivities in different ways, perhaps by crossing disciplines. The historian's subjectivity imagines and produces historiography, even when it is revisionist. The language of historiography is enunciated and repeated, authorizing systems of thought, which are not tested; nor do they interrogate the subject who utters privilege and authority. As Spivak reminds us, "the production of historical accounts is the discursive narrativization of events,"[3] and the assumption that the historian will tell "what really happened" in "value-neutral prose,"[4] if theory is disregarded, is itself a subject position which contributes to the discursive formation of a historiography that claims purity, the purity of knowledge, as if the documents speak for themselves.

In this essay, I am concerned with tracking discursive formations of feminism during a nationalist moment, acknowledging my own subject position as a Chicana feminist historian with historical materialist tendencies. I want to contrast women's voices with men's voices as both articulated a nationalist revolution in Mexico from 1910 to 1920, but more specifically I want to address the gendered narratives constructed at the pedagogic congresses, the Yucatán Feminist Congresses of 1916; and I also want to scrutinize the ways in which working women contested the revolution's reforms through their voiced grievances. This is all a way of querying systems of thought. As the Yucatecan women spoke, a kind of "dialectics of doubling" yielded a politics of contradiction, a contradiction to and with male-centered policies, which, I argue, articulated third space feminism, within and between dominant male discourses.[5] It is as if women and men became each other's doubles, "doubling" or even repeating each other's rhetoric, especially as both were confronted with neo-colonial political dynamics in their nation. The Mexican Revolution, as it was imported into Yucatán by General Salvador Alvarado, became the space for interstitial feminist acts under the eyes of male leaders whose nationalist vision for women was quite specialized. Aware of male discourses as they dominate nationalist rhetoric, cultural critic R. Radhakrishnan asks, "Why does the advent of nationalism lead to the subordination or the demise of women's politics?"[6] In a sense, he is conceding that women should create a new and different space inside nationalisms. Historical events such as the Mexican Revolution show that women's politics may have been subordinated under a nationalist paradigm, but women as agents have always constructed their own spaces interstitially, within nationalisms, nationalisms that often miss women's subtle interventions. I would like to refer to the intervention as third space feminism-in-nationalism, where "doubling" is the performative act.[7]

Within this "doubling," this "double signifier," theorizes Homi Bhabha, a particular politics of the postcolonial is created. For my purposes here, I believe that the postcolonial remains a hopeful utopian project. The time lag between the colonial and postcolonial during this historical moment—the Mexican Revolution—can be informed by the decolonial imaginary. Through the decolonial imaginary, the silent gain their agency. To locate these women's voices, I argue that the decolonial imaginary becomes the tool that will write these feminists into history. Third space feminism, then, becomes the practice that implements the decolonial imaginary. For Mexico, one might argue that neo-colonial socioeconomic conditions were in place. In other words, Mexico had not entered its postcolonial moment. While Mexico had won its independence from Spain in 1821, two years later the United States made it known to the world that Mexico was within the U.S. "sphere of influence." A few decades later, Mexico's dictator Porfirio Díaz welcomed the United States' corporate giants, selling them land at ten cents an acre. Minerals such as copper, silver, and oil were extracted from the land, and trains were built to transport these riches to the United States. Many Mexicans protested this neo-colonial relationship; hence, toppling the dictator Díaz would excise neo-colonial compromises with the United States. The women and men of Mexico who protested Díaz's nearly thirty-five-year regime conceded that they wanted Mexico for Mexicans.[8]

A kind of doubling was in play for women and men in this specific nationalist movement as they allied politically, yet even within that "doubling," women's purpose was discursively constructed as they became symbolic representations for a nationalist cause. Women were left out and could speak only within and from interstitial spaces. There was no space for fusion or integration. Instead, feminism-in-nationalism would have to be articulated as the "intervention of the Third Space."[9] "It is that Third Space, though unrepresentable in itself, which constitutes the discursive conditions of enunciation,"[10] and it was in that third space that the women of Yucatán found themselves reiterating, reassigning, and rehistoricizing their symbolic place in the revolution.

Elite male ideologues of the nation, such as Gamboa, spread rumor and anti-feminism in Mexico just as revolution began to stir. How was feminism going to be reconciled with the Mexico that would forge a new constitutionalist government? Would women's "femininity" become a symbol foregrounded in the construction of the new nation? Would women be relegated to traditional, gender-specific roles? How would women be included in the nationalist agenda? As an addendum? The Mexican Revolution, after all, was a constitutionalist revolution, in which feminist activities were by no means promoted. Women, such as those in Yucatán, may have attempted to reconfigure the nation-state, but they were restricted by the structures of the male-centralist itinerary for the revolution. In other words, the male leaders of the revolution envisioned a discursive order that bound women to "femininity." That is not to say women held back or were passive. Women spoke, even if they were regulated and impeded by systems of thought enunciated by male revolutionaries. Could women have done more to disrupt these discursive formations? Were they not also part of a social design that provided a forum like the feminist congresses to them? And how about the working women who filed grievances against a revolution's government which still neglected women's needs?

The women who attended the feminist and pedagogic congresses were, for the most part, middle-class like the leaders of the revolution, but the domestic servants, the workers, were anything but middle-class. While the male leaders generated women's arenas, women's agency cannot be ignored. The Yucatecan women created their own discursive agenda within that preconstructed domain. And given the political complexities of Mexico's history, its postcolonial relation to Spain since 1821 and its neocolonial relation to the United States since 1823, with the advent of the Monroe Doctrine, perhaps there were interstitial spaces in which the women and men of the nation met, concurred, and spawned a new constitutionalist government. But again, despite the interstices of agreement, women, for the most part, were excluded from the nation's strategies except where men such as Governor Salvador Alvarado sought their backing. What were his words? How did he represent women and their duty to their nation? First, I'd like to present a brief sketch of Mexican feminist historiography.

In her study on the feminist movement in Mexico, Anna Macías posited that "feminism as it developed in Mexico from approximately 1870 to 1940, had a character all its own and bore only a faint resemblance to the feminist movement in the United States or northern Europe."[11] This resemblance was based on two characteristics: First, an international feminist movement in the late nineteenth century had made its way to some third world countries by the beginning of the twentieth century. Mexico was such an example. The word *feminista* appeared in Mexico by the early part of the century. Mexican women, however, did not became aware of gender-specific issues only through their contact with European feminists. Mexican feminism has always taken its own cultural forms. *Marianismo,* as a form of feminism, empowered women in the household in much the same way that domestic feminism gave women power in U.S. homes in the mid-nineteenth century.[12] Second, the feminism of the era was linked structurally to the Mexican Revolution, a revolution overtly expressed as a nationalist, constitutionalist movement. Despite its socialist proclivities, Governor Salvador Alvarado's nationalist revolution sustained a capitalist economy in Yucatán during his tenure from 1915 to 1918. The feminist movement, led primarily by middle-class teachers, upheld reforms under that economy. The most obvious similarity between Mexican, North American, and European feminism was the shared interest in reforming gender inequalities in a socioeconomic system that bred inequalities. Feminism in Yucatán was inextricably linked to an economy which sought reforms that excluded the voices of those marginalized. This was a modernist feminism with its international scope, while entrenched in a liberal revolution's reforms.

Liberal feminism defined the activities of the feminists of Yucatán, while a governor who called himself socialist enunciated the discursive formations of that activism. In this instance, the nation's ideologues restricted and controlled gendered agendas. Yucatecan women were heard from only under particular institutional circumstances in which they performed liberal, modernist, feminist discourse. What was women's potential for influencing leaders of the revolution who already knew what women should say and do, and how they should react to the revolution?

Yucatecan feminists were in a precarious position. While the predominantly middle-class teachers at the congresses disputed the injustices that women experienced in society, the poor, mostly illiterate female population was kept from engaging in the discussion. They found their own discursive arena, however, by filing grievances in government offices which had previously ignored the state's working class. While Alvarado wanted only literate women to attend the congresses, the Mayas and mestizas who worked as domestic servants were not represented, but instead represented themselves in cases filed against landowners, employers, husbands, and even the Catholic Church. This is not to say that the feminists did not debate vital issues for women. They were indeed acting in their gender's best interest when they advocated education, the vote, divorce laws, and even property rights. Alvarado's moderate socialism braced the middle-class women's measures, and for women he charted a scheme, an order, in which women's rights would be mapped out. He set the stage, building a particular discourse within a specific site, but he also passed reforms that allowed working-class women to voice their own needs. The nationalist movement, bent on liberal reforms, prohibited deeper probes into the country's contradictions, but were they really contradictions? Alvarado's stance, in a way, because it was a modernist stance, did not necessarily contradict his policy to protect women. He had an interest in the protective legislative reforms of a modernist revolution.

In addition to tracking feminist discourse, this chapter reviews Salvador Alvarado's discursive reforms to ask whether the initiatives did improve women's lives. Was the governor's rhetoric about women's traditional place as mothers and teachers restricting them or providing them with more opportunities? His education reforms singled out the female population to encourage them to support his revolution in Yucatán. Did these reforms single out women for the same reason? Did the discursive practices of the revolution serve only to silence women? How did women speak interstitially within the confines of the new laws, the legal reforms that were to liberate them?

ALVARADO'S SOCIALIST ORIGINS

Born in Culiacán in September 1880, the general later moved to Guaymas and then to Sonora, where he worked in commerce. In 1906 he became a staunch supporter of the Partido Liberal Mexicano (the Mexican Liberal Party) when it was still a reform-minded organization whose sole purpose was to topple the dictator Porfirio Díaz. The PLM seems to have provided Alvarado with an ideology that shaped his convictions about revolution. Ricardo Flores Magón, the guiding visionary of the PLM, influenced Alvarado's early doctrines. Through Flores Magón, Alvarado recognized the importance of examining class relations and making distinctions between the working, middle, and upper classes.[13] He learned from the PLM that workers suffered exploitation under capitalism.

Alavarado joined Mexico's Partido Antirreleccionista in 1910, and later endorsed Carranza after General Victoriano Huerta staged a coup and assassinated President Madero in 1913. Carranza sent Alvarado to Yucatán to quell an uprising that had further divided plantation owners and their workers.[14] When Alvarado arrived, neither the working nor the middle class welcomed him. Landowners resisted his policies because the revolution promised agrarian reform, which threatened to upset the hacienda system that had made them wealthy. Alvarado's agrarian reforms, however, demonstrate that he had no intention of redistributing land to the peasants who wanted to live on it communally. Instead, he hoped to create a class of small property owners, *pequeños propietarios*, and sustain rural workers on the plantations. The difference was that the landed oligarchy would find themselves owning less land.[15]

The only groups that might be expected to tolerate Alvarado were exploited peasants, hence Mayas, and disgruntled women, mostly of lower and middle income. It is not surprising, then, that the governor wooed the female population. He targeted women when he initiated many of his social reforms in Yucatán. Although Alvarado, like his socialist contemporaries, understood that capitalism robbed laborers, he condoned socialism for Yucatán only in rhetoric. In practice, he sustained an economic system that was rooted in capitalism, and he sought to improve workers' conditions by reforming the plantation economy. This is not to say that the reforms did not help the disadvantaged. Alvarado experimented by instituting bourgeois reforms for a modernist, nationalist revolution.

But even before Alvarado's arrival in Yucatán, the governor in 1910 initiated legislation on prostitution that reveals a certain discursive production of women's bodies as bodies which, under the law, would be under persistent surveillance. While I do not know how women responded to this law, its discourse exemplified the effort to regulate women—poor women, of course—during the advent of the Mexican Revolution, a revolution which had not yet officially reached Yucatán in 1910.

DISCURSIVE MONITORING OF WOMEN'S BODIES

Prostitution: Article 222 of the Sanitation Code

The regulation of women's bodies became a worldwide cause with the spread of sexually transmitted diseases. Syphilis took so many lives throughout Europe that the Contagious Diseases Acts, passed as early as the 1870s in England, were the first attempts to regulate sexual activity in a confused and panic-stricken society. The acts purposely regulated carriers, as well as those in high-risk categories, such as prostitutes.[16]

On 22 December 1910, Governor Enrique Muñoz Arístegui signed Article 222 of the Sanitation Code for the Regulation of Prostitution. The sixteen-page document outlined everything from the registration of prostitutes to their weekly health exams.[17] What is most intriguing about the document is that on page after page, the government regulated women's bodies and monitored their behavior; hence surveillance was discursively justified. And if women chose to be prostitutes, they apparently relinquished any freedom. After they registered with the secretary of the health department, they were required to carry an identification book with biographical details.[18] The notebooks, or "personal passbooks," assured the government that these "public women" had regular checkups. A prostitute's passbook could not be issued until after a medical doctor had examined her. She paid for these regular checkups herself, and if she did not have them, the health department would not allow her to practice her profession.[19]

The decree also kept prostitutes under heavy surveillance in Mérida. Aside from always carrying her notebook, a prostitute had to turn it over to anyone who asked to see it. The law prohibited her from greeting people in public places unless they greeted her first. She could not leave the brothel in "showy" or immoral dresses. What was immoral, however, was not defined.[20] If a woman wanted to retire from prostitution, she had to register with the health department, which kept her under surveillance for three months to ensure that she was not practicing clandestinely. If she was working again, she was required to register with the health department.[21] The document stated, "This surveillance will be performed in a way that will not harm or impair the woman, and which will not give away her past condition."[22]

How the health department conducted the surveillance remains unclear. One might wonder if the officials enforced surveillance; if so, did they harass or blackmail women, thinking they could make extra money from those who had no legal rights? The regulations in Article 222 consistently demonstrate that women who practiced prostitution were public charges, and they remained under surveillance whether or not they continued in the profession.

Governor Muñoz Arístegui's office made outrageous demands upon women practicing prostitution in Yucatán, but no more than the politicians and moralists of other countries. The regulations monitored and controlled women's bodies, keeping them under constant surveillance. Many of the rules, such as prohibiting prostitutes from greeting people on the street or from wearing "showy" clothing, spoke to the officials' enforced notions of morality. These stipulations hardly protected people from contracting social diseases. When a woman carried an identification notebook, she did so for the benefit of male clients who wanted to protect themselves. They more than likely checked her medical history, which was noted by an examining doctor. If a male client was infected with a contagious disease, she had no way of knowing. Men with syphilis were not required to register with the health department; nor were they expected to carry notebooks that tracked the progress of their health. The social double standard practiced in this case implied that prostitutes were held liable because they were in a profession that constituted a health risk. The administrators of Yucatán—male, of course—protected Yucatán's population from contagious diseases by placing the burden on women. Neither prostitutes nor wives of male carriers were protected, however. Instead, discursive moralizing was imposed through a law that benefited the men who had made it.

Governor Alvarado immediately amended Article 222, devised under former Governor Muñoz Arístegui, by eradicating the more exploitative precepts in Article 222.[23] He eliminated the financial abuses imposed upon prostitutes when he voided their taxes and debts. He separated sanitation policies from the municipal government; thus a prostitute's fees for medical exams and registration went to departments that could no longer collude with each other. Alvarado separated the health department from the police department, both of which earned profits by monitoring women's bodies in the name of social hygiene. The new governor determined that the former government officials had taken advantage of the women they policed. He declared a radical stance when he said, "prostitutes are given sole freedom under the condition that they protect themselves from venereal disease."[24] To prevent the spread of syphilis without constantly peering into the women's lives and bodies as Governor Muñoz Arístegui's officials had done, Alvarado decreed, "A major punishment is established that will penalize men and women who purposely transmit venereal disease."[25] The difference, again, was that Alvarado did not point to women, policing their bodies as if they were the sole carriers of sexually transmitted diseases. Men, too, were held liable, by being penalized if they knowingly spread the spirochete. Could this have been the new governor's own third space, his interstitial political stance? Was his a feminism in the gaps that sought to hold men socially responsible as women's bodies were being discursively monitored for men's benefit? In a sense, the decree was a harbinger of Alvardo's political movement, in which he opened a space that made women's interstitial feminism a feminism that could be voiced, even heard.

SALVADOR ALVARADO:
RECONSTRUCTING "FEMININITY"

Less judgmental of women than Ignacio Gamboa or Governor Muñoz Arístegui before him, Alvarado seemed to want to grant women a space in the revolution, a space which I believe became women's seemingly silent third space as a feminism-in-nationalism. During his administration, moderate socialist governor Salvador Alvarado championed women's rights. From 1915 to 1918, the general convened feminist and pedagogic congresses, at which issues such as suffrage, literacy, and higher education for women were debated.

To Governor Alvarado, education symbolized achievement, growth, and advancement for Yucatán's population. His gubernatorial career focused on a variety of reforms, but public education was in the forefront. Throughout the nation, the Mexican Revolution had pushed education reforms forward. Antonio Manero, a member of Constitutionalist leader Venustiano Carranza's administration, initiated rhetoric about women that leaders such as Alvarado appropriated. Manero stated, "Woman is the best educator of childhood and for that veritable ministry she ought also be instructed and prepared."[26] He charged that "education should commence, then, in the good constitution of the home" to fulfill the "general temperament of the races which form a nation."[27] In essence, the Mexican revolutionaries expected women to be the moral guides of the nation.

Salvador Alvarado's education policies fill the pages of his study *The*

Reconstruction of Mexico. He published the volumes in 1919, just as the violent phase of the Mexican Revolution was coming to an end. Having just stepped down from office, the former governor had used his position to shape ideas and experiment with them in the state. In the first volume, Alvarado outlined concepts for a renewed Mexico. In volume two, the governor concluded, along with Antonio Manero, that "It is necessary to elevate the Mexican woman for the reconstruction of the country."[28] He further insisted that the country's national pride rested in the "civilization" of the home. Classroom guidance, therefore, could serve to improve women's skills as homemakers, mothers, wives, and even teachers—all for the good of the country. An emphasis on women's femininity in the reconstruction of the nation apparently guided the former governor's vision for Mexican women and their future.

Alvarado's philosophy about women's "emancipation, independence, and citizenship" was a liberatory discourse which foregrounded his core beliefs—that educating women would, in turn, make them better homemakers. "We live in an epoch of women's emancipation," he began. "If a woman is to complete her responsibilities, and if she is to exercise her rights, then, SHE MUST BE EDUCATED."[29] With that education, she was destined to achieve two social functions: "To be the foundation of the family as she unites with a man to make a home. To be a producer and a worker before she unites with a man to make a family."[30] The first function was the more important of the two, he claimed, because at home her true personality was revealed.

In a section entitled "The Homemaker," his male-centered discourse burdens the wife to sustain romance in marriage while she fulfills multiple roles to suit her husband's needs:

> The bride ceases to be a bride the day after the wedding. However, if the bride is sustained in the wife, if the lover, the friend, the companion, the partner, the sister, mother, and daughter are cultivated, then all that is feminine, everything sweet and beautiful in a woman, will also be part of the wife. She and she alone will be her husband's mistress, absolutely and unquestionably.[31]

How did Alvarado intend to cultivate the ideal wife and the perfect marriage? He proposed that a man's home would not and could not be complete unless his wife could achieve equality with him—a radical proposition for an early-twentieth-century thinker and leader. But equality, marked by Alvarado and his cohorts, assigned women to gender-specific roles. For example, Alvarado professed that it was a husband's prerogative to look elsewhere if his home was not in order and if his wife did not stimulate him intellectually. Education was Alvarado's remedy. Education would improve a wife morally and intellectually for her husband and the nation. More important, the home was the first school for children; therefore, a mother must learn the rudiments of domestic economy. She would be responsible for sending sons into society who would make good citizens and countrymen.

This plea for women's education reduced women to only one space in the revolution's new society: heterosexual marriage. Within that space, a woman was free to embrace multiple identities: wife, mother, companion, sister, lover, mistress, friend, partner, and daughter *to* her husband. With so many possible mobile categoric identities, how could women request much more from the revolution?

As Alvarado reiterated throughout his two volumes, "We will educate the woman, then, so she can rise to the level of her proper mission, which is conferred by EMANCIPATION, INDEPENDENCE, AND CITIZEN-SHIP."[32] Education for Alvarado might guarantee some civil rights for women, but heterosexual marriage, his nation's thread, would continue to weave specific gender roles at home.

BACKGROUND: EDUCATION

When Governor Salvador Alvarado spoke at the Second Pedagogic Conference in Yucatán, he resolved to educate women. Educating women meant forcing them to break from the influence of the Catholic Church. It meant exposing them to rationalist ideas—ideas that promoted the Mexican Revolution. To the governor, women served a purpose. Both he and the Constitutionalist leader Venustiano Carranza agreed that women should be routed into teaching. The leaders sought to impress women with the rhetoric of the revolution. Teachers would then indoctrinate children in the classroom.[33] Reforms, before and during Alvarado's government, shaped teachers' lives in Yucatán. Did the education reforms improve women's lives? Did the rhetoric restrict women?

Throughout Mexico, before Alvarado's governorship in Yucatán, leaders and philosophers had already written their opinions and proposed plans about the kind of education that best suited women. One such writer, Agustín Rivera y Sanroman, echoed the nation's sentiments when he asked, "What should women be taught?" Taking the question from a North American newspaper, he addressed the theme in an essay.[34]

Rivera described duties that bound women to the home. "First, give them a good solid elementary education," he noted, "then show them how to sew, wash, iron, embroider, make dresses, and cook well."[35] Economizing—that is, showing them how to spend less money—was a priority, he thought. After a woman had mastered housework and cooking, she could then devote herself to piano, painting, and the arts. These skills were only "secondary to her education."[36]

He resolved that women needed instruction in hygiene, domestic medicine, and literary, intellectual, and moral education to provide them with "faith, hope, and charity."[37] Rivera expounded that a woman must "dismiss vanity and hate lies."[38] So "when it is time to marry, she will realize happiness is more important than the fortune or social position of her husband."[39]

In his writing, Rivera quoted European philosophers and prominent Latin American thinkers who were also influenced by Europeans.[40] Rivera's ideas typified the era. These philosophers extolled motherhood and marriage, believing that education prepared women for these institutions. The bourgeois thinkers of Mexico restricted women to traditional roles. Alvarado and Carranza were no exception. By encouraging women to become teachers, they coerced them into a gender-specific profession. It is fitting, then, that the majority of women who attended the feminist congresses were, in fact, teachers.

Statistically, Yucatán had not fared well in training women to be teachers.[41] In the Republic of Mexico, more than 9,000 women held jobs as primary school teachers.[42] Since the Porfiriato, women had been routed into primary school education. The census reported that in Mérida, 312 of the 470 public school teachers were women, and only 158 were men.[43] These numbers differed from the state's average, according to which men outnumbered women, at least in primary schools. In 1910, the primary schools employed 257 men and 197 women in the entire state of Yucatán.[44]

Statistics also showed that the state boasted 363 public schools in 1910, 148 of which were schools for girls. Private schools numbered only 54, split evenly between those for girls and those for boys. Seven private schools were coeducational, a rarity in 1910. No coeducational schools existed in Yucatán from 1910 to 1915.[45] Alvarado intended to change that.[46] The public schools enrolled more than 18,000 students, of whom more than 7,000 were girls. More than 4,000 students were enrolled in the private schools, one-third of whom were females.[47]

In 1913, the average annual income of a teacher in a public school was 720 pesos. Rural teachers and evening school teachers earned considerably less, while instructors in small towns made only 360 pesos a year. According to the report by the General Treasury of Yucatán, women and men in teaching received equal pay. Women held fewer posts as administrators and directors, however. Directors earned 1,200 pesos yearly, while assistant directors earned 960 pesos. Women were more likely to be the administrators at girls' schools, and men at boys' schools. In the surrounding towns, directors averaged 480 pesos. One small town listed an income of 780 pesos for a male director and only 600 pesos for a female director assigned to similar tasks. Unequal wages between men and women clearly existed.[48]

As a point of comparison, the governor of Yucatán in 1913, Nicolás Cámara Vales, was being paid 12,000 pesos a year. His officials could earn as much as 2,100 pesos, twice the income of a public school administrator, and more than twice what a teacher received.[49]

Alvarado's administration brought the most prominent changes in education since 1910. The census confirms the dramatic increase in women educators. From 1910 to 1920, the number of female teachers in Yucatán's primary schools more than doubled, from 197 to 579. The number of male teachers nearly doubled, increasing from 257 to 474. In private schools, the numbers did not rise by much at all.[50] The schools were most often Catholic, and they separated boys from girls in classrooms. Alvarado discouraged teachers from working at private schools, not only because he criticized Catholicism, but also because he was a proponent of coeducation.[51]

One of his military commanders took advantage of the governor's stance when he prompted Alvarado to use a church under construction as a public school for girls because the one in the city required too much renovation.[52] The anti-clerical governor surely consented. To demonstrate further the disapproval of private, Catholic education, from 1910 to 1920, the number of women teaching in Yucatán's private schools rose only from 31 to 56. This was considerably less than the number of women pushed into public schools.[53]

The number of public schools also increased between 1910 and 1920. While the number of schools for boys decreased, public schools for girls were eliminated. Instead, the number of coeducational public institutions rose from zero to 421.[54]

Governor Alvarado kept the promise he had made at the Second Pedagogic Congress when he opened the doors to coeducation.[55] The statistics firmly attest to his commitment, despite disgruntled parents frightened of permitting their girls and boys to learn in classrooms together. But the issues of coeducation and sex education ignited the controversy that challenged feminist Hermila Galindo at the feminist congresses, and it was the teachers from Yucatán who overwhelmingly disputed her position.

HERMILA GALINDO, "LA MUJER MODERNA"

Mexican feminist Hermila Galindo was exposed primarily to European feminists, less so to North American. Curiously, the title of her magazine, *La Mujer Moderna* (The Modern Woman), which published essays applauding vociferous feminists from these continents, echoed the title of Ignacio Gamboa's scathing essay about feminists.[56] Could she have been aware of Gamboa's essay? Was hers a refutation? Probably not, but the construction of the "modern woman" attracted society's attention, and while Gamboa sketched stereotypes about feminists, Galindo was, in her own way, constructing the "modern woman's" feminism by publishing such a magazine. Before the journal is examined, more about Galindo must be disclosed.

Hermila Galindo was born in Durango. In 1911 she moved to Mexico City, where she joined a liberal club. The liberal clubs were organized strictly to oppose Porfirio Díaz. As her club's orator, Galindo delivered a welcoming speech to Venustiano Carranza when he arrived in the capital after General Victoriano Huerta's fall. Impressed with her oratorical skills, Carranza asked Galindo to join his constituents in Veracruz, where he stationed himself before solidifying his presidency in 1917. Galindo's career took an interesting turn. She became the private secretary and propagandist to the liberal, reform-minded Carranza. Having won his trust, she proceeded to lobby for the rights of Mexican women.[57]

Before her involvement in both feminist congresses of 1916, Galindo's career with Carranza proved to be rewarding. With his assistance, she published her magazine, *La Mujer Moderna*, in 1915. The magazine's content ranged from literary essays to Paris's latest fashions. An essay on kissing hygiene appeared on the same page as the editors' endorsement of female suffrage, a politically volatile issue. The article exemplified Galindo's and other middle-class women's position on suffrage. The writer, Clarisa Pacheco De Torres, asserted that in the North American states where women could vote, they had demanded and won legal reforms. With the vote, Mexican women could do the same. The magazine's collaborators were women who captivated an audience like themselves: literate, fashion-minded professionals who attended the opera, read Plato and Aristotle, and, most important, sought women's suffrage.[58]

Galindo's convictions must have become known throughout Mexico when Carranza instructed state governors to subscribe to the magazine. The governors responded dutifully and requested fifty subscriptions for each of their respective states. Governors from the northern states of Sonora and Chihuahua, to the coastal areas of Guerrero and Veracruz, and throughout the interior of the country bought this magazine, which published essays promoting women's rights, especially their right to vote.[59] By this time, Galindo and Carranza had established a mutual understanding. A doubling of sorts was being negotiated.

THE FEMINIST CONGRESSES, 1916: THIRD SPACE FEMINISM

A year before the congresses in Yucatán, while studying in the United States, Professor María Martínez had declared to a Boston journalist that women in Mexico were not interested in pursuing the franchise for themselves; instead, they wanted to improve upon their education.[60] At the first and second feminist congresses, the women of Yucatán determined that some were prepared to demand voting rights for women, at least in local elections. Although interested in the contribution of women to the country, Carranza's government was not prepared to recognize that contribution by granting them suffrage.

Governor Alvarado, on the other hand, a promoter of women's rights, called the feminist congresses in Mérida to provide women a stage for debating issues as controversial as the franchise. Alvarado intended to muster a population who would favor his reforms. He turned to the middle-class teachers of the region, ordering Profesora Consuelo Zavala and some other female educators to organize the first congress in Mérida. Held from 13 to 16 January, the conference restricted attendance, at Alvarado's instructions, to literate women with a grade-school education. Since illiterate women were not welcome, the attendance narrowed to middle-class teachers.

The governor also faced obstacles when he introduced socialist ideals such as rationalist schools to a middle-class population. The majority of women at the congresses disagreed with Alvarado's extreme proposals. Many held moderate beliefs, while some preferred conservative measures. The governor's discursive impositions served only to disappoint him later.[61]

Amid confusion, three political factions emerged at the First Feminist Congress. Hermila Galindo, who did not attend, represented the most radical faction. Her controversial statement, read by one of Carranza's education administrators, Cesar González, recommended sex education for women, divorce, and anti-clericalism, topics that pleased the governor. Galindo, perhaps going beyond the boundaries that Alvarado or other women dared to tread, interrogated the male double standard as practiced in Mexican society for centuries:

> When a woman, mesmerized, surrenders herself to her lover, compelled by the ineluctable sexual instinct, the man stands before society as a kind of daredevil. . . . But the wretched woman who has done no more than comply with one of the demands of her instinct, not denied to the lowest of females, is flung into society's scorn: her future cut off, she is tossed into the abyss of despair, misery, madness, or suicide.[62]

The response was anything but favorable. A conservative group of women mobilized immediately to ban her speech from the congress records.[63] Francisca García Ortiz, representing the conservatives, confronted Galindo's stance:

> Let us pay slight attention to women's education, but a lot, a great deal of attention, to the education of men, and above all to their enlightenment. . . . Let us never forget that the woman should always be the delight of the home, the gentle comrade of man; she may indeed overcome him through her love and sweetness. But let her not dominate him with her intellect or with her learning.[64]

Also a teacher, García Ortiz expressed a sentiment that the attending educators defended. Her political stance had its own rationale. She asked,

"What social means should be employed to emancipate women from the yoke of tradition?"[65] She answered her own question and maintained that twentieth-century women did not have to embrace nineteenth-century images. "That yoke is disappearing, and we can make it vanish completely, by educating society."[66] Challenging the participants further, she asked, "Who forms society? Men. Well, then, let us educate men."[67] And finally, she concluded that by educating men, women too would be educated, because society on the whole would begin to change.[68] She also summoned men to accept a new enlightenment:

> Today many men are afraid of the intellectual woman. Why? Because they understand that she improves herself every day; that each day her mind advances. Should men be afraid? No. Men should make sure they are not at a disadvantage. And to do this a man must be more and more enlightened.[69]

How did García Ortiz intend to educate men? Like Antonio Manero, Carranza's administrator who idealized women as pillars of society, she also claimed that mothers should educate children, beginning in the home. The professor proposed that the mother could most influence her sons' education. "She will see to it that her sons respect women's advancement, that they look favorably on a woman's being intellectual."[70] A feminist blueprint, such as it was.

Not a mother herself, García Ortiz called upon the mothers at the convention to assist the "young idealist ladies," including herself. She concluded, "May men become worthier and better men."[71] She hoped to educate women, who would in turn educate men so as to improve society for women—an indirect means to equality, and perhaps a futile one.[72] Again, women are the social signifiers placed in binary opposition to men, yet representing, for men, the women men need. Woman is the sign that will construct "enlightened" men.

According to historian Anna Macías, Consuelo Zavala held a more moderate position than either García Ortíz's or Galindo's.[73] Zavala did not quarrel about ideological injustices; rather, she posed solutions to the inequalities that women experienced in Yucatán. She was, in fact, a practitioner. She pushed for civil code reforms and property rights, tangible requests that the convention could take to the governor.[74] Zavala did not overstep boundaries by demanding the vote.[75] She took small steps, assured of what women could win.

The governor trusted Zavala. He appointed her to organize the January meetings at the Peón Contreras Theater.[76] To her credit, Zavala recruited 620 delegates to the first meeting. During the congressional debates, the teacher vowed to improve education for young women.[77] Women were visibly absent from professions in medicine, law, and engineering, for example. In 1910, less than 1 percent of the female population in Yucatán held jobs in such occupations.[78]

Zavala united the moderate and radical factions to reform the 1884 Civil Code, which deprived women of their legal and property rights. Macías points out that this reform led to President Carranza's Law of Family Relations in 1917. This new law allowed women to make contracts and file legal suits. They were also given the same rights that their husbands had over their children.[79]

Perhaps the most extreme demand at the congress was made by the radicals, who, unlike the conservatives or moderates, asked that women be allowed to vote in municipal and local elections. Despite protest from many women, a petition passed, pleasing Governor Alvarado, who called for a second congress.[80] Alvarado, however, wanted women to vote in national elections. He aspired to be president of Mexico, and therefore needed *his* female constituents.[81]

The Second Feminist Congress, held from 23 November to 2 December, was not as well attended as the first. Consuelo Zavala failed to appear, and Hermila Galindo again could not make her way from Mexico City.[82] The radical group took over the Second Congress, but unfortunately for Galindo, she was not present to lead the group with whom she was most in agreement.[83] She sent a representative to submit a twenty-five-page essay, a rejoinder defending her first speech, "The Woman of the Future." The second speech was titled "A Study by Hermila Galindo with Themes That Should Be Resolved at the Second Feminist Congress of Yucatán."[84] In the essay, Galindo asked,

My work is immoral? And how? Because I dare to expose the problems in our society . . . ? Is it immoral because as a perfectly intelligent and scientific woman, I have challenged men by demonstrating the intelligence of my sex, therefore showing that we too have equal rights with men?[85]

She insisted that her studies reflected those of the European philosophers August Bebel and Immanuel Kant, both of whom justified sex education as one of women's rights.[86] She was not, therefore, the originator of such thoughts about women. Galindo firmly believed that this alone should have proven to her female audience that she was a "scientific woman" making rational assessments about the female gender.

Galindo recommended Carranza's revolution, and she wrote almost as Governor Alvarado would have. We are left to wonder only what went unsaid by Galindo herself. Her speeches at the feminist congresses demonstrate, once again, how the interior of Mexico attempted to administer in every region of the country. Was this revolution only from above, and not at all a grassroots movement? That the Yucatecan feminists denounced Galindo certainly shows a grassroots insider response to outsiders. Moreover, this was not a national feminist congress.[87] Most of the women who attended were from Yucatán. A few came from Mexico City, but only those from Yucatán would decide what they would do for women of Yucatán.

Even the radical faction at the second congress had its own issues to promote in the interests of Yucatecan women. But again, these predominantly middle-class women negotiated on their own behalf. Property rights, the right to legal suits, and education benefited a small group of elite women. The majority of the female population could not exercise such rights.

Yucatán was split between the wealthy and the poor. Alvarado's revolution hoped to create a larger middle-income group, especially after initiating agrarian reforms and nationalizing the henequen industry.[88] Perhaps Alvarado expected too much from such a small group of middle-class women. Given their circumstances, they did debate critical issues, but they failed to mention the Maya women blocked from the congresses, a marginalized group who, as I will show later, could contest the government only by filing grievances with the Departments of Justice and Labor. But at the feminist congresses, there were no resolutions to address the needs of women who were, for the most part, domestic servants, while some were surely prostitutes. In 1910, 57 percent of Yucatán's female population worked as domestic servants.[89] They were neither present nor represented.

Hermila Galindo, an outsider like Alvarado, wanted to use the congresses to reconceptualize equality between women and men—equality that reached into the classrooms to teach young girls the same subjects offered to boys, equality that gave women the franchise reserved for men, equality that defied sexual double standards. Galindo continued her career as a propagandist for President Carranza, and she even published a book in 1919 in support of a politician whose career was almost over in Mexico. She wrote *La doctrina Carranza* at a time when the leader's diplomatic relations with the United States were disintegrating.[90] In the book she proclaimed that if Mexico was to be successful, it had to break its ties with its northern neighbor. Politically, she took a stand against the United States when she deconstructed the Monroe Doctrine to accuse the United States of racial arrogance for instituting a doctrine that benefited only Mexico's neighbor to the north.[91] Carranza's willingness to sever relations with the United States impressed Galindo, who argued that Carranza's doctrine was "the doctrine of the future, the one for humanity."[92] The Monroe Doctrine, on the other hand, had given the United States a neocolonial stranglehold on Mexico. A woman such as Galindo, familiar with politics from a young age, was aware of Mexico's precarious relationship with the United States.

In her writings, Galindo expressed her confidence in Carranza's Constitution of 1917, which in itself promised social revolution only on paper. She wrote that suffrage was ineffective as long as workers and the bourgeoisie remained divided; for her, Porfirio Díaz's regime had made that grave mistake.[93] Galindo recognized that the vote alone would not free the people of Mexico. Like so many other Mexicans, she believed that Carranza would make the most revolutionary articles of the constitution a reality, such as redistributing land to the peasants. Of course, he disappointed even his most avid advisers. By the time he escaped with the nation's treasury, later to be assassinated in his sleep by men he trusted, Carranza had become the nemesis of the revolution.

In 1919 Hermila Galindo published *Un presidenciable*, endorsing General Pablo González, Carranza's choice for president.[94] When Alvaro Obregón was elected in 1920, not only had she promoted the wrong man, but the new administration had no more use for her. She married in 1923 and fell silent.[95] Her career in politics ended.[96]

A radical feminist for her era, Galindo was not heard from again. She lived out the rest of her life without publicly voicing her political views. She surely was disillusioned with her country and its nationalist agenda, which in the end made limited inroads for women, whether middle-class or poor. But Galindo's political interests found her backing a presidential candidate who was Carranza's choice. The corruption in Carranza's cabinet was already obvious to most. What could his candidate possibly have offered Mexican women in their own country? Galindo, however, wrote a pamphlet endorsing Carranza's man, an essay which had little or no impact, but significant in that it was written by her, a woman who dared to go beyond traditional boundaries to embrace politics usually reserved for male nationalists. Women, after all, could lecture about education for themselves and their children, but they could not decide who should be a political candidate for president—at least not until they won the franchise.

But while Hermila Galindo and the Yucatán feminists Francisca García Ortiz and Consuelo Zavala were debating the franchise for women, working-class women, domestics, Mayas, and poor women were speaking their own kind of revolution—one that did not necessarily transform their lives, but one in which they spoke, whether invited or not.

INTERSTITIAL SUBJECTIVITIES: WOMEN SPEAK "IN TONGUES"

The grievances brought before the Departments of Justice and Labor from 1915 to 1918 exposed social and cultural prejudices that had been brewing for centuries in a remote region far from the center of Mexico City. In a case I will discuss below, a Maya woman confronted a government official who could not speak her language, and so she protested against a system that had held her people linguistically captive for centuries. Complaints such as this confirm "interstitial subjectivities" in which "women speak in tongues, from a space in-between each other."[97] Here, in that interstitial space, women did not passively accept injustices, but instead filed grievances against men and upper-income women who, the women believed, wronged them. The following are only a few examples of women's "interstitial subjectivities" in a revolution that had not been prepared to appease so many women. Women spoke among the nationalist revolutionaries for women's own urgent needs. The manner in which these grievances were settled shows how the revolution responded and reacted to an otherwise silent population. But from the gaps and silences, we can know only that which the women chose to say; and we are also limited by what the officials recording their words chose to record.

In a case involving a Maya against a *Ladino*, the Maya woman failed to win against the "white" landowner.[98] She filed her grievance with the Department of Justice in 1915.[99] That the Department of Justice may have handed down more rigorous decisions than the Department of Labor, and that this case was filed early on in the revolution's government, may account for its failure. Perhaps Alvarado's administrators felt more self-assured by 1918 when deciding on behalf of Mayas, laborers, and poor women against the ruling landowners. In any case, the revolution did not act on this woman's behalf. The Maya woman who filed the case was Casimira Palma, a widow from Tekax, who professed that the military commander of that town had ruled against her in a grievance against Señora Manzanilla. She said, "He reprimanded me and accused me of not being able to speak his language, *Castellano*. But he cannot speak Maya which is my language."[100] Before the governor, Palma alleged that Severiana Manzanilla had stolen Palma's jewelry and pawned it without permission. "The military commander will not give me justice. Well, the poor people of this town can only turn to the authorities for help."[101] She requested that the governor require the military commander of Tekax to reopen the investigation regarding her jewelry.[102]

The Department of Justice examined her quarrel against the official, but after carefully analyzing her case, it ruled that she did not have enough proof against the military commander.[103] Palma lost in both instances—in her case against the woman who had allegedly stolen her jewelry, and in her complaint against a government official who had reprimanded her for speaking in her native tongue. Ordinarily, translators were hired to ease tensions between the Mayas and "white" *Ladinos* who faced language barriers. For a government official to reprimand an Indian because she did not speak Spanish reveals the injustices suffered by Mayas in Yucatán even at a time when the revolution was supposed to alleviate differences. Palma, on the other hand, was not silenced, even though she was not really heard. Whether or not she won her case is inconsequential. She promptly pointed out the new government's shortcomings and expressed pride in her language when she defended herself.

Cases involving marriage or divorce settlements demonstrated how working-class women reproached their husbands, or men who might have been husbands. Señora Benigna Gám, for example, alerted the governor that she was disenchanted with her husband, Señor Tomás F. Velasco. Señora Gám could neither read nor write, so a government official drafted the letter. She testified that she had married Señor Velasco on 8 August 1914, and that "he abandoned me after two months without even saying good-bye."[104] Exactly one year after their marriage, Gám argued, "I do not wish that he return for me. I only want my honor to be restored."[105] The governor's office responded that it would investigate the matter further and resolve it on Gám's behalf.[106] While Señora Gám did not seek reconciliation or a divorce, she did demand honor for her name. As a woman abandoned after only two months of marriage, she may have felt unwelcome in a community where only married women and widows won respect. She fit neither of the categories.

A divorce case evinced how some women manipulated the revolution to their advantage. Cornela Padrón, who was suing her husband for divorce, also complained because he had kept her sewing machine. Padrón alleged that her husband, Zacarías López, had abandoned her and their three children. He "threw us out on a rainy night," causing her one-year-old daughter to die of pneumonia.[107] This case was filed in January of 1916, the same month the first feminist congress was held. But the congress could not have made any difference to Padrón, who asserted that her husband acted abusively toward her and their children, and she also made it known that "he lives publicly with another woman."[108] The estranged wife demanded her sewing machine from their house. It was her only livelihood. Arguing on behalf of the husband, López, Silvero Santos testified that "the sewing machine was not the property of either husband or wife."[109] López's father had purchased it, so if it belonged to anyone, it belonged to López's mother.[110] Cornelia Padrón did not gain possession of the machine, but the government ordered López to pay her 25 pesos monthly until the divorce was final.[111] This amount may have been just enough to feed and clothe her and her two children. After the divorce, Padrón's income remained uncertain.

In another case, Demetria Centeno, a widowed domestic servant, demanded justice from the father of her sons, Camilo Zavala, to whom she was not married. A widow for seven years, Centeno argued that her children, aged one and four, deserved "to enjoy all of the rights and privileges that the laws provide for someone of his class."[112] As a domestic worker, she obviously considered Zavala, a single thirty-one-year-old who worked in a harness shop, to be from a class above her own. He was more than likely a skilled artisan who may or may not have owned his own saddle shop. She wanted him held responsible for his sons despite the fact that he was not legally bound to her. He complied without resistance, and when the thirty-six-year-old domestic servant hired tutors for the children, he also complied. Why Zavala and Centeno did not marry is neither mentioned nor clarified.[113]

Another widow wrote to the governor demanding justice for her sons who had lost their father to the revolution. Inez Manzanilla declared in a letter to Governor Alvarado that her two sons, José Fernando and Aquiles Herculano, seven and six years old, cried for their father, who had courageously fought for the governor's cause. She said, "Poor children, they are left without a father, without a home and without bread."[114] In her letter, the thirty-eight-year-old widow acknowledged that the immortal men of the revolution, "Madero, Carranza, yourself, and Paredes Esquina," her husband, had dedicated themselves for love of their country.[115] Women like herself, she argued, were left with the responsibility of raising and educating fatherless children for the cause. Finally, she requested an unverified sum of money for her sons' education and their living expenses.[116] How the governor's office settled the case is unknown, but significantly, this widow argued on behalf of the mothers of the revolution who had not received compensation after their husbands' deaths.

In a peculiar family squabble, a twenty-two-year-old woman sued her brother-in-law for 2,000 pesos. Engracia Avila insisted that Ramón Moguel Bolio owed her the inheritance from her deceased father's estate. Her father, Ambrosio Avila, had died in 1900, leaving behind his widow, María Nieves San Miguel, and seven children, one of whom was Ramón's wife.[117] The military commander from the nearby town of Maxcanú ruled that Ramón owed Engracia the money she requested. Ramón appealed the decision and urged the governor to overturn the ruling, on the basis that the plantation laborer had been named the executor of his father-in-law's estate. Ramón contended that when Don Ambrosio died, he left only two houses and a number of debts. He professed, "I don't know where I'll get such money with my family responsibilities."[118] He further implored, "Governor, I ask for your justice. Resolve that I am not obligated to pay her for the simple reason that I have never owed any of Don Ambrosio's debts."[119]

Unfortunately for the brother-in-law, the governor's office certified that he owed Engracia Avila the debt. He was incarcerated for three days until he could pay her. His mother-in-law, Señora San Miguel, also mother to Engracia, paid her daughter the 2,250 pesos on behalf of Ramón.[120] The governor's office acknowledged that the debt was paid and released him from his legal obligations.[121] Why Señora San Miguel elected to clear her son-in-law by paying her own daughter is unclear. Perhaps she had kept the inheritance that belonged to Engracia, or perhaps she did not want to see her other daughter's husband in jail and incapable of supporting his family. This is yet another instance in which women's actions speak to us historically and interstitially, between and among the ironies of a revolution that promised so much. In any case, the family finally settled the dispute.

The grievances filed by women, many of whom were poor, show how they intervened in a revolution that often promised much more than it delivered.The cases are examples of women's interstitial subjectivities. These women may not have been avowed feminists, but their spoken language seemed feminist enough as they complained against a governor and his socialist agenda.

From 1915 to 1918, women protested their social reality by contesting a revolution which claimed that it would take them seriously. They tested its seriousness through the Departments of Justice and Labor. Women, whether domestics, Mayas, estranged wives, or widows, complained to the governor when they felt wronged. Some won and some lost, but the women asserted themselves and coaxed the revolution's government into addressing gender issues for these working-class Mayas and mestizas. These grievances exposed inequalities between women and men. The new government did not drastically change gender, race, and class relations, but it did expose discursive practices unfair to the underclass. The feminist congresses, on the other hand, provided a forum for middle-class women.

Avowed feminist Hermila Galindo enunciated from an interstitial space in which the congresses became the discursive territory. She voiced differences as a woman who had lived in Mexico City most of her life and was genuinely interested in social change for women, even though women of her class would benefit most from the reforms. Who was this subaltern voice who spoke between and among the elite, the middle classes, the socialist men, the counterrevolutionaries, and the Yucatecan feminists? Can we really know? Does it matter that we have only a few of her speeches and scant information about her life? It is unfair to characterize her as merely a carrancista with bourgeois ideals. She was incriminated at the feminist congresses for challenging a sexual double standard, but she was probably feared because she dared to throw sex into the discursive arena.

Galindo represents much more at a moment in the nation's history when few women were orators and few women wrote and published essays about their country's international policies. Her outsider/insider status in Yucatán created enormous tension between the spokeswoman and the Yucatán feminists. Perhaps the Yucatecan women were annoyed that Galindo did not show herself at either conference, instead sending a representative to read her position papers. Her stance was not so far removed from those of the Yucatecan feminists. She believed in women's education, but perhaps it was education *for* women that so disturbed the conservative faction—an education *for* women that did not emphasize their femininity or their relegated roles as wives to the "nation," but instead an education that finally probed women's sexual conditioning.

However, three years later, in *La doctrina Carranza*, she acquiesced, echoing García Ortiz, that women were the moral guides of the nation, destined to educate their children at home. Perhaps Galindo tempered her earlier stance to recruit women to champion Carranza's doctrine.[122] How much of his doctrine was her own? How much was she speaking, again, from and within an interstitial space?

The Yucatecan women's construction of a feminism-in-nationalism during the Mexican Revolution seemed to mimic the nationalist leaders' hegemonic discourse. What Carranza and Alvarado outlined was reiterated by Galindo and the teachers of the Yucatán congresses even when the factions disagreed. Only Galindo stands alone in the end, daring to invite women's sexuality into discourse. However, "the rhetoric of repetition or doubling"[123] constructs the political discourse of feminism-in-nationalism. Although "things said" were a "sameness-in-difference,"[124] by whom these things were said makes some "difference" in retrospect. As Teresa de Lauretis points out,

> The movement in and out of gender as ideological representation, which I propose characterizes the subject of feminism, is a movement back and forth between the representation of gender (in its male-centered frame of reference) and what that representation leaves out or more pointedly, makes unrepresentable. It is a movement between (the represented) discursive space of the positions made available by the hegemonic discourses.[125]

In this instance the feminist congresses and the filed grievances were the spaces made available for women.

> Those other spaces both discursive and social that exist, since feminist practices have (re)constructed them, in the margins (or between the lines, or against the grain) of hegemonic discourses . . . coexist concurrently and in contradiction.[126]

No fusion, no integration for such third space feminism.

Voices were seemingly identical, yet at odds. Alvarado's hegemonic narratives represented women in a particular way; feminists such as Galindo, García Ortiz, and Zavala (who did implement reforms) moved in and out of the male-defined representations, interstitially, congruently, yet often at variance with a seemingly identical discourse on women's rights. After all, women had something to gain if they voiced discrepancies from the margins, if only to disrupt hegemonic discourse interstitially. The nationalist agenda did not do much to improve or change women's social conditions; women's grievances are testimony to that. The changes were differential by degrees, but a forum was held, grievances were filed, and the women voiced a third space feminism-in-nationalism.

Chapter 3

THE POETICS OF AN (INTER)NATIONALIST REVOLUTION

EL PARTIDO LIBERAL MEXICANO, THIRD SPACE FEMINISM IN THE UNITED STATES

Marx doesn't exist.
—Michel Foucault, *Power/Knowledge* (1980)

Foucault no existe.
—Amigo de Armando Pereira, *La herencia de Foucault*
(1987)

If the colonial imaginary hides something, then the decolonial imaginary teetering in a third space recognizes what is left out. To locate third space feminism, I will broach the Partido Liberal Mexicano, an anarchosyndicalist, transnationalist organization, and subsequently evaluate how the women in the PLM practiced third space feminism. Archaeology asks that disciplines and their categories be exploded, confronted, inverted, and subverted; genealogy, on the other hand, recognizes how history has been written upon the body. In this chapter, "things said" will be reconstructed as an exercise to show how words are practice; hence, the women practiced the words of third space feminism. I have chosen that practice to import the decolonial imaginary, a critical apparatus that transcends the colonial to sit somewhere in that time lag between the colonial and the postcolonial.

First, what is the relevance of the Mexican Revolution to Chicana history? What is the revolution's significance to Chicana identities, Chicana feminisms, Chicana voices? Apart from the socialist experiment in Yucatán that opened a space for women to voice a feminism-in-nationalism within the boundaries of the country, the Mexican Revolution on the U.S. side of the border embodies the historical moment when thousands of Mexicans left their homeland and crossed a rather small, sometimes dry river to become a "colonized" diaspora in a region formerly Spanish and Mexican. Socioeconomically, Mexicans were relegated to an inferior status affecting all areas of their lives in the region that became the Southwest.

I am interested in the rhetoric of the revolution, river or no river, on both sides of the geopolitical border; hence my reason for tracing Yucatecan feminists. I do not accept fixed notions of Chicana history that confine, stifle, obstruct, obligate, and limit studies to the boundaries of the continental United States as the center of the Americas. For many historians, Chicano/a history materialized only after 1848, and any probing back into Mexico is illegitimate, or should I say "illegal." Chicana/o history from Mexico that tries to cross the U.S. border is detained there as only Mexican in origin. Our "undocumented" history is barred by a political border, as if that imagined boundary can erase centuries of Spanish-Mexican domain.[1]

The discourse of the revolution knew no boundaries. Language, words, corridos, and concepts crossed back and forth along the Mexico–U.S. border as easily as the renowned revolutionary Francisco "Pancho" Villa. The Partido Liberal Mexicano was an anarchist organization that carried slogans back and forth from Mexico City to Laredo and Los Angeles, as well as along the Baja California coast and the U.S.–Mexico border. Many women wrote for the Partido's newspaper, *Regeneración*, on both sides of the border, but mostly in Los Angeles, where the group came to be based after 1910.[2] Women such as Sara Estela Ramírez in Laredo, Texas, the Villarreal sisters in San Antonio, and Blanca Moncaleano, Teresa Arteaga, and Maria Talavera in Los Angeles all contributed to the revolution's agenda as revolutionists, activists, and journalists. The revolution, then, created a kind of renaissance during which women wrote essays and edited their own magazines, newspapers, and journals. Many of these women, who sought political exile in the southwestern United States, wrote prolifically, criticizing the dictator Porfirio Díaz and championing the revolution as a revolution for women.[3]

I am concerned with tracking discursive formations of feminism during a nationalist moment. I am not necessarily concerned with origins, but instead with parallels, continuities and discontinuities, acknowledging my own subject position as a Chicana feminist historian with historical materialist tendencies. This is a way of theorizing present-day Chicana feminisms and finding parallels with contemporary Chicano nationalisms. History is, after all, our understanding of the present through the past.

One way to track discourse about feminism during the revolution is to probe publications by the women and men who wrote about women's rights. While a cross-section of ideologues conceptualized women's place in society as well as their contribution to the revolution, perhaps one of the most prolific and controversial was Ricardo Flores Magón, the Mexican anarchist leader of the Partido Liberal Mexicano (PLM). I am intrigued by the extent to which Flores Magón's treatises affected Mexican revolutionaries, but since then his works have also been taken up by Chicanos/as in the sixties and again in the nineties. (This work falls within the first category of my paradigm: "Chicanos are also intellectuals/heroes.") The text to which I will be referring, albeit briefly, is *Sembradores: Ricardo Flores Magón y el PLM* by historian Juan Gómez-Quiñones.[4] This is all the more reason to look again at Flores Magón, his writings, and his discursive framework, which often reduced women to stereotypes—not because he did not believe in liberation or revolution for women, but because the historical moment ascribed to a particular politics and knowledge about women, their rights and their inherent biological traits. The PLM and its leaders were in many ways ahead of their time in their effort to transcend a society that only debated women's rights.

I would like to accomplish three tasks. First, I will invoke the discourse that addressed women. Second, I will argue that the gendered discourse created a particular poetics for the nationalist cause which became internationalist in scope. This poetics tied women to gender-specific roles, at the same time erasing women's activities, activities which were significant interventions in a masculinist revolutionary rhetoric. Women, however, expressed third space feminism. (This practice is its genealogy.) A "dialectics of doubling" was in play for them, as it had been for the Yucatán feminists.[5] Just as Governor Alvarado's socialist revolution opened a space for women to articulate third space feminism-in-nationalism, Ricardo Flores Magón and his cohorts, men and women, opened a space for a feminist politics within the (inter)nationalist agenda. The group genuinely believed that women belonged in the revolution, doing everything and anything for the larger cause. Unfortunately, some men voiced personal judgments about women's place in the revolution. Contradictions that placed women in a less than favorable light were common.

My third and final point refers to the writing of history, or rather the manner in which this women's history has been written. For me, PLM rhetoric demands attention because it has served as a foundation for contemporary Chicano nationalist discourse, without recognizing the PLM's transnational impetus, and where, again, Chicana activists are relegated to the margins and their history becomes the history of male activists and their priorities.[6] In a comprehensive study of the Chicano movement in Los Angeles in the sixties and seventies, Ernesto Chávez provides a fresh perspective when he identifies the masculinist discourse that framed Chicano nationalism.[7] I believe that the masculinist rhetoric contributed to a colonialist history, thus making the decolonial imaginary and impending critique necessary to locate third space feminism both in the contemporary movement and during the revolution. I would also like to clarify that while historians are interested in tracking change, I would like to trace repetition, the manner in which rhetoric is repeated to serve similar kinds of purposes.[8] This chapter will not lend itself to tracking repetition as much as I would like. I will, however, provide examples from a contemporary Chicano nationalist journal that indicts feminism to show how these indictments resemble those by the PLM against feminists of their era.

The story of the Partido Liberal Mexicano is not unique. It is a story of oppositional history, in which men and women trusted a revolution that would free them. The retelling, then, must be narrated with caution. Another perspective must be called upon, a decolonial one: decolonial in that, as a historian, I look back eager to assign new meaning to a group who understood the binary functions of evil against good, the bourgeoisie against workers, capitalists against anarchists, socialists, and communists, and finally even men against women; decolonial in that this imaginary allows for the in-between, for the shades of gray, for the voices unheard between and among those who were evil and those who were good.[9]

Ricardo Flores Magón and his brother Enrique Flores Magón wrote a number of essays addressing women's rights and their duty to the revolution. They were concerned with the evils that had burdened women's lives, the evils of capitalism. One of the more prominent essays was "A La Mujer" by Ricardo. It first appeared on 24 September 1910 in *Regeneración*, the newspaper of the Partido Liberal Mexicano.[10] Since then, it has been reprinted in books and journals that recognize the party's significance to Chicana/o history. "A La Mujer" typifies the radical leftist ideology of the moment. The PLM, along with other socialist, anarchist, and leftist labor movements of the era, voiced similar rhetoric about women. For many of these organizations, the subjugation of women resulted from an exploitative social structure in which capitalism condemned working-class women and men to the lowest rung of the socioeconomy. The Industrial Workers of the World, the Socialist Party of Eugene Debs, even union organizer and IWW member Elizabeth Gurley Flynn expressed similar convictions in writings and speeches.[11] Eugene V. Debs wrote essays titled "Man," "Woman," and "Child," in which he outlined his ideas about the perfect socialist family. The essays were published and reprinted in the Socialist Party weekly, *American Appeal*.[12] In her study "Rebel Girls and Union Maids," Ann Schofield showed how the American Federation of Labor and the Industrial Workers of the World fostered an ideology that restricted women's roles in leftist organizations and unions in the early twentieth century.[13] Michael Miller Topp, on the other hand, examines masculinity in Italian-immigrant syndicalism, focusing the debate on gender roles in which male-centered politics is consciously interrogated.[14] There was, then, a general idea among leftists in the early twentieth century about how women would serve a socialist society, a leftist union, and a revolution.

DIALECTICS OF DOUBLING

In several articles, *Regeneración* made public the rhetoric of the party while forecasting the PLM's hopes and desires for the women who would be revolutionaries. Two aspects of the rhetoric require explanation. The first is its relationship to the organization's larger political goals and ideals. *Regeneración* helped to politicize Mexican women in the Southwest, but women were politicized to serve a nationalist cause—the Mexican Revolution. In essence, the male leaders idealized nationalism and in the name of revolution laid out duties for women. Implicitly, however, the future movement was envisioned to be a transnational one, in which women along with men would join the workers of the world. The second aspect of the rhetoric that demands explanation is the manner in which women expressed their agency. A kind of "dialectics of doubling" was in play for women, who may have supported the "nationalist" cause of the revolution, but they intervened interstitially with their own rhetoric about their place and meaning in the revolution. The group's ideology about women was challenged as women's participation in the Mexican Revolution transformed them. The women of the PLM may have mimicked men's ideas, in essence, agreeing with the greater cause of the revolution, but many female members performed activities in their own way, often expressing an interstitial feminism—that is, a feminism which intervened subtly as men harangued women to engage in the larger movement.

POETICS OF NATIONALISM

The poetics of history for Hayden White alludes to the making of history, its construction through human consciousness. That consciousness is expressed through the four tropes borrowed from literary criticism. White explains the making of human consciousness as the historical interpretation derived from the tropes to inscribe the narrative.[15] What, then, would the poetics of nationalism be? How do we interpret the making of nationalism?

Rafael Pérez-Torres decodes how the Chicano nation is manifested through Aztlán, the mythic homeland, by the prominent Chicana/o poets of the movement. He offers us a way of traversing Aztlán—both inside and beyond an imaginary nation where poets quite literally invented the nation.[16] The poetics of nationalism, then, refers to the poets who literally and symbolically chiseled the Chicano/a nation—Aztlán. Aztlán is not an empirical space. The Chicano nation has been framed linearly, but

Aztlán, when taken out of the past, becomes a culturally constructed nation written into the present imaginary by poets, historians, and social scientists.

But what was the meaning of nationalism, its poetics, for these leaders of the revolution? And how does that kind of nationalism coincide with the contemporary notions of Chicano nationalism arising from an understanding of Aztlán as homeland? The nationalism of someone in Mexico in 1910 may have been different from the nationalism of Chicanos in the 1960s, yet how much do the ideologies coincide, parallel each other in a kind of poetics of nationalist revolution and tradition? How has the language (discourse) of revolution historically been produced? Moreover, how has the language (discourse) of nationalism historically been produced?

The PLM, according to Gómez-Quiñones, transcended the nationalist principles of Mexico's revolution and instead ascribed to an international workers' movement. Their rhetoric showed an allegiance to anarcho-syndicalism as a worldwide movement. One can argue that during a historical moment when Mexico was changing its bourgeois leaders, the anarchist group entertained a modernist politics, one that would unite the workers of the world. One may even say that this was a harbinger of postcolonial hope for Chicano history. The PLM opened a space for a different kind of nationalism, a transnationalism that moved beyond land, beyond geographic space, beyond the boundaries of Mexican identities. It is as if breaking through borders produced a new kind of political movement, but their notions of feminism still coincided with "modernist" Marxist tenets, as is illustrated in the leaders' writings—that is, the leaders and members who found themselves on the other side of the border beyond Mexico, and beyond the socialist experiment in Yucatán.

RHETORIC OF (INTER)NATIONALIST REVOLUTIONARIES

The PLM, a leftist party with anarchist convictions, began their work in Mexico City in 1900, when Ricardo Flores Magón and his brother Jesús published the first issue of *Regeneración*. In 1904, the central figures of the group—Ricardo Flores Magón, his brother Enrique, Camilo Arriaga, Juan Sarabia, and Santiago de la Hoz—sought refuge in the United States. For six years, the *junta* traveled from Texas, Missouri, Canada, Arizona, and California, publishing *Revolución* intermittently with *Regeneración* while they eluded Pinkerton agents, imprisonment, and Porfirio Díaz's loyalists. By this time Jesús had abandoned the revolutionary cause, and he later betrayed his brothers.[17]

In 1910, amid social and political turmoil, most of the group settled in Los Angeles. Through their newspaper, the PLM reached an audience throughout the Southwest. Its circulation, which rose to 30,000, reflected a growing influence in the Mexican community on both sides of the border. *Regeneración* earned its success in the face of fierce opposition. Often smuggled from the United States into Mexico, the paper sometimes cost those distributed it their lives; among the casualties was a young boy shot by federal soldiers in Mexicali.[18]

To aggravate anti-Mexican sentiments, *Los Angeles Times* owner Harrison Gray Otis encouraged ridiculous cartoons and scathing editorials against the revolutionaries. Otis had purchased land at ten cents an acre from Diaz's government, and he used the daily to protect his Mexican investment. When the *Times* was bombed on 1 October 1910, Otis and his supporters accused labor leaders, leftists, and anarchists of the terrorism. The city was clearly unwilling to welcome the party when the overall sentiment was that Los Angeles already harbored undesirable socialists, anarchists, and militant laborers.[19]

The Mexican government, too, feared the rising militancy of the organization and its newspaper. Initially the anti-Díaz publication had favored reforms for Mexico instead of revolution, but on 3 September 1910, Ricardo Flores Magón declared the party anarchist and announced a radical platform. Influenced by the writings of Pierre Proudhon, Peter Kropotkin, and especially Spanish anarchist Francisco Ferrer Guardia, as well as works by Karl Marx and Frederick Engels, the leading members unfurled their own style of anarcho-syndicalism. Their platform demanded violent revolution, called for workers' rights, and professed equal regard for land and liberty, "Tierra y Libertad."[20] But their idea of land and liberty transcended a nationalism that demanded a Mexico for Mexicans. ("Tierra y Libertad" was the call of the followers of Emiliano Zapata in the southern state of Michoacán.) The Partido Liberal Mexicano called for a worldwide workers' revolution.

In addition, Flores Magón committed the party and the newspaper to frequent discussions of women's social equality. In its first month, *Regeneración* published Ricardo Flores Magón's celebrated essay "A La Mujer."[21] The author confirmed the PLM's commitment to women's issues and, more importantly, delineated the organization's ideology about women. More than any other essay, "A La Mujer" elucidates the PLM's ideological contradictions. Flores Magón's most frequently quoted work illustrates his perceptive yet flawed examination of women's social condition. He begins the essay thus:

> You constitute one-half of the human species and what affects humanity affects you as an integral part of it. If men are slaves, you are too. Bondage does not recognize sex; the infamy that degrades men equally degrades you. You cannot escape the shame of oppression. The same forces which conquer men strangle you.[22]

Flores Magón reflected on women's suffering, linking their social conditions to men's. Warning women of the upcoming battle, he ordered, "Your duty is to help the man; to be there when he suffers; to lighten his sorrow; to laugh and to sing with him when victory smiles."[23]

Noting that prostitution was a crime against women, the philosopher and activist also equated marriage with prostitution. He said:

> When it is motivated by economic security instead of love, marriage is but another form of prostitution. . . . That is, a wife sells her body for food exactly as does a prostitute; this occurs in the majority of marriages. And what could be said of the vast army of women who do not succeed in finding a husband?[24]

Flores Magón's convictions echoed those of most anarchists. Anarchists generally denounced marriage at the same time that they held certain ideas about women's "natural" duties and desires. A leading theoretician of anarchism, Peter Kropotkin, attributed to women an instinctive desire to nurture and to remain in the home. Proudhon and Kropotkin, both of whom influenced the Mexican anarchists, believed in women's instinctive bond to the domestic sphere.[25] Interestingly, precursors of anarchism had held similar views. As early as the thirteenth century in France, the Amalrikites "preached not only a community of goods, but also a community of women." Amalrikite principles surfaced in the sixteenth century in the Zurich Highlands, where men also held "wives and property in common."[26] Influenced by Kropotkin and other philosophers of the era, Flores Magón accepted the home as woman's destined sphere, but he faced a dilemma. He realized the need to expand her duties beyond the private sphere if the revolution was to be won. He ordered, "Demand that your husbands, brothers, fathers, sons, and friends pick up a gun. Spit in the face of those who refuse to pick up a weapon against oppression."[27]

In November, only two months after the publication of "A La Mujer," the Mexican Revolution erupted. After a decade of agitating for revolution and informing the public about Díaz's horrible crimes in Mexico, the PLM found its authority heightened. During the revolution, women's strengths were recognized if not always rewarded. Still more articles asking women to champion the cause appeared in *Regeneración*. The editorial staff wrote most of the essays. The writers included the Flores Magón brothers, Librado Rivera, Antonio I. Villarreal, Anselmo Figueroa, and Praxedis Guerrero. Ethel Duffy Turner, the only woman as well as the only Euroamerican on staff, edited the English section for six months, but did not seem to share the other writers' interest in women's issues. Turner, who adamantly supported the party, often reiterated themes raised in *Barbarous Mexico* by her husband, John Turner. Turner's book, which has been reprinted repeatedly since its initial publication in 1910, revealed slave-like labor conditions in Yucatán and pointed out how plantation owners became wealthy on the blood and sweat of Mexican peasants. His book became a popular treatise for revolutionists who opposed Díaz, since it showed the conditions of the poor as a result of the dictator's policies.[28]

The staff of *Regeneración* printed at least one essay on women, their rights, or their subjugation in almost every issue of the newspaper from its initial publication. The essays do not all require scrutiny, since they echo the maxim in Flores Magón's "A La Mujer." I will provide a few more examples, however, to demonstrate how other leaders of the group followed Flores Magón and the socialists, leftists, and unionists of the era who articulated an international movement of workers, both women and men.

Regeneración published "La Mujer" (The Woman) and "Las Revolucionarias" (Women Revolutionaries) by Praxedis Guerrero, the PLM field commander who died in combat in 1911, during the early years of the revolution. Before its publication, Guerrero delivered "La Mujer" before a Los Angeles audience. It closely resembles Flores Magón's essay in format, content, and ideology. Sketching PLM policy, Guerrero discussed and denounced feminism, a controversial topic in 1910. In his opinion, feminists wanted not to equal men, but to *be* men: "Because she cannot be a woman, she wants to be a man; and in the name of rational feminism she wants to embark upon the ugly duties that are only for men."[29] He pursued this line of reasoning:

> Feminism is the fundamental antagonism to women's emancipation. [Furthermore], there is nothing attractive about a masculine female who is divorced from her sweet mission as a woman; there is nothing desirable about a woman who prefers to be manly instead of womanly.[30]

By making a distinction between feminism and women's emancipation, Guerrero persuaded those who resisted equality between the sexes to accept the party's stance on women. To reinforce his position, and as if to convince more conservative party members, he argued in the last paragraph of "La Mujer,"

> Equality between the sexes will not make men out of women; instead it will enforce equal opportunities without disturbing the natural order between the sexes. Women and men must both fight for this kind of rational equality because without it there will only be tyranny and misery.[31]

Guerrero, like his leftist contemporaries, believed in a "natural" order between women and men. Essentializing women's roles and their duties, the revolutionaries of their epoch defined the natural place for each sex, defying the social construction of gender. Women's behavior was believed to be intrinsic to their sex, biologically determined. It is interesting to note how often women's "sweet mission" was debated by ideologues from the era, whether revolutionaries or defenders of the status quo. Even as far away as Yucatán, the "sweet" nature of women was contemplated by the anti-feminist women who attended the feminist congresses in 1916. As early as 1910, there had already been debates in Yucatán about whether feminism was responsible for creating lesbians. It was as if woman's sweet mission were a universal language that required no definition. (I often wonder how anti-feminist rhetoric has simply slid across decades, to reappear in the late twentieth century to be repeated in the rhetoric of contemporary Chicano nationalists.)

Like Flores Magón, Guerrero summoned women to inspire their husbands, lovers, and sons to join the battle. He concluded "Las Revolucionarias" with the same demand made by Ricardo in "A La Mujer": "Revolutionaries, the day you see us hesitate to fight, spit in our faces."[32]

The two leaders shared a fascination with sexuality, and even used it to condemn members who did not follow party policies. Just as Guerrero had accused the wrong kind of feminists of being "manly," Ricardo made similar kinds of accusations. In an angry commentary, Ricardo denigrated a former party member, accusing him of unnatural and unmanly behavior. Antonio I. Villarreal, an activist and writer who had once shared a prison cell with Flores Magón, abandoned the PLM and enlisted in Francisco Madero's growing army shortly before the wealthy landowner assumed the presidency. Intentionally humiliating Villarreal, the party leader reproached him in an essay, "Que Hable el Maricón" (Let the Faggot/Queer Speak):

> I have made serious charges against Antonio I. Villarreal. I have called him a pederast, an assassin, and many other things, yet he stays so calm. Why doesn't he answer? . . . Silence does not exculpate; and in his case silence accuses him. . . . Everyone knows that he is silent because the accusations ring true. He is not a man but a . . . pederast. Villarreal does not have a right to face any man. Villarreal should be spat upon by every man and woman.[33]

Whether or not Villarreal was a pederast is inconsequential. The essay reeks of ill feelings between a party leader and a former member who had failed his leader. Flores Magón then made incriminating charges debasing Villarreal's masculinity. Even this kind of anarchist, who for the most part sanctioned free and spiritual love, had limitations.

But the PLM, like other leftist organizations that were attempting new social-sexual roles for women and men under a new society, still assigned sex roles to women which were consistent with traditional expectations of women. The larger and better-known Socialist Party and Industrial Workers of the World (IWW) mythologized women in the same way. They glorified working-class heroines, yet commanded them at home and at work. As Socialist Party leader Eugene Debs explained, "If the hand of man is magical with accomplishment, the small white hand of woman has even greater magic in that it soothes and blesses ever."[34] Even the IWW song "Rebel Girl" modeled after labor organizer Elizabeth Gurley Flynn, honored women's courage, yet minimized that courage by insisting that women serve men.[35] Penned by Joe Hill, the martyred troubadour who wrote and sang songs for the IWW and leftist causes, "Rebel Girl" was dedicated to Flynn.[36] The lyrics stressed:

> That's the Rebel Girl, That's the Rebel Girl
> To the working class she's a precious pearl
> She brings courage, Pride and Joy
> To the fighting Rebel Boy. . . . [37]

Flynn was proud of the Joe Hill song, just as she had been proud of Joe Hill. In her own way, however, she intervened with criticism of women's expected household duties.[38]

Female membership in the PLM is impossible to calculate. Equally difficult to estimate are the number of women who read *Regeneración*. But the statistics are not necessary in order to examine the group's expectations or the women's responses to them. Like socialist and anarchist women in the United States, the *magonistas* were trapped between the imaginary rhetoric that declared their freedom and the imagined reality that ignored it. Although they subscribed to worker solidarity as manifested in *Regeneración*, they did not stay at home to do so. The women stretched their functions beyond an alleged natural sphere to join a public one; but even in the public arena, work was categorized by gender. The following examples show central female figures and the problems they faced in the organization. What is most intriguing is how the women responded to the specified gender roles. After having invoked how the ideologues thought and wrote about the women, who in the male party members' eyes were destined to be "nurturing" revolutionaries, I would like to move on to my second point—that despite the men's artificial rhetoric about women's duties, the women themselves practiced interstitial feminism. It is my contention that the women of the PLM, just like the feminists of Yucatán and the women revolutionists of Mexico, expressed a dialectics of doubling in which on the one hand they agreed with the male revolutionaries and their (inter)nationalist cause, but as feminists, on the other hand, they intervened with their particular agenda about what that revolution meant. The following examples trace a genealogy of women's interstitial feminist activities. The *magonistas* included journalists, soldiers, organizers, and companions to the male party members.

THIRD SPACE FEMINIST ACTIVITIES

Two soldiers from Baja California, Margarita Ortega and her daughter, Rosaura Gortari, often smuggled supplies hidden under their skirts to revolutionaries across the border. Gortari died in 1911 while she and her mother were fleeing from Mexican federalists. Two years later, when General Victoriano Huerta's regime gained power after Francisco Madero's assassination, his militia captured, tortured, and murdered Margarita Ortega in Mexicali.[39]

María Talavera and Teresa Arteaga, companions to Ricardo and Enrique, remained PLM loyalists throughout their lives. Arteaga joined the *junta* in 1905 after leaving her home in San Pedro, California.[40] María Talavera, frequently arrested and imprisoned by U.S. federal agents, was harassed not only because of her activities for the revolution, but also because of her intimate involvement with Ricardo Flores Magón. Announcing the dangerous revolutionists on the front page of the 19 September 1907 edition, the *Los Angeles Times* publicized the relationship in an article titled "Murder-Plotting Letters Found on the Mexican Revolutionists." The newspaper printed a front-page story indicting María Talavera as Magón's "accomplice" on the basis of a letter she had smuggled out of jail for him. The article warned that Talavera was a "brilliant and bold woman anarchist who dared more than any of the men."[41] In an illustration that seemed to have been drawn without Talavera's likeness in mind, her face resembled that of a woman whose profile might be carved on a cameo pin. Nothing in the drawing indicated that this was indeed María Talavera. Ricardo's mug shot appeared on the same front page. A caption under a letter written by Ricardo, which connected the images, specified María's willingness to "kill a tyrant" if necessary. The *Times* cited the letter as proof that she was an "expert assassin" who had plotted to kill President Theodore Roosevelt and the dictator Porfirio Díaz.

The love letters from María to Ricardo demonstrate a commitment to Ricardo, the party, and the revolution. She was Ricardo's compañera, but she was also an activist who dared to take risks for the sake of the PLM's vision, a vision she also held. But the *Times* highlighted her role as lover to Ricardo, a dangerous Mexican revolutionist, and it was this relationship that made her capable of being an "expert assassin." The *Times* further described María as "a quiet housewife, intent on cooking *frijoles*. But in her fry pans she was seeing men fighting; hearing in the sizzle of the grease the crash of arms, the pound of horses' feet and the din and commotion of a nation's government overthrown."[42] Interestingly, María was depicted as a housewife and assassin in the same breath, her dual roles in the revolution. María did, in fact, risk her life for the party. Ethel Duffy Turner recalled that while she and María Talavera were visiting Ricardo in a Los Angeles jail, "María picked up a paper from the floor of the jail cell where

Ricardo dropped it. The paper had plans for the 1908 revolution. María sent it to the border, but it was captured."[43] Federal agents retrieved the scheme, and the *Times* circulated it on the front page of the paper.

In 1914, Talavera, along with Ricardo, Enrique, and Teresa, settled on a communal farm near Los Angeles. Although they lived there only until 1916 with other members, the group practiced their ideals for the first time. Women and men shared field work but not housework, and as the men generated articles for *Regeneración*, the female members cooked, cleaned, and rolled newspapers for distribution.[44] When they moved to the commune, the editorial staff temporarily halted the newspaper's publication because they lacked funding. To help the journal, the PLM chapter Luz y Vida (Light and Life) organized fundraisers. Exclusively a women's chapter, Luz y Vida was founded in Los Angeles in November 1915 by María Juárez, Micaela Grijalva, Elisa Martinez, Carmen Mendrano, and Benita and Carmen Talavera. The women, believing that they had a responsibility to the revolution, agreed to serve it. The chapter planned benefits and dances, at which they sold "tamales, refrescos, and sandwiches," then donated the proceeds to *Regeneración*.[45]

THIRD SPACE FEMINIST ESSAYS

During the revolution, essays appeared in *Regeneración* that reaffirmed the PLM's intent to politicize women. Articles written by women and men who shared similar views on women's issues include "La Mujer Obrera Bajo el Burgués" (The Working-Class Woman under the Bourgeoisie) by Antonio de Pio; "La Mujer Esclava" (The Woman Slave) by René Chaughl; "Que Luchen" (Let Them Fight) by Paula Carmona de Flores Magón; "La Mujer Pide Guerra" (Women Demand War) by Antonio I. Villarreal; and "Para Ti, Mujer" (For You, Woman) by Blanca de Moncaleano.[46] The essays by women are critical because they demonstrate how a few women were affected by—and in turn transformed—the Party's ideology while writing their own rhetoric. The female journalists associated with the organization included writers living in Mexico, Texas, and California. Teresa and Andrea Villarreal wrote for their own newspaper in San Antonio; Blanca de Moncaleano and Paula Carmona de Flores Magón wrote for the Los Angeles group. Juana Gutiérrez de Mendoza, Elisa Acuña y Rosetti, and Sara Estela Ramírez were writers involved with the early *junta*. Sara Estela, who died at the age of twenty-nine, taught in Laredo, Texas, where she met Ricardo and Enrique. Accompanied by Juana, Elisa, and other supporters, the brothers crossed the border for the first time and stayed with Sara Estela.

In Laredo, the women grew disillusioned with the group's bickering; the discontent caused Juana and Elisa to return to Guanajuato, where they resumed publication of their own newspaper, *Vesper*. The two women also joined Emiliano Zapata's agrarian movement. Unforgiving of what they saw as disloyalty, the *junta* spread slanderous rumors to discredit Juana and Elisa, alluding to their reputations as improper women. Ricardo Flores Magón and other PLM members accused the women of being "indignant women—one of whom abandoned her husband and the other engaged in obscene practices frequently." "Obscene practices" meant that a woman was more than likely an autonomous female, something even the most radical of male anarchists would not tolerate, it seems. A party member from southern Mexico squelched the lies in a letter to Ricardo and reminded him that both Juana Gutiérrez de Mendoza and Elisa Acuña y Rosetti were valuable and influential revolutionaries in Mexico.[47]

In their essays, the women took a different approach from the men's and disputed, although implicitly, the PLM's ideology on women. Through their active feminist agenda, the female journalists conveyed a doubling—that is, an explicit agreement with the male leaders—when as feminists they endorsed an (inter)nationalist revolution, but by advocating their own agenda, the women wrote and spoke third space feminism. In "Que Luchen," for instance, Paula Carmona de Flores Magón, Enrique's former wife, expressed her own expectations of women, expectations that seemingly mimicked the men's:

> Comrades, Mexican mothers: Push your husbands to fight. . . . We should all fight, men and women. Many times a woman is at fault when a man abstains from taking part in the great struggles for liberty, but she too is degraded along with men. Slavery does not dignify us, nor does misery improve our status.[48]

Teresa and Andrea Villarreal responded identically to Flores Magón's and Guerrero's messages to women when they summoned men to revolt. In the headlines of *Regeneración* they asked, "Que Hacéis Aquí Hombres?" (Men, What Are You Doing Here?) and then ordered, "Go, go to Mexico to conquer for us and for our children: LAND AND LIBERTY."[49] And of themselves, the Villarreal sisters announced, "We are women; but we are not so weak that we will abandon the struggle. . . . We have the right to demand strength from those who hesitate to fight."[50] Besieging men, the Villarreals emphasized women's strengths over their weaknesses, perhaps as a way of intimidating and coercing reluctant revolutionaries.

Based in San Antonio, Texas, the journalists published *El Obrero* (The Worker) and *La Mujer Moderna* (The Modern Woman), edited by Teresa and Andrea, respectively. In the "combat" newspapers they embraced the party's fundamental tent—international worker solidarity.[51] Originally from Coahuila, the sisters fled to Texas, avoiding persecution by Porfirio Díaz. Their denunciation of Díaz led to Teresa's mistaken kidnapping and arrest in Mexico. Releasing her almost immediately, Mexican officials reported that they had intended to capture Andrea, the more outspoken of the two sisters. Andrea's rebellious speeches fueled her reputation. She, however, protested her notoriety: "It is not good to call me the Mexican Joan of Arc because I cannot go to Mexico on a horse at the head of my soldiers and I cannot fire a gun, my hands are too small."[52]

Blanca de Moncaleano, a journalist from Mexico, ardently supported both the revolution and women's rights. Her articles exhibited a formidable feminist stance, one that none of the male writers on the staff had ever expressed. Formerly a journalist for *Tierra*, a leftist weekly published in Mexico, she had arrived in the United States after her husband, PLM member Juan Moncaleano, pleaded with the readers of *Regeneración* for donations to bring Blanca and their children from Mexico to Los Angeles.[53] Blanca de Moncaleano published her first essays for *Regeneración* in 1913. In an article printed that same year, she criticized women's subjugation in the family: "Do not forget that a woman has rights equal to those of a man. She is not on this earth only to procreate, to wash dishes, and to wash clothes."[54] By acknowledging and naming women's confinement in the family, de Moncaleano intervened with a feminism that spoke to the social conditions that the male leaders such as Flores Magón and Guerrero accepted as natural for women. Both leaders expected women to encourage men to join the battle. In their minds it was women's duty—their "feminine" duty—to coddle men, nurture them, and dare them into becoming revolutionaries. Blanca de Moncaleano, by contrast, ordered women from their prescribed functions entirely.

De Moncaleano also inspired mothers in "Para Ti, Mujer" to send their children to *La Escuela Racionalista*, located in La Casa del Obrero Internacional (The International Workers' Home). Along with her husband, Juan, an educator from Colombia, Blanca promoted the home they helped to establish in Los Angeles in 1913, shortly after she arrived in the city from Mexico. The International Workers' Home, which reflected the internationalist spirit of the party, became the PLM headquarters. At the school, instructors lectured party members' daughters against the "bonds of female slavery" and its sons against the "fetters of imperialist wars."[55] The school itself mirrored the principles developed by the Catalán anarchist Francisco Ferrer Guardia, who argued that education was the key to emancipation of the working class. La Casa del Obrero Mundial (The Home of the Workers of the World), the anarchist headquarters in Mexico City, followed Ferrer Guardia's doctrine and served as a model for the home in Los Angeles.

Juan Moncaleano was instrumental in founding La Casa del Obrero Mundial in Mexico City and the newspaper *Luz* in Monterrey. Essays in *Luz* supported the PLM and glorified Ferrer Guardia. The newspaper was similar to *Regeneración* in format and ideology.[56] Numerous anarchist and socialist newspapers were published throughout Mexico at this time, indicating an internationalist perspective on the part of revolutionaries who were not just promoting a nationalist Mexican Revolution. Some of the newspapers included *Tribuna Roja, Trabajo, Aurora Social, Nueva Solidaridad Obrera,* and *Avanté.* All reflected views on women's liberation similar to those held by the PLM male leaders who wrote for *Regeneración.*[57]

La Casa del Obrero Internacional (The International Workers' Home) was located at 809 Yale Street, near Alpine in downtown Los Angeles. It had formerly been the Los Angeles Orphans' Home, housing orphans in the city as early as 1880, when the social programs of the Progressive era began to make their way to the West Coast from Chicago and New York. Upon hearing about the group who had taken over the home, the *Los Angeles Times,* exhibiting its usual anti-Mexican sentiments, sensationalized in March of 1913 that "Mexican Revolutionists Establish Armed Camp in Los Angeles."[58] The armed camp, however, was nothing more than a spacious house where workers and their children could seek free lodging, cultural activities, and lectures. An application submitted to the Department of Buildings in March 1914 shows that the house was subdivided into thirteen two- and three-room apartments to accommodate the growing number of inhabitants.[59] The Workers' Home in Los Angeles is a testimony to the party's internationalist commitment.

Blanca's feminism may have challenged *Regeneración*'s audience, but so did other women's issues pertinent during the era. Birth control, for example, was the topic of an article published in 1917, shortly before the newspaper's demise. The essay showed that the Partido Liberal Mexicano may have been modifying its ideology, but only to a small degree. Its author summarized:

> While a social and economic redemption cannot be expected from the practice of birth control, the annihilation of the pernicious and brutish idea that a woman is not the sole owner of her body, to do with it as she pleases, is refreshing enough while we are on our way to bigger things.[60]

Interestingly, the author, who may have been male or female, focused upon a woman as the owner of her body, an idea as radical in 1917 as it seems to be today.

From 1910 to 1918, *Regeneración* echoed images about women that encouraged the formation of revolutionary, internationalist identities for these early Chicanas. One of many leftist journals that endorsed specific gender roles, this weekly is an excellent vehicle for analyzing gender and the manner in which nationalist ideas became internationalist; yet women still intervened with their own thesis about the revolution while mimicking men's rhetoric. Unlike other controversial newspapers, this one endured for two decades. And in spite of the social upheaval, *Regeneración* retained most of its original editorial staff. Ricardo Flores Magón, the Partido Liberal Mexicano's guiding visionary, sustained his romantic ideals about the revolution and contemplated gains for working men and women—not only in Mexico, not only in Texas or California, but throughout the world as he envisioned a transnational movement. Both the U.S. and Mexican governments considered Flores Magón an international threat until he died in Fort Leavenworth in 1922. Ricardo was serving a twenty-one-year sentence for violating the Espionage Act, which targeted those who were members of anarchist, socialist, and communist organizations. Choke marks on his throat led many to believe that he had been strangled in his Kansas jail cell.[61]

For all their radicalism, the PLM's male leaders did not move entirely beyond their traditional views of women as nurturers. The men's nationalism seemed to be in sync with that of the Mexican revolutionaries of Mexico; however, the PLM expressed an internationalist nationalism. The women, however, were caught between the imaginary and the real. Were they to ascribe to imagined "natural" rights as the nurturers of male revolutionists, or were they to ignore the reality that compelled them to join men on the battlefields? Women such as María Talavera seized Ricardo's plans for revolution from his jail cell, while mother and daughter, Margarita Ortega and Rosaura Gortari, were murdered for their PLM activities. These activists personify the doubling of duties. The PLM women intervened interstitially, seemingly broadening the party's platform to fit their own agenda. They pleased their male party leaders, and they engaged in revolutionary activities as they saw fit.

REPETITION OF RHETORIC

Finally, the "official" Chicano movement of the 1960s and 1970s, like the Mexican Revolution, spoke to women—but only on certain terms, as exemplified in the male rhetoric and in men's expectations; "real" activities on the part of two of the early women activists, Juana Mendoza and Elisa Rosetti, caused controversy because they defied the male leaders' agenda.

Gómez-Quiñones invoked the PLM to identify implicitly ideologues who impressed Chicano movement leaders. Like Flores Magón, the historian envisioned a transnational Chicano/a movement, one that would travel beyond the borders of Aztlán, one that would call for alliances of workers, both women and men, beyond the United States, beyond Mexico, into the world of workers. Gómez-Quiñones was aware that Flores Magón had jettisoned his nationalist stance after 1910, when he left Mexico, and realized that an international workers' movement would be the paramount goal for the PLM. What did this mean for women, for women's rights? As we have witnessed, women, too, had a duty to follow an internationalist philosophy that joined all the workers of the world. Women had to tread the space between the rhetoric and their activities. Women such as Blanca Moncaleano asserted a caustic critique against ideologues who tethered female revolutionists to housework as their assigned duty to the "nation" and its revolution. For Moncaleano, the home was not the place where revolution would transform anything, much less gender roles. Housework did not connote revolutionary activity.

By resurrecting the PLM, Gómez-Quiñones, himself a radical leader of the Chicano movement of the 1960s and 1970s, put forth an oppositional history. His commitment to telling the story, to narrating the PLM's internationalist nationalism, was a significant historical move, one that has been noted but overlooked for its intent. That is, the PLM, more than any other organization during the Mexican Revolution, was in many ways mimicked by the leadership of the Chicano movement of the 1960s and 1970s. Posters of Emiliano Zapata and Ché Guevara decorated the homes of college Mechistas, and "Tierra y Libertad," also the slogan of Zapata, reflected the revolution's vision, a vision of the past now imaged for contemporary Chicano leaders. Ricardo Flores Magón repeatedly voiced the words "Land and Liberty." As Pérez-Torres reminded us about Aztlán, a land that was once tangible becomes an intangible, imaginary, mobile space for contemporary Chicano/a nationalists. Can we argue, perhaps, that the PLM, with an internationalist perspective, began to enunciate an imaginary "land and liberty" for all the workers of the world? Or was land only a geographic, spatial category that could not be questioned until the modern social movements of the 1960s and 1970s began to be challenged? Gómez-Quiñones himself was caught between modernist and postmodernist perspectives, where a decolonial imaginary best explains the history of past leaders and intellectuals. He elected to valorize a modernist moment and its radical leaders—the Mexican Revolution and the anarchists of the Partido Liberal Mexicano—yet by doing so, he brought them into the present, where the colonial imaginary may exist as a backdrop to our writing of history, but the decolonialist project forces an intervention.

To bring this further into the dilemmas of the late twentieth century, since history is about the present, to quote Foucault and White once again, a repetition of rhetoric also haunts contemporary Chicano/a movements. It is intriguing how often the rhetoric of the Mexican Revolution and the leftist organizations of the early twentieth century is reiterated by the "radicals" of the 1990s. I am referring to an anonymous southern California group that published a newsletter under the name *Regeneración*. Almost word for word, the author of an essay enunciates the rhetoric that was spoken by Ricardo Flores Magón and his cohorts. Homophobia, antifeminism, women's natural role in the home—all are set forth in the 1993 essay. It is almost as if the dialectics of history has failed us. Is it any wonder that revolution remains a dream and postmodern revolt is our next summons? In yet another publication, *La Verdad* by Unión del Barrio, which also appeared in 1993, the collective of authors critique Chicana feminism, "women's, gay, or Lesbian rights," as "nothing but another form of white power."[62] Remember, Praxedis Guerrero in his essay on "La Mujer" denounces feminism as a bourgeois notion whereby women act "masculine" to negate the "natural order" between the sexes. The collective, anonymous group arguing against Chicana feminism as the divisive factor that will only hurt the nationalism of the 1990s, not unlike Guerrero and his notion of revolution, further expound:

> Any valid response to the mistreatment of Chicanas/Mexicanas must be rooted in the understanding that the end of oppression of Chicanas/Mexicanas can only be brought around through national liberation.[63]

Again, the rhetoric of "nationalism" is condoned as the all-encompassing answer to all oppression—racial, sexual, psychic, and any other differences will be overcome through a commitment to utopian nationalism, the modernist fantasy.

> Once we have concretely placed nationalism as the guiding force within the Chicano/Mexicano movement, we will then begin to develop the means to challenge sexism and all other forms of exploitation as we march to free Aztlán.[64]

The last paragraph borrows its rhetoric from the socialists, anarchists, unionists, and revolutionists of the early twentieth century who were convinced that a class-based movement must place gender, race, sexuality, and any other differences on the back burner while moving on to more important issues. Interesting, though, is that while the Mexican Revolution had its "nationalist" paradigm to take it into the twentieth century, Flores Magón was attempting an "internationalist" worker movement. Again, class took precedence, gendered issues became less significant, but the idea of internationalism was probably Flores Magón's most revolutionary premise—but one that was buried in the rhetoric of nationalism.

To free Aztlán, to identify Aztlán, to pose this as the political project of contemporary Chicano nationalists in all their masculinist rhetoric, whether women or men are speaking from a masculinist position, is unimportant. Masculinist rhetoric is not practiced solely by men, after all. What does this mean, then, for the making of nationalism, its poetics? Who or what is being served and/or serviced? At the same time, is there a third space feminism practiced by women (and men) of contemporary nationalism? I would argue yes, and therein lies the challenge. Feminist activists intervene with this doubling and its dialectics. Patriarchal nationalism has permitted only one kind of in-between intervention. By definition, nationalism defies difference, hence feminism. Nationalism must be patriarchal in all its modernist trappings, yet third space feminist practice within a decolonial imaginary will deconstruct a masculinist trap.

The Partido Liberal Mexicano fit a modernist paradigm of binarisms in which evil was identified rationally and simply—the bourgeoisie who resisted revolution. Good was also easily named—the workers of the world in an international movement who united to overthrow evil capitalists. The 1960s, while following the rhetoric of Marxist, socialist, and anarchist philosophers of the early twentieth century, would reassert modernism's simplicities, but complexities abounded. I will address some of the complexities in my last chapter, on the technologies of sex, desire, gender, and identities; but in the next chapter, I want to illustrate how the immediate post-revolution era transformed the identities of Chicanas/Mexicanas in Texas during the 1920s and 1930s, a new immigrant generation which was not so new. Mexican immigrants fused culturally with Tejanas and even became Tejanas along with those who had been in Texas for many, many generations. The process of "tejanaization" paralleled the anarchist and socialist movements just outlined—perhaps not as vehemently, but with its own rhetoric and style.

Chapter 4

TEJANAS

DIASPORIC SUBJECTIVITIES AND POST-REVOLUTION IDENTITIES

¿Acaso no se parace tu tejido a la vida de tu madre?
Todo está conformado por arroz y cadenas; puntos al
derecho, puntos al revés, bastas, nudos . . . Arroz
cuando se casara; cadenas en su matrimonio; nudos
en la garganta. Puntos al derecho para ella y puntos
al revés para ti y para tu padre. Basta. No, en esta
vuelta no hay bastas, sólo puntos al revés como los
tuyos. . . . Puros puntos al revés en esta vuelta . . .,
puros puntos al revés.

—Rosina Conde, "Arroz y cadenas" (1994)

I did not deny history, but held in suspense the general empty category of change in order to reveal
transformations at different levels; I reject a uniform
model of temporalization, in order to describe. . . .

—Michel Foucault, *The Archaeology of Knowledge*
(1972)

THIRD SPACE FEMINISM: THE DECOLONIAL PROJECT

History, although it is studied and written diachronically, then exemplified in grids, is not necessarily a documentation of progress through
time. Perhaps all that progresses is our notion of time, Western time, which
moves in grids and categories, ordered with names of eras and epochs. The
hands of a clock move in circles, completing cycles, not unlike Maya beliefs
of time as cyclical. But we are confined by and to Western time, Western
space; the dialectic of the future has condemned us to believe in progress

simply because technology, like fool's gold, assures us that we must be moving ahead, and quickly at that. The narrator in Rosina Conde's short story says that often there are only "puntos al revés," a moving backwards where progress is defied and movement is repeated, and words are spoken again and again with no hope for resolution. The repetition of struggles, of oppression, seems endless, as if never to gain movement forward into another future, one where change would be hopeful or better. Perhaps all one can really hope for is survival.

Estela Gómez's story is one of movement. She traveled across a spatio-temporal border to arrive in Houston on 1 April 1920, when she was about eight years old. She left behind a home in the rural village of Piotillo in San Luís Potosí, a home that had been ransacked repeatedly by *federales.* When her father was taken to the plaza to be executed in front of a firing squad for withholding his support from the government agents, the young girl joined her two sisters at the plaza early the next morning to plead for his life. Having barely survived, Melesio Gómez accepted a contract for a job with the Southern Pacific Railroad, just as many men like him had done. Within a year, he sent for his wife and daughters. Like many other Mexican male workers recruited by the Southern Pacific Railroad, Melesio Gómez was offered an opportunity for progress. In fact, the Gómez family earned prominence in early Houston when Señor Gómez opened the first tortilla factory and the first Mexican restaurant in what would become the Mexican business district of Houston in the 1920s. This was an era of prosperity throughout the country, and Houston's Mexican American community was as much a part of that prosperity as immigrants in eastern or midwestern urban centers. Both the tortilla factory and the restaurant proved to be such a success that when his three daughters grew up, they all opened businesses. But before then, when Estela was a teenager, she helped to organize a young women's social club, el Club Feminino Cha-pultepec, and it was in this organization that she would learn about racism in the United States, about the struggle to survive in a place where she and others like her forged modern identities of survival.[1]

The revolution was the impulse that compelled Estela Gómez's father to abandon his home in Mexico. Work may have been the incentive that permitted the ease of movement from San Luís Potosí to Texas, but community organizations became the source of cultural survival for the Mexican diaspora. Organizations were practically transplanted from Mexico to the United States. Liberal Clubs, which had served as anti-Díaz groups in the early years, were replaced by social and cultural groups that took on regenerated functions in the new homeland. The clubs and organizations served as a strategic means of survival for the diasporic who came and subsequently changed "the history of a nation."[2] The young Mexican American women who organized clubs were themselves transformed in their efforts to assist their communities. Their parents, escaping the carnage of the revolution, had brought them across the border to live, to work, and above all to survive.

Were these organizations spaces where women expressed third space feminism? How much did diasporic subjectivity shape women's post-revolution identities as they participated in club activity? In this chapter, I address the discursive formation of women's identities by pursuing the diasporic as an avenue that may elucidate identities within specific diasporic cultures.[3] As Mexican women became immersed in U.S. culture, they also transfigured an unfamiliar homeland with Mexican language, habits, and customs brought from Mexico, or already dispersed in a region formerly Indian and Spanish-Mexican. Diasporas have a long history in the region of Texas. Some Native Americans may have been indigenous to the land, like the Tejas tribe, while others traveled through and around what became Texas, from the Comanches to the Apaches, who roamed the land for centuries before their near-extinction, and certainly before the land shifted beneath them.[4] Women and men from the northern states of Mexico became the new diaspora after a revolution that forced many families to abandon their homes. Everyone seemed to enter a diasporic configuration in a land where coloniality foisted yet another identity upon migrant populations. A kind of colonial diaspora emerged, created by colonial relations historically inherited in the Southwest. In other words, populations dispersed through a land named, renamed, bordered, mea-sured, mapped, and fenced to restrict more movement, whether dictated by Spanish colonialists, Mexicans, or Euroamericans—all have mapped and demarcated with artificial lines land where travel persists through time.[5] Identity itself transforms as diasporas weave through historical moments. The unmarked identities of the diasporic become ordered and categorized according to the named and renamed geographic spaces on which they travel.[6]

I am being tentative in a precarious, loose application of diaspora. I am not adhering to a strict definition. I can already hear objections to my experimentation as applied to Chicana/o histories. But I am not dismiss-ing noteworthy interpretations of history by way of borderland or immi-gration studies.[7] We cannot dismiss borderland studies, especially if we consider how borders and diasporas fuse spatially as borders themselves move with populations on the go, taking with them cultural expressions thought to exist only on a distinct geographic border. James Clifford's essay "Diasporas" argues that border and diaspora overlap and therefore "bleed into each other."[8] While I agree with Clifford, I do not propose that we replace border and borderland studies or immigrant studies with diaspora studies, but instead suggest that an analysis of the diasporic may elicit different questions concerning the identities of these travelers/migrants. I toss into the debate "diaspora" to interrogate "immigrant," a concept that has meaningful historical junctures for European immigrants who are mostly of white, assimilable, ethnicities.[9] Again, I would not dismiss immigration studies for Mexicans; rather, I augment the analysis with "diasporic subjectivities" to implement a subjectivity sensitive to gender and race. Both remain unmarked under the category "immigrant."

A diasporic subjectivity may differ from "immigrant" in a number of ways. For one, "race" may not be so easily erased from diaspora. Diasporic subjectivity would not deny the culture of race, but instead would open a space where people of color—in this case, Chicanos/as—could negotiate a raced culture within many kinds of identities without racial erasure through assimilation, accommodation, adaptation, acculturation, or even resistance—all of which have been robbed of their decolonial oppositional subjectivity under the rubric of immigrant. The colonial imaginary imprints Chicano history when the category immigrant remains the privileged signifier. Immigrants are expected to become part of the dominant culture; they are urged to adopt its habits and forget their own—to erase. Diasporas, on the other hand, intervene, construct newness, and "live inside with a difference."[10] The decolonial imaginary would call upon these complex diasporic subjectivities that live the many differences.

The diasporic subject reminds us that Aztlán, the mythic homeland, shifts and moves beneath and around us. The mythic homeland is longed for, constructed, and rewritten through collective memories. Time is traversed, and a mythic past entwines with a future where a decolonized imaginary has possibilities. If diaspora, loosely defined, is a "history of dispersal coupled with myths and memories of a homeland," where "alienation in the host country" often fosters a "desire for eventual return" while a collective memory reconstructs the alienated group's history, whether real or imagined, then Chicanos/as are appropriately diasporic.[11]

The culture of an imagined nation such as Aztlán is not a linear, horizontal thing that can be traced through time, its movement and lineage tracked from the old world to the new.[12] And yet Mexican "immigrant" culture has been theorized in this way. Its dispersal, its travel, is often impossible to trail. If nation is conceptualized as "dissemination"[13]—that is, traveling and shifting through time and place, dispersing culture across time and space—then Chicanos/as take their "nation" with them beyond the Southwest and throughout the United States to invent Chicano/a nations as they disperse. Origins are, therefore, refutable. Mexican immigration studies erase a diasporic pre-twentieth-century past and target Mexico to imply a single temporal-spatial origin, forgetting mixed-race Chicanas/os, and forgetting Chicanas/os with Indian ancestors from the mythic region of Aztlán, or from the "real" region of the Southwest.[14] Immigration, therefore, is not only a move from the old world, Mexico, to the new, the U.S.; if one dares to examine pre-twentieth-century movements of people traveling, dispersing through regions with no political borders, then one also begins to think about nation and culture in different ways. The "imagined community" of Aztlán was initially given an "essentialist identity," but if it is rethought as traveling culture, then its identity depends upon its social construction, in which memory and forgetting are as much a part of the history as the myth.[15] As Stuart Hall posits, "diaspora identities are those which are constantly producing and reproducing themselves anew, through transformation and difference."[16] Although seemingly adaptive, diaspora's transformative mobility is in actuality its most creative oppositional function. Unlike adaptive immigrants, transformative diasporic subjects travel and "live inside with a difference." In the difference is the diasporic subject's mobility through and about, weaving interstitially, to create, always create, something else, whether music, food, clothes, style, or language.[17] The diasporic ushers in an adaptability as only one of many ways to keep moving, to keep weaving through power, to grasp and re-create culture, to re-create oneself through and with diasporic communities. The diasporic subject is not only here and there, is not only Mexican or American, or Mexican American, or even Chicano/a, but more, much more, is always re-creating the unimagined, the unknown, where mobile third space identities thrive, and where the decolonial imaginary gleans the diasporic's subjecthood.

The nation, its culture, has been historicized and conceptualized linearly—as if time itself moves without the past always already encoding the present. As historians, our project is to decolonize the writing of history to create a decolonial imaginary of the future. But why use diaspora, then? For me, the Mexican immigrant has been staged as the twentieth-century modernist man or woman seeking a cure, and the cure was to assimilate into dominant culture, but history has shown that race has precluded the Mexican immigrant from assimilating. Racism experienced by the tejanas of Houston created its own diasporic culture through social and cultural club activities. And what is dominant culture? It has become as dispersed as the populations that have disrupted its purity, but even at the turn of the century, southern and eastern European immigrant populations, along with Asian and Mexican, so muddied the purity of northern European immigrants who named themselves "nativists," believing they were the only real Americans, that these "old" immigrants also forgot their own mixing, or mestizaje. Diasporic subjectivity is always in movement, disrupting, re-creating, and mobile in its representation, converging the past with the present for a new future.

If we consider the production of knowledge that has constructed Chicana history, then how have women fit into the categories of "immigrant" and "Mexican American" generations? For the most part, male immigrant experiences have been written in such a way that they seem to be the normative experience, thus denying and negating women's experiences and their difference. "Diasporic experiences are always gendered,"[18] whereas universalizing immigrant experiences for Mexicans and Mexican

Americans leaves gender unnamed. The categories of "immigrant" and "Mexican American" generations have been posited by Chicano historians who argue that the Mexican Revolution brought Mexicans who still wanted to preserve "lo Mexicano," but by the late 1930s and into the 1940s, the community no longer looked southward but began to look north, toward the United States, as home for its survival and success.[19] Women's clubs and social activities seemed to indicate that they initially looked south to Mexico, and then the next generation, born in the U.S., turned their eyes north to succeed in North American institutions. Learning English, going to business college to learn secretarial skills, running one's own business, entering professional occupations such as nursing and teaching—all required attending North American institutions, and therefore learning skills to survive and succeed. Whether women entered an American generation willingly or from necessity is not as important as how they intervened and how they re-created themselves through diasporic subjectivities. At the same time, not all Mexican women were recent immigrants; some were part of a diaspora who had traveled the region of Texas-Coahuila for centuries before the Mexico–U.S. political border of 1848.

ASSIMILATION: THE TOOL OF THE COLONIAL IMAGINARY (SOCIAL HISTORY OF THE OTHER AS THE SAME)

"The time for 'assimilating' minorities to holistic and organic notions of cultural value has passed. The very language of cultural community needs to be rethought from a postcolonial perspective," claims Homi Bhabha.[20] In the same vein, James Clifford has duly noted that "the new immigrations of non-European peoples of color disrupt linear assimilationist narratives"[21] where racial exclusion makes assimilation difficult, impossible, and often undesirable.

What does assimilation mean in cultural and socioeconomic terms? Can one argue for assimilation or acculturation as definitive and teleological? Isn't there a weaving between cultures, between worlds, between borders? Is there ever a complete process of assimilation? In a capitalist patriarchal society, is it really assimilation that is desired, expected, and striven for from the bottom? Critically assessing assimilation is important, because as historians we have inherited its use. Historians, having written extensively on the topic through the decades, have theorized Eurocentric perspectives about racial/ethnic minorities assimilating into a mainstream dominant society.[22]

In his study on Houston, Arnoldo De León writes about the "internal dynamics" of that city's Mexican American community as it underwent a process of Americanization over the decades. He argues that "patterns of oppression" may explain Mexicans' adaptation to U.S. culture.[23] That is the point of departure in my work. Agreeing with Bhabha's postcolonial perspective—a way of perceiving, seeing, grasping silences and interstitial communities—I too believe that Chicano/a communities must be rethought beyond the limits of assimilation, beyond the hopes of cultural adaptation, and instead reinscribed with an agency that is, like Chéla Sandoval's differential consciousness, at once oppositional and transformative.[24] In this case, I am proposing that diasporic subjectivity is the oppositional and transformative identity that allowed these women to weave through the power of cultures, to infuse and be infused, to create and re-create newness. The argument that Euroamerican, white dominant culture is the alternative opted for by Mexicans, who will haplessly enter that dominant cultural terrain only to be Mexican once in a while—on cultural holidays such as cinco de mayo and on occasional visits to a Spanish-speaking grandmother—is an intriguing modernist argument in which bicultural binarism rules the arrangement. Historian Mario García argues that Americanization of Mexicans was too slow in the 1920s to be of any consequence, and that the same was true of the 1930s. He calls those decades the Mexican generation. World War II then ushered in an Americanization of Mexicans never before witnessed in the United States; hence the Mexican American generation was born. Other Chicano historians have followed García's lead in documenting racism.[25] In the end, many seem to say that some form of assimilation is inevitable—a generational inevitability. It will happen.

Few have probed how assimilation may be a tactic, an interstitial move for survival. Why must we call upon assimilation at all? Why not examine this population for its diasporic character: Leaving home because the socioeconomic conditions there force migration, thus traveling to a host country/region that may offer some economic and political reprieve, but at the same time racism and discrimination, compels these new cultural survivors to be as creative as possible as they move through power. Choices were few for women in an urban settlement such as Houston, where big business took priority over the worker, whether female or male. I would like to posit that women's activities, their spoken words, have been overdetermined as assimilationist even when scholars have detected opposition and resistance. Yet these women may have been using what was available to them to intervene with their own tactics as diasporic subjects claiming survival. To say yes to speaking English, to say yes to an American education, to say yes to participation in organizations such as the YWCA—these were interstitial moves for survival. The contradictions women faced compelled them to accept existing structures and to create their subjecthood within those structures. Moreover, women did not live comfortably within a patriarchal order, whether in the old country or the new.[26]

Other historians have asked, "What path does acculturation take?"[27] Again, I think that women alter the historiographic debate. Vicki Ruiz persuasively demonstrates how the daughters of Mexican immigrants adopted new cultural forms while also "blend[ing] the old and the new, fashioning new expectations, making choices, and learning to live with those choices."[28] To (en)gender history, as I have argued in the first chapter of this book, means to transfigure questions that have been assumed to be universal. The issues differ, perhaps because women, whether working-class or middle-income, are merely adjusting to another patriarchy. Statistically, the majority of women were not assimilating into the institutions of dominant culture; that would have been a luxury and a privilege. Instead, they were working in the factories of Houston or in the fields of the surrounding rural areas during the first decades of the twentieth century. And statistically, the majority of daughters were working alongside their mothers in factories and fields, attending school only during the off-season. As soon as they were older and able to work full-time to supplement the family's income, the young girls quit school. Professional and proprietorial women, along with semi-skilled clerical workers, were the minority in Houston from 1900 to 1940.[29] It is possible to discern an assimilationist voice from Mexican American women if one is looking to name their strategy for survival assimilation. I am not.

The voice of an emerging middle class was not the single voice of the community. Conflict coexisted. Contradictions arose. Race wars, gender wars, class wars—all were characteristic of diasporic communities in the early-twentieth-century United States. The Great Depression of the 1930s had its detrimental effects upon an already poor community. How did women survive those years? How did they feed themselves and their families? Yet even the emerging middle class voiced anger in a country that made its fortune through racist practices. I will discuss some of those women who were members of social and cultural clubs in Houston.

Because so little has been written about the Mexican American community of Houston, especially the Mexican American female population, I would like to give a brief background of the Euroamerican settlement before I move on.

BACKGROUND TO TEXAS

Houston was officially settled in 1836 by Euroamericans who had migrated from the East, but initially most of its population came from southern states. Southerners looking for fresh land on which to grow cotton moved to Texas, bringing enslaved African Americans with them. Despite protests from northern legislators, Texas became a slave state. But even before the region became a territory of the United States, Mexico passed a colonization law in 1824 to encourage foreigners to settle in the sparsely populated area, hoping it would serve as the buffer between

Mexico and the U.S. In one decade, the colonization law attracted as many as 30,000 Euroamericans, who greatly outnumbered the small population of 5,000 Mexicans in the northern Mexican region. The new immigrants, resentful of Mexican laws and governance, wanted to break with Mexico. The war of 1836, most famous for the battles of the Alamo and San Jacinto, won Texas its independence, thus forming the Republic of Texas for the next decade. It was then that Mexicans were compelled to learn to coexist with a population that disparaged them.[30]

While most Tejanos lived in rural areas and in Spanish-Mexican settlements such as San Antonio throughout the nineteenth century, rural Tejanos moved into urban areas such as Houston in the early twentieth century. Houston became industrialized in the early twentieth century with the discovery of oil, with the rise of the textile industry (cotton cloth), with the emergence of railroad lines such as the Southern Pacific, and with the construction of Houston's port. The Mexican population was lured into Houston, where men worked in the railroad yards and women worked in the textile industry.[31]

In 1910, the Mexican Revolution caused a population explosion on the U.S side of the border. Mexicans from the northern states of Coahuila, Nuevo Leon, and San Luís Potosí arrived in droves in a region that had been a U.S. state for only half a century. According to U.S. immigration statistics, 18,691 Mexican entered the U.S. in 1910, and by 1920 the number had risen to 52,361.[32] In Houston, the Mexican population numbered only 500 in 1900, while Euroamericans numbered more than 40,000. By 1910 the Mexican population rose to 1,000, but by the time the violent phase of the Mexican Revolution came to a close in 1920, 6,000 Mexicans lived in the predominantly Euroamerican city. By 1930 the population had more than doubled, with 15,000 Mexicans living in Houston.[33]

The character of Houston's Mexican community did not develop until the late twenties and thirties precisely because the population did not reach a significant size until then. Even at that time there was no single Mexican barrio, but instead a number of areas where Mexicans could be found. While the early business district was located near downtown on Congress and Franklin, the Mexican population was located near there and spread out as far east as Magnolia Park, a subdivision of Houston.[34]

TEJANA/O IDENTITIES:
"TO LIVE INSIDE WITH A DIFFERENCE"

Staying within their social class was important to Mexicans who arrived in Houston shortly after the Mexican Revolution. Maria Villagomez pointed out the cultural differences between Mexicans in Magnolia Park, located in outer Houston, and the tejanos in the Second Ward, an inner-city neighborhood. The tejanos spoke a "slang version of Spanish." "Most of those people were from here"—meaning, of course, that tejanos were born in the United States, in Texas, many in Houston: "Tejanos, as we used to call them." She further implied, "We were a different people from the people in the Second Ward; now this is just in my mind," Villagomez qualified. "And they were different, their ways were different, their language was different. We were Mexicanos, you see, so there's quite a difference. A tejano will have a lot of corruption in the language; they will say, for example, 'boyla' for 'boiler.'" Her brother, Rafael, agreed, providing another example of how tejanos constructed their own language. "They called a railroad 'el traque.' That offended us because that wasn't the right way to say it." Qualifying his remarks, perhaps to illustrate that he had no intention of offending the more native tejanos, Mr. Villagomez remarked, "They were people." Maria Villagomez, agreeing with her brother and speaking in retrospect, claimed, "I suspect that we did have a tendency to look down on the tejanos. I think so, because we thought we knew better."[35] The Villagomez family emigrated from Morelia, Michoacan, in April 1918. Both sister and brother maintained that the revolution claimed jobs and left Mexico's people impoverished.

A social life beyond one's own neighborhood was not common. While the tejanos of the Second Ward attended "El Teatro Azteca," located in their inner-city neighborhood, the Mexicanos from Magnolia Park often stayed in their own district, feeling uncomfortable among tejanos.[36] The Houston city directories indicate that the population that was referred to as tejano by the incoming Mexicans had lived in that part of town for only a decade or so.

THIRD SPACE PERFORMATIVE ACTS

Women's social and recreational clubs carved their identities in the post-revolution Southwest. Women came together in these organizations to plan dances, balls, dinners, and a variety of entertainments that brought Mexican families together outside the home. Two prominent clubs exclusively for young women were the Club Femenino Chapultepec and the Club Terpsicore.

Club Femenino Chapultepec

In 1931, less than twenty Mexican American women gathered under the auspices of the Young Women's Christian Association in Houston to formally organize a club.[37] It was to be the first organization of its kind exclusively for young Mexican American women. The Club Femenino Chapultepec, as the women named it, had been meeting informally since 1928.[38] It originated as an athletic, recreational, and social organization, but in time it would come to serve other purposes.[39]

The YWCA offered the club a meeting spot and helped to recruit women from the community.[40] Estela Gómez (also known as Stella Quintenella), the secretary, said, "We wanted to show the Anglo American community that we could be good Americans, not just Mexican girls."[41] Frustrated because they had tried to rent halls downtown for their dances and were refused by the white owners, the "girls" decided it was time to address the hostility. As members of the YWCA, they held dances, meetings, and other functions in the YWCA building. But as attendance at their dances increased, and because they wanted to stay until 1:00 A.M., after the YWCA's closing hours, the club decided it was time to rent other ballrooms. The YWCA sponsors agreed that they could do so as long as they did not use the YWCA's name in connection with the club.

The group again faced difficulties when the white owners of ballrooms would not rent to them. In the minds of most of the Euroamericans of Houston, Mexicans did nothing but get drunk, have knife fights, and cause trouble. English-language newspapers such as the Houston *Chronicle* and Houston *Post* reported news about Mexicans only when knifings, murders, and criminal acts were committed, and since most Euroamericans did not read Spanish, they did not know that the Mexicans in the community were not all criminals; the vast majority were upstanding citizens who wanted to sponsor their own social activities.[42]

Some of these young women were daughters of the diaspora who had crossed the border with their parents during the Mexican Revolution. Others, however, had been born in Texas, or had migrated long before the revolution. The club's name, Chapultepec, still looked southward, honoring the historic castle and avenue in Mexico City where the "niños héroes" had plunged to their death in defense of Mexico against the U.S. invaders in 1847. The young women had also considered calling the club Azteca; both names acknowledged a tie to Mexico. Estela Gómez commented, "We wanted to keep our own culture, not lose it."[43] The members even debated whether to hold meetings in English or in Spanish, but loyalty to both Mexico and the United States encouraged them to speak both languages. They decided that they would conduct the meetings in English one week, Spanish the next, in an effort to sustain their bilingualism.[44]

Establishing a social club in the United States and giving it a Mexican name seems a bicultural act. When Estela Gómez said "We wanted to keep our own culture," she apparently invoked all things Mexican, "lo mexicano." But in taking from "lo mexicano" to name a social and cultural club, Chapultepec, in the United States, were these women merely transplanting the old to the new? Or were they re-creating, reassigning much more? A third space intervention, perhaps?

The club comprised the following members: Esther Andrews, Josephine Andrews, Magdalena Andrews, Margaret Andrews, Emilia Bell, Pura Castillo, Carmen Cortez (who would later become president of League of United Latin American Citizens [LULAC] Council #22),[45] Anita Davis, Henrietta Davis, Lupe Dominguez, Matilde Guerrero, Cuca Guevara, Eugenia Guevara, Estela Gómez, Rosie Mendizabal, Esther Pascoe,

Mrs. Mary Pascoe, Eva Pérez, Mary Ramirez, Delfina Ramirez, and Mrs. Olivia Ypiña. Any member who missed four meetings was dismissed from the club. At least five members were expelled for this reason. But young women continued to join throughout 1932, and the membership grew to at least twenty-seven, including Mamie Olivares, Lucia Morales, Lucia Juarez, Marie Fernandez, Carmen Garza, Evangelina Ramos, Santos Habitud, Bertha Medina, Mamie Olivares, and Esther Luna.[46]

Once a week, promptly at 7:30 in the evening, the young women met at the YWCA. They called roll, and when necessary elected members to the offices of president, secretary, treasurer, and reporter. Business discussed included when to hold fundraisers, as well as the possibility of staging plays for their community and family. By 8:00 P.M. they were dressed and ready for gym.[47]

By 1932, a year after its inception, the club was still holding business meetings, electing officers by ballot, and discussing plans to earn funds; the members had unanimously agreed to pay dues of twenty-five cents a month.[48] The group also continued to discuss campaigns to recruit members and to raise more money. The fundraisers were usually suppers at which the Mexican American community could gather and socialize; families met and became friends through these club socials.[49] The members also organized art exhibits, and the club once sponsored the 16th of September celebration, because it was the only organization during the Depression with the funds needed to stage the festivities in Houston.

Members were recruited by word of mouth, and they were usually high school graduates. Every year the club sent invitations to the upcoming graduating class, encouraging them to join. As younger groups of single women joined each year, the women's ages diversified. While members who married were not automatically excluded from the club, they often left, because marriage brought with it demands that single women had not had to meet. Some of them moved out of the inner city, making it difficult to attend meetings at the downtown YWCA.[50]

Every Mother's Day, the members would invite their mothers to the YWCA. In addition, the Mexican consul often spoke to the young women at the club's invitation. One member recalled that they wanted to demonstrate to the public that "there were Mexican girls at the Y planning their own activities."[51]

THE CONTROVERSIAL "LETTER FROM CHAPULTEPEC"

Six years after the members had begun meeting and raising funds through dances and dinners, they decided it was time to do something of importance for their community. They wrote a letter entitled "Letter from Chapultepec," which seemed harmless enough at the time. Stella Quintenella (Estela Gómez)[52] and treasurer Carmen Cortez drafted the controversial document.[53] In it, the group stated that it was time to address Anglo racism against the Mexican community. They outlined ten separate points, in which they elucidated the problems as they saw them in Texas:

1. Texas is next door to Mexico and there are border town problems to be considered, historically as well as present.

Texas history is founded on troubles, oft created by Texas, to get land and cattle from the Mexican people. [N]ow the problem of stolen automobiles is causing the same problem and also the water power of the Rio Grande River is causing hard feelings.

2. Texas cannot, due to the Chamber of Commerce and patriotic society activities, forget that Texas lost a tragic battle at the [A]lamo in San Antonio and won a battle at San Jacinto. This causes teachers to preach a patriotism not kind to Mexican children. Mexicans have been known to stay out of school [in Houston] when that part of history was being taught because of abuses inflicted by pupils and even teachers.

3. Mexicans in [a] desire to get ahead have at times denied their nationality calling themselves French, Italian, and Spanish. This induces the Mexican colony's disfavor. Nationalistic spirit [is] being cultured at present [and] this of course can be as dangerous an attitude as the denial [of] one.

If they should move back to Mexico they are considered traitors for having lived in Texas.

4. They do not take out citizenship papers because those who have are still called Mexicans and treated as such.

5. The Mexican people find it impossible to rent or buy in any decent section of town and are forced to live in dirty crowded conditions in houses out of which Americans have moved.

6. Playgrounds and parks show distinct distaste to their presence on them and in some cases they are ordered off or forbidden on. This problem is caused by the youth and not the recreation leaders.

7. Falsely accused of many crimes in the city and because of some difficulty with the English language they are taken advantage of frequently.

8. Mexican people are paid less in wages on all jobs and a great many jobs and industries are closed to them.

9. Mexican lawyers receive no respect from other lawyers nor even from our judges. It is a well known fact that a case is practically lost if a Mexican lawyer handles it. Justice is very one-sided, and they have had some rather serious cases recently.

10. They are called "brown people," "greasers," et cetera and of course want to be called white.[54]

The letter was signed by Stella Quintenella, Carmen Cortez, and Olive Lewis, an Anglo woman who served as sponsor to the club at the YWCA.

In the letter, its authors argued that Mexican girls and women in Texas faced these problems of racial discrimination despite the fact that "they were American citizens," and many in their group came from "an excellent cross section of the Mexican colony in Houston." They also stated that there were "many high school graduates in the group and of course every year more Mexicans are staying in school until graduation"; they noted that dropout rates were declining, if only minimally. They added, "Minority groups elsewhere in the United States face some, though not all of the same problems."[55]

The letter was addressed to Miss Leona B. Hendrix of Kansas City, Missouri, probably the representative of the National Business and Professional Girls Council there.[56] Dated 11 June 1937, it was published only a week after two Anglo policemen had been acquitted in a murder case against a Mexican man, Elpidio Cortez.[57] Perhaps responding to this case, and certainly to many other cases in which Mexicans were brutalized, the club was anxious for social change in a racist Houston where Anglo and Mexican relations were particularly strained during the Depression. Gómez, Cortez, and their supporting members agreed to publish the final draft of the "Letter from Chapultepec" in the *Negro YWCA* newsletter.

Despite its reasonable tone, the letter caused considerable controversy. Olive Lewis, who had sent the document to the newsletter, was fired as a result, and was forbidden to contact the club. The members never heard from her again. Mrs. Rocco, their new sponsor, was expected to guide the young women, and in so doing to discourage them from contesting racism in Houston again.[58]

The secretary who had helped draft the letter, Estela Gómez (Stella Quintenella), soon received the first of many visits from the FBI, who questioned her activities. Houston in 1931, like the rest of the country, had just undergone the "Red Scare" of the 1920s, an anti-communist sentiment that targeted new immigrants from eastern and southern Europe. The city was also hostile to Mexican women and men who were willing to claim American status. Even when women such as these attempted to voice their concern against a racist society, they were silenced with harassment. But these women were neither silent nor powerless.

A document such as the "Letter from Chapultepec" is a gem for a Chicana historian and for scholars who study women of color—women who are so well hidden from history. Documents are rare and difficult to find, either because they were not recorded or because archivists have not actively sought materials by women of color. When we do find evidence of women's activities, it is often overlooked. The additional significance of this letter is that through its ten points, it reveals the racial construction of systems of thought in a city that was becoming populated with "unwanted" Mexicans.

The social unrest resulting from the Depression would soon be forgotten as World War II approached. The war gave rise to widespread blind patriotism, while many others were afraid to criticize the government for fear of being targeted as communists. The "Red Scare" of the 1920s lingered into the Depression era, even though the bottom had fallen out of a once-prosperous society that had promised so much to its incoming immigrants. The women of Club Chapultepec were censored after the letter's publication. Although they wanted to address the kinds of problems posed in their letter, they also wanted to continue drawing correlations between the plight of Mexicans in the Southwest and the social conditions of people in Latin American countries. Mrs. Rocco advised them against speaking negatively.[59] At a youth conference, the "letter" itself was accused of having communist sentiments, thus implicating the members, especially those who had drafted it.[60]

Estela Gómez Reyes continued to be harassed by the FBI until 1942. She reported that in 1937, two men who identified themselves as FBI agents began to visit her at her store, the Mexican Spice and Curio Shop. They refused to tell her why they were keeping her under surveillance, but they proceeded to interrogate her about her religion, her belief in God, the schools she had attended, her friends, the organizations to which she belonged, and the literature and newspapers she read. Gómez assumed that the letter had prompted the visits. Frightened, she told no one about the FBI, but she later realized that her neighbors had also been questioned. A woman who worked in Melesio Gómez's tortilla factory asked Estela if indeed she was a communist. It seemed that even the employees at her father's factory had been interrogated. Estela recalled that the FBI never asked her if she was a communist, but their frequent visits and questions kept her fearful for years. In 1937 they descended upon her store at least four times. After that year, they paid a call twice a year, often parking their car across the street from her curio shop. Gómez claimed that she never discussed the visits with any of the club members, fearing repercussions from the agents.[61]

The censoring, however, was not limited to the FBI. Members of Estela Gómez's own community attempted to silence her. When she was invited to speak before *La Federación de Sociedades Mexicanas y Latinas Americanas de Texas* in Galveston in August 1941, a year when she was still being watched by the FBI, she consented. Founded in 1938, the FSMLA brought together Mexicans and "Latin American" citizens to discuss discriminatory practices directed against them in Texas. The organization worked closely with the Mexican consul, Luis L. Duplán,[62] who made an effort to meet the differing needs of both Mexican-born immigrants and Mexican Americans from Texas.[63] It is ironic that the consul who encouraged delegates to offer solutions to community problems, particularly racism, was the same one who would suppress Estela Gómez Reyes.

As a representative of Club Femenino Chapultepec, Gómez had been asked to give a speech about "Mexican problems." Aware of the "Letter from Chapultepec" published four years before the conference, the FSMLA was impressed with the social work the club members had done. By ferreting out racism in schools, on playgrounds, and in neighborhoods that would not rent to Mexicans, the women of Club Chapultepec had targeted the most serious of problems for the Mexican American, Mexican, and Latino communities of Texas. A group of Mexican consuls from Corpus Christi, San Antonio, and Houston attended the August 1941 meeting. The more prominent social and recreational clubs in attendance were Club Mexico Bello and LULAC, as well as religious assemblies. With two hundred people in the auditorium, Gómez was prepared to read a speech she had written in Spanish, which expanded on the "Letter from Chapultepec." But just as she was to begin her presentation, she was approached by Duplán, who advised her not to give the speech. In his mind, her list of grievances might be interpreted as anti-American, thus possibly causing subsequent problems with the U.S. government.[64]

Just a year before, Duplán had announced in a statement to the Houston *Chronicle*, "In some parts of Texas they [Mexicans] are being discriminated against. We are going to try to solve this problem and [achieve] better conditions for Mexicans and Latin Americans in Texas."[65] In the speech she had planned to present, Gómez reiterated Duplán's sentiments and asserted that it was time to take measures to resolve the community's justified complaints. She proposed that an "Abogado-Consultor" (Attorney-Counselor) be named in Houston to "protect and defend" Mexicans of the city. Houston, she argued, was a city of "great commercial and industrial importance," and yet Mexicans were useful there only as exploited workers.[66] Gómez criticized a wealthy urban region that had done little to advance economic conditions for Mexican workers and yet had built much of its wealth on their sweat. Two particular points in her declaration stressed workers' rights in Texas: She promoted legal services to help fight for equal salaries for workers, salaries that would conform to the Texas law; and she noted that Mexicans should not be excluded from office jobs usually reserved for the Anglo community.[67] In the conclusion to her speech, she proposed that hers was an effort to fight for the rights of Mexican nationals and Mexicans born in the United States.[68]

Why Gómez's words were considered disloyal and too radical to present before the delegation in Galveston is unclear. Her own statements were no more extreme than those of Duplán, who had himself criticized the social, political, and working conditions of Mexicans in Texas.

Gómez responded to Duplán's censorship by vindicating herself. Despite harassment from the FBI, she believed she had not betrayed her new country. Prepared to speak before the FSMLA delegates, she finally felt unafraid. She defended her statements exposing the injustices against Mexicans and Mexican Americans in Texas.[69] But being silenced by her own community was indeed a disappointment. In many ways, Estela

Gómez was not unlike Mexican feminist Hermila Galindo, who negotiated within a male-centered nationalist moment to voice her own concerns. Gómez may not have been arguing for feminist propositions, but her intervention was a woman's voice, from a women's club concerned about the limitations of a society in which they all lived—a racist Houston where discriminatory practices against Mexicans and Mexican Americans were common.

Club Femenino Chapultepec survived about four more years after the Galveston meeting. The war interrupted future meetings, and many of the members married and moved away. During the war, however, those who remained sold war bonds on Main Street in Houston. One of the club members was credited with having sold more war bonds than any other girl in the Business Girls' Department.

By 1944 Gómez had stopped attending meetings, and in 1945 the group dissolved. Since its first meetings in 1928 and its inauguration in 1931, Club Chapultepec had maintained a cultural enclave for the Mexican American community. In many ways, the group brought the community together by holding dances and enchilada dinners, sponsoring the *fiestas patrias*, and even confronting racism in Houston and Texas. But like so many clubs that somehow managed to provide a semblance of unity during the Depression decade in Houston, this one too fell apart during World War II. Other organizations took its place. A prominent one which was revived after the war was the women's auxiliary to the men's group Club Mexico Bello. But there was another women's organization which did not serve as auxiliary to a men's group. Club Terpsicore was an unusually exclusive, almost elite club for upstanding high school women from Houston's rising middle-class families.

CLUB TERPSICORE

El Club Terpsicore was created in 1937 by some young women who had recently graduated from high school. Like Club Chapultepec, Club Terpsicore functioned originally as a social club where these young Mexican American women could ally with other women like themselves. One of the founding members, Catalina Sandoval, explained that they were primarily a dance club, meeting to organize dances in the Mexican community. "Now in the '30s and '40s, this is very important because in Houston, there were no places like clubs or bars as we know them today. So if the community wanted to go to a dance, they had to wait until one of these organizations held one in a local hotel or room that they rented."[70] Club Terpsicore served this purpose by sponsoring exquisite dance formals. By invitation only, they often were held at the lavish Rice Hotel and featured well-known Mexican orchestras. Although not wealthy, these young women's families were striving lower-middle-income families. The club maintained an exclusivity by allowing only thirteen members. And not just anyone could join. A prospective member had to wait until one of the thirteen resigned. The remaining members took applications and discussed the candidate's credentials. The young woman's family and how she was perceived by her peers determined membership.

One would not think that such an exclusive club would have existed in Houston during the Depression years, but these young women clearly were expressing pride in their Mexican American heritage by organizing and joining Club Terpsicore. The club, in a sense, was a kind of interstitial survival mechanism whereby emphasizing social standing in the United States perhaps opened doors usually closed to Mexican Americans in Houston society of the 1930s. Sandoval herself remembered that after she and her family arrived in the United States from Aguascalientes in 1927, they experienced racial discrimination. In school, for example, they were the only Mexicans, and "at that time there was a lot of discrimination; we were beat up and harassed."[71] In her own way, Sandoval constructed an identity for survival when she told her schoolmates that she was an Aztec princess. She claimed that she and her family had fled people in Mexico who wanted Moctezuma's treasure. It seemed that the family knew where this treasure was. After she told the story, no one in the school yard harassed her again. In fact, Sandoval was later crowned a princess in the May Day parade, the first Mexican American to hold that honor.[72]

Like Club Chapultepec, Club Terpsicore ended during the war. In keeping with its philanthropic goals, the members raised money through their dances and donated it to hospitals for beds.[73] But more important, the club was a way for these young women and their families to create and re-create cultural identities through social functions such as exclusive dances in extravagant hotels usually reserved for the Euroamerican community. It was as if these rising middle-class Mexican Americans ignored any racist obstacles and decided to construct their own cultural organizations, which helped them to feel proud of their race and their community. They were indeed weaving oppositional and transformative identities in a new home where they had decided to make themselves welcome despite racial and socioeconomic barriers.

CLUB PAN-AMERICANO DE LA YWCA

The Pan American of the YWCA was established around 1919, earlier than any of the other Mexican American clubs in Houston. The coalition of Euroamerican women and Mexican American women who had been expressly recruited by Euroamericans was located at the YWCA on Rusk Avenue and functioned, like Club Chapultepec, under the auspices of the YWCA. Antoneta Rivas recalled that her mother had been active at the YWCA and therefore encouraged her daughter to join the association, which sponsored parties, dances, teas, picnics, and socials to gather community members.[74] The members—Stella Holt, Bernice Bates, Peggy Aldridge (her mother was Mexican American and her father was Euroamerican), Olga Pérez (Ripley when married), Antoneta Rivas,[75] and Elvira Luna (Mrs. Fernando Salas)[76]—were all around eighteen years old and from the north side of Houston.[77] Many of the young women stayed in the organization until they married, then promptly dropped out.[78]

In the early twentieth century, the Pan American attempted to improve relations between the Anglo and Mexican communities, perhaps believing that social events would produce good neighbors. At the teas, "girls dressed in clothes from other countries and invited consuls."[79] At the formal dances held by Club Mexico Bello, the president of that club would honor the president of the Pan American by inviting her to begin the march that kicked off the event. Then each member of Mexico Bello would select a member of the Pan American for the celebrated march. As president in 1935, Antoneta Rivas marched that year in the formal event, which brought together the men from Club Mexico Bello and the women from Club Pan-Americano.[80]

The Pan American did not have a booming membership. While the members of Club Terpsicore reasoned that their lucky number was thirteen, the Pan American was small because of a lack of interest. Why did so few women join an organization that helped promote Anglo–Mexican relations in Houston? This may have been a testimony to the strained relations between Euroamericans and Mexicans in the city during the early decades of the twentieth century. Yet even though Mexicans and Mexican Americans were not enthusiastically joining clubs and organizations with Euroamericans, the diasporic subjects were certainly interested in re-creating their own cultural enclaves in the United States.

Maintaining social standing for the newly arrived diaspora seemed to be the purpose of many of the clubs. Clubs that were not as popular included Club Mitla, a theater group for both women and men that operated out of Rusk Settlement. The members, marshaled by Josefina Rosales Ypiña, Rivas's mother, were active as early as the 1920s.[81] Los Machetes Pandos, also a social club exclusively for Mexican immigrants, sustained a nostalgia for their homeland and reclaimed spaces for their activities.[82] Members included both women and men, who wore a pin made of a machete with a ribbon of red, green, and white for the Mexican flag. It was customary for members from the men's clubs to marry young women from the women's clubs, and "they tried to recruit from that same social level."[83] In other words, the clubs recruited Mexican immigrants from a higher social class than the tejanos, Mexican Americans born in Texas who were often poor and could not speak Spanish well. "We always tried to stay within our own social class," recalled Mrs. Rivas, who affirmed the seriousness of speaking correct Spanish. Having emigrated to the United States from Mexico in 1918 when she was five years old, her parents impressed upon her the greatness of Mexico, its culture and language. Her father had insisted that the family speak only in Spanish when they ate dinner together. As a result, Rivas learned to speak proficiently in Spanish and English.

CLUB FEMENINO MEXICO BELLO

The first club of the 1920s to add a women's auxiliary was Club Mexico Bello, the oldest of the social and cultural fellowships of Houston. Created in 1924, the men's club was composed of young Mexican American men who agreed that their newly arrived community must celebrate Mexican holidays such as el cinco de mayo (the fifth of May) and el 16 de septiembre (the sixteenth of September).[84] Other activities included playing baseball, performing musicals, and holding dances. The club was famous for its black and white dance balls, which were exclusive formal dances held in Houston's most prestigious hotels.

The women's auxiliary, however, was not established until 1936, more than a decade after the men's club was founded. The early organizers of the auxiliary were Mrs. Crespo, Olivia Ypiña, and Mrs. Gustavo Ypiña, who had been a member of Club Chapultepec in her teen years. Mrs. Fernanado Salas, Elvira Luna, was also a member of the auxiliary. During the Depression, Club Mexico Bello lost members, like so many other groups. No one could afford the monthly one dollar dues. When the women's auxiliary began marshaling support in the midst of economic hardship, the men's club felt an incentive to reemerge, but the Depression was unrelenting, and most members could not meet the dues. During World War II, ten members were active in the men's club, and the women's auxiliary all but disbanded. After the war ended, entrepreneur Félix Morales phoned one of the original members, Isidro García, in hopes of reorganizing the Club. "Yo te ayudo con lo que sea" (I'll help with whatever you may need), Morales told Isidro, to which Isidro responded, "Sí Félix, una cosa es ayudar y otra cosa es hacerlo" (Yes, Félix; it's one thing to help, and another to do).[85] Morales proceeded to take on the challenge, announcing the reorganization of the men's club on his radio station, KLVL, the only Spanish-language station in Houston.[86] When the men's club regrouped, the women's auxiliary also came back to life, but not until the 1950s, when postwar prosperity transformed the lives of so many.

Club Femenino Mexico Bello may have not scrutinized racism in Houston as Club Chapultepec did, but the women's auxiliary still represented a quest for cultural survival in a city hostile to Mexicans and Mexican Americans. Club Mexico Bello was its very own imagined community in a new country where Mexicans were fusing a variety of cultural elements from their homeland and their new home.

LADIES' LULAC

In May 1935, the first women's auxiliary to the League of United Latin American Citizens was constituted. LULAC itself had been founded in Corpus Christi, Texas, in 1929. The league represented rising middle-class Mexican Americans in Texas who sought to battle racism and any discrimination against Mexican Americans. Fundamentally, they also wanted to improve educational opportunities for their children. The league believed that reforms would rectify any injustices that people of Latin American descent might suffer in the United States. Certainly, most had faith in the capitalist socioeconomy, and they had no intention of fomenting revolution. The league did not support strikes, marches, or protests.[87] In Houston, LULAC Council #60 was chartered in November 1934, a late date considering that LULAC chapters had existed for years in south Texas and San Antonio. Historian Arnoldo De León argues that because Mexicans did not settle in Houston until the twenties, entrepreneurial and professional associations did not appear until the 1930s. The Mexicans and Mexican Americans who provided services such as neighborhood stores, community pharmacies, and local restaurants did not become prominent in the city until the mid-1930s. They were the group most likely to become LULAC members.[88]

Six months after LULAC Council #60 was chartered, the women's auxiliary began outlining plans for the Ladies' LULAC Council #22. Not officially activated until the 1950s (with former Club Feminino Chapultepec member Carmen Cortez as its president), Ladies' LULAC #22 owed its inception to Houston's first women's auxiliary to the league.[89]

SOCIEDAD MUTUALISTA OBRERA MEXICANA

One of the founders of the women's auxiliary to the mutual aid society Sociedad Mutualista Obrera Mexicana, established in the mid-1930s, was an influential Mexican American woman, Angie Morales. In 1932, she moved with her husband, Félix Morales, from San Antonio to Houston. The couple opened the first Mexican American funeral home in the city, a nine-room house with two chapels and a reception room, at 2701 Navigation Boulevard. Angie Morales could claim the unique distinction of being the first woman in the city of Houston to become a certified embalmer. In an oral interview, Morales explained that she would persuade the Mexican community to utilize her services by telling them, "If your mother dies, I'm the only lady embalmer in Houston, so no man has to touch her." "And that was a good selling point," she proudly concluded.[90]

The Depression, Angie Morales said, prevented the community from burying their dead. The expense was simply too much. In 1935, Morales estimated that funeral costs ranged from $18.50 to $75.00, depending upon the casket.[91] To alleviate the burden, the county allocated funds to any funeral home that bid low enough for a contract to bury indigents in the city. The Moraleses bid such a low price—ten dollars to be exact—that they won the contract. By building their own caskets and sewing burial clothes, the husband-wife team began a lucrative business in an industry that had not been open to any other Mexican Americans. The Moraleses knew that winning the county contract would mean that they could now bury Anglos, formerly impossible in a racist Houston. But the contract was not won easily. According to Morales, the editor to the *Houston Press* wrote a column protesting that the county had awarded Mexicans a government contract, but the county commissioner and the county judge had to turn the contract over to the lowest bidder.

> They couldn't find anything against us . . . even though they didn't want to give it to a Mexican. . . . We were citizens. We were born here, and they called us Mexicans because they wanted to call everybody Mexican, but we were really Americans born in the United States. I've never been a hyphenated Mexican. I'm an American.[92]

The Sociedad Mutualista Obrera Mexicana, however, provided the funds for burials of the Mexican American community, a community that did not want to be buried in the county graveyard, Powder's Field, with Anglo indigents. Angie Morales remembered that if a family did not have money, they were allowed to dig a grave in the county graveyard, but "Mexican people didn't want Powder's Field; they were leery of it."[93] The mutual aid society stepped in to help "people who could not afford to bury their dead."[94] During the Depression, La Sociedad's Mexican American community pooled their financial resources and acted as a bank by lending and giving money to needy society members.

Angie Morales, who had been instrumental in creating the society's women's auxiliary, publicly expressed her discontent with La Sociedad. The male members of the mutual aid society had voted to have one of the men be present at each of the women's auxiliary meetings. Morales, angry at their distrust, remarked,

> The men did not trust the ladies too well. They always had to have a man at all of our meetings. It used to irk me because sometimes we wanted to discuss things and we did not want men there, but they were always there as sort of watchdogs, to see that we performed right, I guess. But this time, the man there said that our group was so small that we had to be under them, and that day he was talking about our small group, we had ninety members present. And their group hadn't had but about thirty or forty present. I told him that I thought our group had to send a woman to their smaller group.[95]

This self-affirming quote, by the same woman who exclaimed that she had "never been a hyphenated Mexican," spoke to women who willingly separated from men's agendas to make their own. Even though theirs was a women's auxiliary to a men's organization, Angie Morales recognized that they were not just comadres meeting to gossip; rather, they were Mexican American women congregating to deliberate upon their own convictions in their own way.

LA CRUZ AZUL MEXICANA

La Cruz Azul Mexicana, the Mexican Blue Cross, was a volunteer organization that provided medical care to the Mexican community on the U.S. side of the border. La Cruz Azul was often the only source of medical attention for the Mexican diaspora throughout the Southwest. Active in Los Angeles, the organization assisted many families in the 1920s, particularly during the Depression, when medical attention was difficult to obtain. Women volunteered to visit barrio residents who could not afford a doctor, but the volunteers found themselves making house calls especially to those who feared deportation in the 1930s. One of many chapters in the Southwest, the Mexican Blue Cross was affiliated with the national association based in Mexico.[96]

In the 1920s, when Houston's Mexican population was rapidly multiplying, La Cruz Azul had already established an office in the Mexican consulate. A young woman who had emigrated with her family from Aguascalientes in 1918 volunteered for La Cruz Azul a few years after their arrival, contributing her time to the association throughout the 1920s. Josefina Rosales Ypiña, eager to serve her community in the United States, was of a generation that re-created and seemingly duplicated Mexican organizations in the U.S. In La Cruz Azul, however, her duties included encouraging clients to learn English. She also visited homes to teach Mexican women how to diaper and bathe their babies while instructing housewives how to maintain sanitary conditions in their homes.[97] A major concern of the new country was the cleanliness of its potential citizens. The Mexican Blue Cross, perhaps on behalf of the Mexican consulate, seemed to be preparing Mexicans for the cultural and social values of the United States.

I have focused my attention on this rising middle class, however small, whose clubs and societies took an interest in the working women and men of the Southwest. Confronting racism, battling discrimination, affirming cultural pride through social activities—all were vital to these young Mexican American women, just as protests or marches against low wages, long working hours, and exploitative conditions in fields and factories were crucial. Certainly, LULAC was against protests of any kind in accepting reforms for social change. In many ways the women's clubs were no different. The only club that brazenly impugned widespread, violent racism in the United States, Club Femenino Chapultepec, was promptly censored not only by the Euroamerican community but also by its own Mexican community, which feared retribution from the United States government.

These groups may not have been the majority population in Houston, but they were indeed an emerging middle class, a class determined that they and their children would gain access to more privileges in North America. I found that most Mexican and Mexican American women in the 1920s and 1930s worked in the factories and fields of Texas. They usually did not have the time to affiliate with clubs or societies. Most were busy eking out a living, often as migrating farm workers. Texas's history of economic exploitation kept women from moving far and fast up the occupational ladder.

This chapter focused on the smaller population of women, some of whom were from the middle class, who worked for social change in different arenas. Many were very young women who organized cultural activities as second-generation teenagers; many came from working-class origins; others were middle class. Certainly, Club Femenino Chapultepec, with its small membership, incited concern when its members assembled to write a letter that unabashedly confronted racism in Texas, and especially in Houston. LULAC, on the other hand, would become one of the most powerful organizations in Texas and counted among its members women who would become influential leaders.[98]

That women commingled and designed associations similar to the clubs and societies in Mexico for their cultural survival in a hostile new home seems apparent. It also seems reasonable that they, like their husbands, brothers, and uncles who invented and imagined organizations such as Club Mexico Bello for men in the 1920s, were also re-creating little Mexicos in the Southwest—little Mexicos cross-pollinated with cultural differences, whether tejana/o, or whether Mexicans from a higher social class who spoke "proper Spanish," or whether already American and not "hyphenated Mexicans." Did women only mimic categories reduced to immigrant and Mexican American generations? Or was their effort to survive a strategy of interstitial weavings through varying power bases by this colonized diaspora? I argue that it was. Racism, along with gender discrimination, precluded any opportune movement up hierarchical ladders. What precisely was the movement forward into a better life for the colonized diaspora? How much was their movement only a repetition of an old familiar struggle, whether immigrants, Mexican Americans, or diasporic subjects traveling in old and new terrain? For how many women was movement only "puros puntos al revés," a movement without progress inside the United States? How much were these diasporic subjects merely weaving the old with the new for cultural survival?

Part Three

GENEALOGY:

HISTORY'S IMPRINTS UPON
THE COLONIAL BODY

Chapter 5

BEYOND THE NATION'S MATERNAL BODIES

TECHNOLOGIES OF DECOLONIAL DESIRE

Interpretation blandly begins with what we can happen upon just about anywhere, Freud tells us, but it
also reveals in the present time and in every day life
the most bizarre conclusions. History is a form of this
"uncanniness."

—Michel de Certeau, *The Writing of History* (1988)

[T]he personal desire and the sexual and proprietorial instincts must be those of men, who are then the
term of reference for desire, sexuality, property.

—Teresa de Lauretis, *Alice Doesn't: Feminism, Semiotics, and Cinema* (1984)

In this chapter, I expand my argument about the power of sexuality and
how its discourse circumscribes historical studies. Elsewhere I articulated
and named genders, sexualities, queers, and any other differences that
constitute our communities.[1] Here I offer a genealogical exposition of
specific cultural bodies, pleasures, and desires. Genealogy as a method
thematizes the body, power, and social institutions where fictive truths
and values are enacted upon the body.

Through the juxtaposition of four cultural bodies—La Malinche, the
translator for and alleged lover of Cortés in sixteenth-century Mexico;
Silent Tongue, an Indian woman, the fictional character in a film by the
same name; Delgadina, the object of desire in a popular corrido that
forecasts bleak consequences for women if they do not embrace patriarchy
and femininity; and Selena, the slain Tex-Mex singer who exhibited a
particular Chicana feminist agency—something of India/Mestiza/Chi-
cana desires and their technologies may be discerned. All four cultural

bodies can show that when they are read from a third space feminist perspective, an analytical shift is made. The shift unveils women's desires through their own agency. Feminists have remade La Malinche into an agent of her own desires, and not just Cortés's whore. Perhaps a diachronic leap from La Malinche in 1519 to Silent Tongue in 1873 as each other's cultural double can help us trace the technologies by which power often molds desire. I suggest that Silent Tongue is a modern, nineteenth-century Malinche set against the backdrop of the Euroamerican "West." I will also consider the relevance of the colonial primal scene and its utility for Chicana feminist history. I am tracking the colonial object of desire by invoking a third space feminist analysis to locate the decolonial subject. Malinche is the colonial object who has been decolonized by feminists; Silent Tongue is the colonial object, yet becomes decolonized when she runs from her abductor/rapist/husband. Delgadina is the colonial object whose own father tries to seduce her. She chooses death, and only in death is she free. For Silent Tongue's mixed-race daughter, Aubonnie, death is the other space, that other world that cannot be invaded by the colonizer/ husband. Finally, I will turn to Selena. Is she a colonial object? I believe she represents decolonial desire; that is, she authorized her desire through third space feminist practice by deliberately fashioning a sexed body for public consumption. Selena Quintanilla Pérez, the Tex-Mex singer murdered by an "obsessed" female fan on 31 March 1995, performed Chicana agency in a way that exuded sexual prowess endemic to a specific cultural woman-of-color feminism.[2]

This chapter has two parts. In the first I offer a critique of *Anti-Oedipus: Capitalism and Schizophrenia* by Gilles Deleuze and Félix Guattari, whose work represents a turn away from psychoanalysis.[3] Some cultural critics and feminists have taken up Deleuze and Guattari to position desire outside of psychoanalytic renderings. I argue that such a position teaches us little about desire, instead repressing its history, its memory. I discuss the theorists of *Anti-Oedipus* because I think their work represents contemporary society's contempt for psychoanalysis. They seek an alternative insight to desire, disputing Oedipus, and complicating desire through the concepts of deterritorialization and reterritorialization, which reaffirm origins in a universalist manner. Again, they defy history and culture. The second part of the essay reinvokes psychoanalysis by way of Teresa de Lauretis's reading of Sigmund Freud via Jean Laplanche and Jean-Bertrand Pontalis, to sketch how fantasies of origin are historically structured, but more importantly how fantasies of origin "structur[e] the subject's history"[4]—and, I would add, how they structure the subject of history. Through the examples of Malinche, Silent Tongue, Delgadina, and Selena, I will carve out the scenarios to unravel colonial and decolonial desire in India/mestiza/Chicana bodies. Finally, I will return to Foucault's power/ knowledge paradigm and its implications for the sociosexual construction of desire. The conclusion is, in a sense, a meditation upon the ethics of scholars who construct our histories.

Adopting de Lauretis's analysis, I appropriate the scenarios of the three fantasies of origin to decipher something of India/mestiza/Chicana sexualities, expressly how those sexualities become racialized, colonial desires, meaning that desire is construed through and by colonialism. The question "Whose fantasies are privileged?" may be contemplated. I will begin by taking a tour through the first original fantasy—the primal scene in which an individual witnesses her/his own origin through parental coitus. Reinscribing the fantasy with coloniality will bring forth the colonial primal scene. Next, I will briefly mention the corrido, or ballad, of Delgadina to explain the seduction fantasy—the origin and emergence of the individual's sexuality—and how that particular fantasy represses the sexuality of Indias/mestizas/Chicanas by expecting them to subcribe to patriarchal rule. Here I will discuss Selena and how the seduction fantasy worked for her and against her. Through her sexualized body and her performance, she seduced her audiences and often defied her father's rigid control over her and her body. She negotiated within the law of the father, her father's patriarchal rule, to gain her own agency, yet contradictions abounded. How much was she really daddy's little girl, as the recent film by director Gregory Nava would have us believe? And how much could she enact her own desires? The last original fantasy, the castration fantasy, exemplifies the difference between the sexes. It elucidates how Indias/mestizas/Chicanas gain their agency. I maintain that women can claim their agency through Malinche, who for patriarchal "nationalists" is the phallic mother.[5] Malinche is the "nation's" nightmare, the betrayer, the sole reason for the loss of the nation as it was. To reinscribe her as a feminist icon, as Chicana/Mexicana feminists have done, is to identify her as an agent of her own desires. For feminists, Malinche is not the phallic, devouring mother, but a woman who was in charge of her own destiny as much as she could be, given her historical circumstances.

I am concerned with unmasking desire in the works of writers and theorists who have meditated about desire's potential to transform us, to revolutionize us, and to challenge that which is repressive in our society. The theorists/activists whose writings conceptualize mutating desires are, for example, Michel Foucault and Teresa de Lauretis, both of whom alert us to desire's inscriptions upon the body.[6] De Lauretis offers a "perverse" reading of Freud, one which I contend can unmask cultural bodies. Foucault laid a foundation for deciphering sexuality through the centuries in Western Europe, and in doing so he traced the emergence of moral engineering and its effects on repressive sex and its desires. Foucault's *History of Sexuality* may be useful to the study of India/mestiza/Chicana histories, coupled with his *Technologies of the Self*, in which he theorized the construction of the body and how that construction was, and is, historically specific.[7] Unwittingly, Foucault's work also addresses colonial/racial desire when one considers Western Europe as global colonizer imposing its authority upon the racialized/colonized other from Asia to Africa and the Americas.[8]

Throughout the chapter, I reassert the relevance of the arguments I made in "Sexuality and Discourse" to history and the historiographic construction of history. In the following section, I want to speculate how the body's desire, through memory, is negated in the anti-Oedipal proposition by the French theorists Gilles Deleuze and Félix Guattari, who are hailed as the new designers of desire by many cultural critics.

DESIRING MACHINES?

It is at work everywhere, functioning smoothly at times, at other times in fits and starts. It breathes, it heats, it eats. It shits and fucks. What a mistake to have ever said *the* id. Everywhere *it* is machines—real ones, not figurative ones: machines driving other machines, machines being driven by other machines, with all the necessary couplings and connections. An organ-machine is plugged into an energy-source-machine: the one produces a flow that the other interrupts. The breast is a machine that produces milk, and the mouth a machine coupled to it. The mouth of the anorexic wavers between several functions: its possessor is uncertain as to whether it is an eating-machine, an anal-machine, a talking-machine, or a breathing-machine (asthma attacks). Hence we are all handymen: each with his little machines. For every organ-machine, an energy-machine: all the time, flows and interruptions. . . . Everything is a machine.[9]

Is everything a machine? What is liberatory about naming organs of the body machines, thereby linking their production to desire? In *Anti-Oedipus: Capitalism and Schizophrenia*, Deleuze and Guattari claim that when desire is defined as production, as a machine, it is no longer driven by psychoanalysis and its drives, that is, the sex drive, the death drive, and so on. Rather, for Deleuze and Guattari, the drive, the motor, is a machine that produces something, anything, but the something that is produced is real, not metaphoric: "something is produced: the effects of a machine, not mere metaphors."[10] They further reflect, "There is no such thing as either man or nature now, only a process that produces the one within the other and couples the machines together. Producing-machines, desiring-machines everywhere, schizophrenic machines, all of species life: the self and the non-self, outside and inside, no longer have any meaning whatsoever."[11]

The preface to *Anti-Oedipus*, by Michel Foucault, is the most promising exposition in the book. Foucault exalted the manuscript as a "book of ethics" that can perhaps rid us of "the slightest traces of fascism in the body."[12] He asked in the preface, "How does one introduce desire into thought, into discourse, into action? How can and must desire deploy its forces within the political domain and grow more intense in the process of overturning the established order?"[13] I thought again about revolution—desire as revolution. How to make a revolution with this desiring-machine that Deleuze and Guattari celebrated became a concern for me once again. But along with desire as revolution, I needed to think about the revolution of desire. Would they help me theorize desire, its components, its distractions, its longing, its craving and hunger within specific historical, political, cultural, colonial, and sexual relations as well as conditions? Moreover, how much does memory inscribe desire, the body's desire, the revolutionary's desire? Memory as history is often the motive for revolution, for transformation, whether the transformation is of society and its collective memory or of the damaged individual who is part of some collective.

In this cursory estimation of *Anti-Oedipus*, I define the more obvious terms in the book: desiring-machines, BwO (body without organs), and Oedipus; then I mull over Oedipus and coloniality by referring to the section of their book titled "Psychoanalysis and Ethnology," in part three, which is called, perhaps ironically, "Savages, Barbarians, Civilized Men"; finally I submit my own critique of *Anti-Oedipus*, borrowing from Foucault, de Lauretis, and Elizabeth Grosz.

In the lengthy quote above, Deleuze and Guattari define desire—desire as a machine that produces that which is real, not metaphoric; desire as a machine of intensities and flows. The machine is desire; desire is a machine, not a metaphor. Movement, flow, and production are all important elements to these mechanic alliances. The body without organs, a core concept for Deleuze and Guattari, is linked to their body with a "thousand plateaus," a fluid, mobile texture affected by a multiplicity of pleasures.[14] They describe the body without organs as an "imageless, organless body, the nonproductive."[15] "[T]he body without organs presents its smooth, slippery, opaque, taut surface as barrier" to resist organ-machines, or a body with organs.[16] The surface, then, becomes the signifier for Deleuze and Guattari, who want us to turn the body over to an "amorphous" fluidity. There are no organs, only surfaces, textures to be touched and fondled, hence no depths. Moreover, "the desiring-machines attempt to break into the body without organs, and the body without organs repels them, since it experiences them as an over-all persecution apparatus."[17] Psychoanalysis, then, and its apparatus, in the name of Oedipus, becomes a persecuting machine for Deleuze and Guattari. But more important, it is precisely the "imperialism of Oedipus" that has dictated a repression of desiring-machines.[18] In other words, Oedipus is the culprit, the cause of problems for Eurowestern society forced to look for the complex, the triangle of father-mother-child, everywhere. The triangulation and the resulting complex create a specific economy of desire in which the dictum "You will not marry your mother, and you will not kill your father" becomes the rule for modern society.[19]

THE ANTI OF OEDIPUS

In "Psychoanalysis and Ethnology," the writers tell us that "We are moving too fast, acting as if Oedipus were already installed within the savage territorial machine."[20] "[T]o our perverted eyes—... at first glance, everything appears Oedipal."[21] At this juncture, *Anti-Oedipus* captivates me precisely because of the *anti* of Oedipus. In other words, Deleuze and Guattari attest that Oedipus is not everywhere, and certainly not in so-called "primitive" societies where kinship systems are not governed by nineteenth-century Western European father-mother-child triangles. To look for Oedipus in these societies would be absurd, but they claim that it is equally absurd to continue seeking Oedipus in Western Europe, where the population has suffered under the imperialism of imposed Oedipus since Freud's case studies. They attempt to convince us that Oedipus does not exist—in fact, never existed. That, precisely, is the *anti* of Oedipus.

But what if it is too late? What if the Oedipal economy has already infused our consciousness so profoundly, whether Eurowestern or not, that the only feasible anti of Oedipus is resistance? For me, the anti of Oedipus is not that it does not exist, but that the anti becomes resistance to Oedipalization when the colonial Oedipus arrives in a colony to transform kinship systems into the Oedipal economy. With that in mind, I can proceed with my assessment of this section.

"[U]nder the effect of colonization," then, according to Deleuze and Guattari, two phenomena occur: (1) "the colonized resists oedipalization" at the same time that (2) "oedipalization tends to close around [the colonized] again."[22] But is resistance successful? Once colonization of a nonwestern society by a Eurowestern society is in motion, there are effects on the colonized other / self as well as the colonial other / self. Resistance itself already patterns different colonial and familial relations. Whether Oedipus is present or not depends upon the mixing, the miscegenation, and the resulting racial, cultural hybridity. Oedipus colonizes and therefore restructures familial relations. Deleuze and Guattari ask, "After all, how are we to understand those who claim to have discovered an Indian Oedipus or an African Oedipus?"[23] In "Sexuality and Discourse," I find Oedipus in the Americas in the culture of Chicanas/os. I find a mestizo Oedipus after the colonization of the Americas by Spain. By devising a model that I called the Oedipal Conquest Triangle (or Complex) with Hernando Cortés, Malintzin Tenepal (La Malinche), and Octavio Paz as imaginary son to the white colonizer father Cortés and Indian mother Malinche, I argued that Oedipus had invaded the Chicano/a consciousness through these imaginary historical metaphors, through this language of conquest. Hence, a colonial imaginary was initiated through the Oedipal Conquest Complex, one that we are forced to contend with and resist. In his writings, Paz disavows his Indian mother, referring to her as "la chingada." The Oedipal arrangement exposes how the metaphoric (yet for some historically real) Indian mother of Chicanos/as is denigrated precisely because Paz and others like him cannot come to terms with the Indian woman who, in their eyes, betrayed the race by embracing the white male colonizer. Yet contradictions proliferate. At some level he is compelled to embrace the colonizer father. Malinche becomes the dreaded phallic mother who will devour him, castrate him, usurp him of his own phallus/power. He must therefore ally with the white colonizer father, but to do so is to ally in ambivalence. This dynamic, I argue, will repeat itself and will be the driving force behind a form of patriarchal Chicano nationalism that repudiates feminism. Malinche, feared as phallic mother, will be despised over and over again.

Deleuze and Guattari ask us to abandon these universalist notions of Oedipus, although by using Oedipus I am not proposing that Oedipus is universal, but rather that Oedipus is installed with colonization. They would have us turn instead to the body without organs. They point out,

> Sexuality is no longer regarded as a specific energy that unites persons derived from the larger aggregates, but as the molecular energy that places molecules–partial objects (libido) in connection, that organizes inclusive disjunctions on the giant molecule of the body without organs (numen), and that distributes states of being and becoming according to domains of presence or zones of intensity (voluptas).[24]

Ultimately, the theorists argue that "Desiring-machines function within social machines" and that "Beneath the conscious investments of economic, political, religious, etc., formations, there are unconscious sexual investments, microinvestments that attest to the way in which desire is present in a social field. . . . "[25] For Deleuze and Guattari, desire, its components, the unconscious, sexuality, and fetishes are determined by social machines. Theirs is a desiring economy in which the body has no organs, and finally no memory—hence no history. Their body has no history and no memory. How can historical erasure be revolutionary?

Deleuze and Guattari take us into the realm of the "real" physical body, but as they do, they defy the past and the memory that holds that past. For them, the body without organs is always living in the present, and it is affected only by the immediate touch on its skin. It is a body that is always in the state of forgetting.

Desire, Teresa de Lauretis argues, is "a psychic activity whose effects on the subject constitute a sort of habit or knowledge of the body."[26] Deleuze and Guattari, on the contrary, maintain that the body can forget what it knows. But how? How can the body forget its habits, its longings? How does the mind forget the past and its imprints upon the skin? The flesh comes to know someone or something in a certain way, whether through a scent or a touch; a gesture seen or experienced will remind the imagination how the body itself has its own memory. Memory as history, as social construction, as politics, culture, race—all are inscribed upon the body. Inscriptions upon the body are memory and history. The body is historically and socially constructed. It is written upon by the environment, by clothes, diet, exercise, illnesses, accidents. It is written upon by the kind of sex that is practiced upon the body and that the body practices. But memory, dreams, fantasy, the imaginary, the lure of fetishes as imaginary, how are these to be explained under the desiring economy of social machines that run desire? And what of the unspoken, the unthought harbored in a memory so brutal that repression is the body's only form of survival?

Elizabeth Grosz, in her favorable explication of Deleuze and Guattari, points out that for the theorists, "sexuality and desire are not fantasies, wishes, hopes, aspirations"; instead they are "energies, excitations, impulses, actions, movements, practices, moments, pulses of feeling"[27]—in other words, surface effects that ultimately have no memory. "Surfaces come together—fingers on velvet, toes in sand. They come to have a life of their own. They have no memory," she informs us.[28]

But how is desire possible without memory? Can the body react to intensities and flows, to touch upon its surface, without being haunted by particular pleasures that it will long for again? And again? Grosz's appropriation of Deleuze and Guattari is a wish for what could be if what had been had not been. In other words, if fingers touching velvet are inscription upon a surface, then the fingers are inscribed by the feel, the softness, of velvet. But for these theorists there is to be no memory, buried somewhere in the unconscious, of velvet in childhood. Perhaps velvet became eroticized because a girl (or boy) you had a crush on wore blue velvet. But the mind cannot remember this, either because it happened so long ago or because some tragedy took her/him away. The psyche buried it. But the body, with its own memory, stirs the imagination. The body remembers. It remembers that it craves the feel of velvet, although it may not know why; it may not even matter why—it just longs for this fetish, velvet. A past, a history, therefore dictates desire, its intensities and flows. Grosz, like Deleuze and Guattari, has a wish, a fantasy, to erase the past to deny the imposition of memory, the body's memory, that which comes toppling forth in the form of a gesture, a scent, a taste that disrupts the body, lingering on the skin. The past, its memories, becomes so much a part of the body's desires that it will attempt to re-create what has come before, the way flesh has been caressed. The memories, even when objectionable—such as sexual abuse, for example—haunt the body. Often the wish is to negate the past and live in the unmarked graze of the present, where the skin's surface can be inscribed with a fresh energy, a new excitement, an impulse each time the surface is skimmed. But what about the haunting feel of velvet? That which has come before reminds the body when it comes again, or leaves it unsatisfied if it does not come again. The body will seek that thing, whether fetish or not, will seek it again in a similar form, or differently; the memory conditions the body to want, to desire, to crave, to long, to hunger, to beg, to plead in specific ways. The body conditions the memory. The memory conditions the body. The body constructs its desire through memory, and it constructs its memory through desire. That which may not yet be—but will be—is the scenario created to satisfy desire, where bodies meet as if they have already met. The body creates how it will crave and how it will satisfy—or perhaps how it will not be satisfied; not to be satisfied is its own craving, its own desire.

Deleuze and Guattari ask us to defy Oedipus, to forget psychoanalysis for its oppressive regime. But what they submit as replacement is a tool for analyzing desire not as it is, but rather as they would like it to be. In other words, they offer a utopian body, one that is not racialized, colonized, presexualized, or abused—psychically and/or physically. They offer a body that does not fantasize, wish, or hope, but instead responds quite superficially to touch, to action, to feelings upon the skin in the present as it happens. The past does not have to be negotiated between bodies. The past will not besiege. It will not have to be repeated to satisfy the body. Not a bad proposal, I think, one that defies memory, history, and even fantasy—the site of desire.[29] More important, to erase memory is to erase history. How, then, can we place desire into thought, into action, into discourse without *desire's history*? The fantasy, the desire for political and social revolutions in which sexed bodies enter a liberatory transgressive regime, may well be one in which Oedipus, once and for all, is forgotten and made useless, but the process itself toward some fantasy of liberation clings to memory.

The thesis of *Anti-Oedipus* is problematic for a number of reasons.[30] For one, the Oedipus of the *anti*-Oedipus remains the trace that is indelibly engraved upon Eurowestern colonial desire. It is precisely this problematic trace that draws me back to the *anti* of Oedipus. It is the trace itself that inscribes the colonial object negotiating for a postcolonial liberatory moment in history. Therefore, the colonial object must defy Oedipus, must be *anti*-Oedipus to become decolonized, to become the decolonial subject and finally enter postcoloniality, that utopian dream.[31] But will desire be the vehicle for that movement from the colonial imaginary to a decolonial imaginary? Another, more obvious problem is that Deleuze and Guattari invoke a transcendental "desire," transhistorical and therefore non-mutable.[32]

To trace desire to memories of origin is a way of tracking it historically. Tracking desire historically invokes the site of fantasy where resistance is possible, perhaps even making revolution possible. The resistance of Malinche, Silent Tongue, Delgadina, and Selena is third space feminist practice that activates a decolonial imaginary to gain a sense of freedom.

Let me backtrack to remind you how I employ the notions of colonial and decolonial imaginaries to discuss desire and its complexities. I argued in chapter 1 that the colonial imaginary in the United States, specifically in the Southwest since the sixteenth century, has been constructed by the imagination of contemporary Chicano/a historians.[33] The decolonial imaginary embodies the buried desires of the unconscious, living and breathing in between that which is colonialist and that which is colonized. Within that interstitial space, desire rubs against colonial repressions to construct resistant, oppositional, transformative, diasporic subjectivities that erupt and move into decolonial desires. (Malinche, Silent Tongue, Delgadina, and Selena are examples.) The imaginary, indelibly marked, thus follows. It follows into new terrains where desires can be constructed differently and regionally. Freedoms are measured by degrees; power is enacted upon the body according to regional morals and laws. The decolonial imaginary remains intangible, unseen, yet quite "real" in social and cultural relationships between the colonizer and the colonized, where the ambivalences of power come into play. In other words, one is left to ask, Who is really the colonizer or the colonized? Who has agency in this political and cultural arrangement? The difference between the colonial and decolonial imaginaries is that the colonial remains the inhibiting trace, accepting power relations as they are, perhaps confronting them, but not reconfiguring them. To remain within the colonial imaginary is to remain the colonial object who cannot be subject until decolonized. The decolonial imaginary challenges power relations to decolonize notions of otherness to move into a liberatory terrain.

SILENT TONGUE: THE COLONIAL PRIMAL FANTASY

I proposed the Oedipal triangle to introduce the repetition of a power dynamic reenacted through Cortés, Malinche, and Octavio Paz. It was a metaphor. An example, the film *Silent Tongue* as metaphor can explain the extended kinship networks that are played out through Oedipus, but also beyond that arrangement into a doubling. Everyone and everything seems to have its double, its "other," to express complexities, to express how there is more than one way to be, and that there are many "in-betweens" to offset the binarism of doubles. The characters in *Silent Tongue* are severely Oedipal, while at the same time they are beyond Oedipus. The family is framed through the father-mother-daughter (instead of son) paradigm, and different familial ties are privileged. Ultimately, the mother and her daughters are central. They are the resistance, the oppositional figures on the colonial terrain. The brother-sister ties are racialized; the father-mother represent a colonial tie whereby rape of the mother by the father creates a hybrid race of daughters who defy the father and will not betray their Indian mother.

How is the primal scenario reframed in the film *Silent Tongue*? How does that original fantasy become the colonial primal scene? While I attempt a textual reading of the film, I also pose questions: How are women of color represented in the film? How might women of color spectators be similar to or different from their representation? How does the colonial object imagine her own desire when it is policed, restricted and constructed through rape, for example? Finally, how does the colonial object become decolonial subject?

Silent Tongue was written by prize-winning playwright, actor, and filmmaker Sam Shepard. He weaves a story about a modern-day nineteenth-century Malinche, yet in doing so quite nearly grants a postmodern wish, with postcolonial hope buried in a fragmented resolution at the end of the film.

Briefly, the story revolves around a Kiowa Indian woman named Silent Tongue (played by the Native American actress Tantoo Cardinal). We learn that she received her name because her tongue was cut out by her own tribe members for lying. The film is staged in the Llano Estacado in 1873, near the northern plains of Texas and eastern New Mexico. Other sources refer to the area as *la jornada de muerte,* the journey of death. The film begins with two white men performing for a traveling medicine show. They sing "Ole Jaw Bone," a song about expelling ghosts from the land. Later it becomes apparent that the white men want to expel the Indians—the Indians are the ghosts they fear.

The proprietor of the medicine show is an alcoholic Irishman named Dr. McCree (played by Alan Bates). I will refer to him as the first Irish father. He sells medicine, an alcohol elixir. In the distant plains, a man on horseback approaches. He is another Irishman, Prescott Roe (played by Richard Harris). I will refer to him as the second Irish father. He brings horses to trade for Dr. McCree's remaining Indian daughter, whose name is Vilma McCree. (She is played by the actress Jeri Arredondo). The second Irish father had swapped with the first Irish father for the first Indian daughter as a wife for his son, Talbot Roe (River Phoenix), who now grieves over her dead body. The first Indian daughter, Aubonnie (Sheila Tousey), died giving birth to "a child I never wanted," she says. Richard Harris, the second Irish father, fears that his son will die grieving for his dead mixed-race Kiowa wife: "he stands over her corpse like a lost soul." He believes the younger sister can comfort and save his son, as if any Indian maiden will do. The first Irish father is quite willing to exchange his second daughter, as he had the first, for horses. His son, however—the first

Irish son (played by Dermot Mulroney)—will not allow the trade. He is fond of his sister, and angry that his father sold the first sister at all. The second Irish father is forced to abduct her, convinced that his son will release the corpse of his first wife for the living second sister.

We have, then, two Irish fathers, two Irish sons, two Indian daughters—all doubles of each other—yet only one Indian mother, Silent Tongue. Man and his doubles, mirroring difference, yet sameness:

SILENT TONGUE

The origin; the mother;
the motherland; the resistance
to the colonial white fathers

1. *First Irish Father*
Leader of medicine
show; rapes Silent
Tongue; father of
two mestiza daughters

Second Irish Father
Trades horses with
first Irish father for first
Indian daughter; abducts
second Indian daughter

2. *First Irish Son*
Son of first Irish father;
half-brother to Indian
sisters

Second Irish Son
Son of second Irish father;
obsessed with first
Indian daughter—his dead wife

3. *First Indian Daughter*
Ghost; daughter of
first Irish father and of
Silent Tongue; married to
second Irish son

Second Indian Daughter
Daughter of first Irish
father and Silent
Tongue; abducted by
second Irish father for second
Irish son

For Silent Tongue and her daughters, the past *does* haunt. Desire, its fantasy, is possible only for the white male colonizer subjects: the two Irish fathers and their two sons. Yet, in a doubling of sorts, the mother and her two daughters are not engaged in the colonizer's desire; instead, as they mirror each other, the hybrid mestiza daughters defy and refuse the colonizer, his desire; even the whiteness they have inherited from their white father is refused. The ghost daughter, Aubonnie, returns to torment the second white son, who will not release her corpse to the spirit world. The first white son will not allow his father to sell his half-Indian sister to the other Irish father. When she is abducted, the second son compels his father to go with him in search of her, on an almost incestuous quest; yet perhaps it is his own origin that the second son seeks.

While son and father roam through the *jornada de muerte* looking for the second Indian daughter, we realize that this son despises his father. At one point he says to him, "It shames me to be your son." We can almost hear the voice of the filmmaker/writer agonizing over the sins of the father that he has historically inherited.

In the mesmerizing next scene, the first Indian daughter's corpse comes alive. Her ghost slowly turns her face to the camera. We see that half of her face is young, alive; the other half is wrinkled, dried, withering. A black line is painted from her forehead down to her chin, as if to accentuate hybridity—two halves, the colonial decayed self and the decolonized free self. The eye in the decomposed half of her face is glazed over with a film as if blinded. She speaks to her husband, the second son: "You're a dog, a low dog to tie me here. You keep me bound here out of your selfish fear of aloneness. I'm not your life. It's you who must release me. Throw this body to the wind." The ghost waits, longing to enter the spirit world, but cannot while this white man still clings to her decaying corpse, hence her spirit. She jeers at him to release her, to throw her into the fire or let the vultures devour her. When he begs to go with her, she responds, "You belong in this world, not mine. You owe me my freedom." Then, taunting him, "Take your own life—place your gun in your mouth and set me free. If you don't do this thing I ask, then a curse will fall on your father." She sneers, "I was sold like a slave. I died giving birth to your child, a child I never wanted." The ghost will continue to haunt and humiliate the second son, the husband who clutches her corpse. She will also appear to the second Irish father in her promise to curse him. But first, let me explain the primal scene.

The primal scene, in Freudian terms, is the first moment when a child witnesses sexual intercourse between her/his parents, thereby realizing her/his origin. The colonial primal scene, for my purpose here, is a re-enactment of the rape of Indian women by white male colonizers/conquerors.[34] In the film *Silent Tongue,* the scene is witnessed by a child—not an Indian child, as we might expect since this is Indian country, but a young white boy. And what he sees is not his own origin, as the primal scene dictates, but rather the origin of his half-white, half-Indian sister.

The film cuts to a scene in which Dr. McCree (the first Irish father) is sleeping. Suddenly it shifts from color to black and white. As spectators, we are witnessing his memory in a dream. On the desolate prairie, an Indian woman, Silent Tongue, is gathering bones—whether human bones or animal bones, we don't know, but she walks in a bone graveyard nonetheless. As they stand on a hill overlooking the prairie, an anonymous white man says to the first Irish father, "Try your Irish luck; she won't scream." The first Irish father, Dr. McCree, gives an order to his son, who is about five years old: "If I catch you looking, I'll thrash you 'til your knees buckle," to which the white man responds, "He might as well see how it's done." McCree chases Silent Tongue, who sees him and runs. He pounces and rapes her. The camera pulls in for a close-up of Silent Tongue's face, and we are shown a mouth wide open in screaming silence. The son has covered his face with his hands, but the anonymous white man pulls the boy's hands away, forcing him to look, to gaze upon this act of sexual violence. And we too are forced to gaze upon an Indian woman raped by a white male colonizer. The first son observes his father raping an Indian woman. He witnesses the origin of his half-sister—a mestiza who will spurn her mixed blood, and hence her white father.

The film now cuts back to the second Irish father, who has abducted the second Indian daughter. Having lassoed her, as he would any animal, he reassures her, "I don't want to harm you." He hopes her kindness will save his son from relentless grief for her dead sister. Upon learning that her sister is dead, she throws her head back, agonized, galloping away on her abductor's horse. Her mouth wide open, she screams loudly, juxtaposing her mother's silent scream. At this moment, we realize that both daughters will perhaps avenge the history that has befallen their mother and now themselves, the unwilling captives of white men. The daughters will become their mother's agency.

The ghost of the first Indian daughter repudiates the white male colonizer, her husband to whom she was sold like a slave by her own white father. (Thus she is not unlike La Malinche, who was sold into slavery, but by her mother, an Indian woman.) She refused to have his child, and she curses her husband's white father. When she sees her younger sister with the same white man who purchased her, the first daughter's ghost reminds her sister, "You like bargaining with white men, then you bargain with me." By now the second daughter has accepted money from the second father in exchange for agreeing to comfort his son. But her sister's ghost proclaims, "I'll cut your tongue out"—just as their mother's tongue had been cut out—"so you will never forget who gave you birth." When the ghost chases the second Irish father, who has abducted her younger sister, the second daughter says to the man who has kidnapped her, "My sister is sending you her thoughts," to which he replies, "Your sister is dead."

> Second daughter: "She is my mother's weapon."
> Second Irish father: "Your sister is dead!"
> Second daughter: "She is more alive than you."

DELGADINA AND SELENA: THE SEDUCTION FANTASY

Were the daughters in *Silent Tongue* seduced by the white colonizer fathers and sons? The seduction fantasy dictates the moment one enters sexuality, its upsurge. We know that the mother, Silent Tongue, runs away from her rapist husband, leaving her half-Indian daughters to contend with the colonial terrain represented in the medicine show. They were probably both on display as acrobatic Kiowa warrior princesses until the first daughter is traded for horses and the second daughter is stolen; hence their sexuality is born from reducing women (mestizas) to objects for exchange. But the daughters, although seemingly belonging to white sons, do not belong willingly. The ghost daughter mocks and scorns her white colonizer husband. She would rather die than be mother to his child, or at least she appears to have willed her own death at childbirth. The second daughter is pursued by her half-brother. We witness only his obsession for her; we never hear or learn of her feelings for her half-brother. It seems that for her, he is nonexistent. As spectators, we have no sense that the second sister has been seduced, or that she is necessarily sexual. She is abducted for a man she has never met, as a replacement for her dead sister, as if the sisters are interchangeable. Any Indian woman will do. Her own desire, her own sexuality on this frontier, is immaterial.

But how do we, the spectators, see? How are women of color, mestizas, represented? Silent Tongue, I believe, represents the motherland—North America invaded and colonized. She has escaped, leaving behind daughters who were born of colonial rape, and who loathe their white father, ignore their white half-brother, and refuse the white husband. The first daughter's ghost returns to retaliate against the colonial white fathers and sons. She would rather be dead than live her life colonized. She yearns to enter the spirit world, a world beyond the colonizers. When her white husband begs to go with her, she responds, "You belong in this world, not mine." And where is her world? Perhaps it is an interstitial space that eludes invasion, a world unseen that cannot, will not, be colonized.[35]

The corrido, or ballad, of Delgadina is an evocative representation of the seduction scene in which the daughter thwarts her father's incestuous sexual advances. The father's desire leads to tragedy for both father and daughter. The lesson, however, is for Delgadina, who had no choice but to guard her womanhood. Entering sexuality is her burden. Her sexual, enticing body tempted her father—she becomes the evil Eve, the temptress who caused her father's ruin. Delgadina, like any other young woman, was supposed to have hidden her sex. She is to blame for having a sexed, female body that a man will desire. Yet as a sexed woman, she enters a double bind. There is no way she can guard her sex enough from male seducers. By becoming a woman, she has already failed; despite the fact that she refused her father, opted for imprisonment, and finally dies, she is still blamed because she caused her father to desire her. The patriarchy is not blamed, however. It is left intact. The father is pitied and the daughter is jailed. She exemplifies what will happen to the daughter who refuses patriarchal seduction. The double messages conflict the daughter: to be seduced, not to be seduced. The patriarchy leaves few options. Oedipal logic guides the corrido. In other words, the seduction fantasy within phallocentric discourse serves to punish women into subservience. Whether women listen or adhere to the cultural message is something else altogether.

I think that a third space feminist perspective permits another analysis. When perceived as agents, women cast their own fantasies. *Silent Tongue* quite closely represents a woman's fantasy. The Indian woman escapes the colonizer, her rapist; her daughters spurn the colonialists' desire or any relation to their colonizers, honoring their mother. The corrido of Delgadina, however, is male fantasy, its construction reified. For it is through Delgadina that patriarchy owns its power, its knowledge; it is through patriarchy that women's desire is silenced. If women as objects of male desire are expected to embrace patriarchy and femininity, then are they realizing their own desires and fantasies? Their own sexuality? The seduction scene in this corrido dictates "the system of exchange instituted by the incest prohibition, where woman functions as both a sign (representation) and a value (object) for that exchange."[36] In effect, women have no agency. They can, however, have their agency within the seduction fantasy. I turn now to Selena.

"Freudian psychoanalysis grants women the power of seducing and of being seduced, being . . . sexed and desiring subjects."[37] Selena, I would suggest, negotiated a symbolic mutual seduction with her audiences, but also with her father as she bargained within the law of the father to assert her agency. Selena can be perceived as a victim who was controlled by her father, or she can be seen as a formidable woman who manipulated her sociocultural circumstances to her benefit. Or we can find decolonial desire in that in-between space where Chicanas such as Selena exhibited an in-your-face, working-class sexuality and did so with pride, not inhibition. A turn in the meaning of Chicana/Latina sultriness as empowerment through self-expression is taking place here, but not without its contradictions.

Although I was not eager to discuss the film *Selena* by director Gregory Nava, I think it is imperative to address it, because the movie represents the most obvious conscious construction of Selena through the lens of the father. It is precisely the law of the father that is authorized in the film. How Selena will be remembered by her fans is also crafted; that is, the memory of Selena becomes, as Gaspar de Alba argues, a man-made construction.[38] The filmmaker dictates *the* Selena that he wants the public to remember. The seduction fantasy as symbolic and mutual exchange between the father and daughter is apparent in at least three critical scenes. I contend that these scenes unveil how Selena's father wrestled with his own compulsion to control his daughter. And many would say that he did control her. She was, after all, living out his aspiration to be a singer/performer and a famous recording artist, with fans on both sides of the Mexico–U.S. border. She surpassed him by becoming the successful star, but through his daughter, whom he also managed, he was able to realize his own dream of success.

The film reconstructs Abraham Quintanilla's past as a singer in Texas who was not permitted to cross racial barriers in the segregated 1950s. It is as if the message for the spectator is that Abraham was as talented as his daughter; he was simply born too soon. Selena, on the other hand, was born at a time when racial barriers had been crossed—a little. It is no coincidence that on the day the young artist records the crossover album that will introduce her to English-speaking audiences, Quintanilla, played by Edward James Olmos, says to her, "You crossed all the barriers. For you they weren't even there." He implies that Selena seemed unstoppable. Her initial fame came from the Mexican and Mexican American audiences who listened to her sing rancheras and cumbias in Spanish—this from a young tejana who could not even speak Spanish.[39] Yet Selena typified the many Chicanos/as in central Texas who grew up listening to popular groups such as the Pretenders, the Eagles, and the Jackson Five along with Madonna and Janet Jackson. Like many tejanos/as her own age, she did not speak Spanish initially; she lived a cultural amalgam of things Mexican, Euroamerican, and Chicano/a, but characteristically tejano/a—a hybridity specific to a region where Tex-Mex is its own "authentic" blend of cultures.

The first crucial scene that calls up the seduction fantasy occurs when seventeen-year-old Selena, performing at the fairground in El Paso, Texas, in 1989, suddenly removes her jacket. Under it she wears a skimpy black bustier. Working the sound stage, her father shouts to his wife, "What is she wearing? She's practically got nothing on. She's in a bra. . . . She can't be wearing things like that. There are men out here." The mother attempts to calm her husband by responding, "It's a bustier. I think she looks cute." He is not convinced, and after the performance we see Selena assuring her father that she was only borrowing from Madonna, who wears the latest fashions. It is a persuasive conversation, with Selena winning his approval.

In the second scene, the family and band members are touring on their bus. The father, who is driving, witnesses a flirtation between Selena and Chris Pérez, the band's guitarist. He stops the bus and throws Chris off, unable to watch his daughter's seduction by this young man. The film goes on to show the two lovers meeting secretly because the father will not permit the relationship to mature. In effect, he cannot let his daughter go. The daughter, on the other hand, has already made that shift. She is already not her father's little girl.

The father's hold becomes even more apparent in the third scene I address here. Having learned that Selena has eloped with Chris, he is a broken man. Quintanilla and Selena have the following conversation in his study:

> Quintanilla: "When I found out yesterday what you had done, I went crazy. I went for a walk on the beach where I used to take you when you were a little girl. I sat down and cried. I cried like a baby. I'm glad you did what you did. I know I forced you into it."
>
> Selena: "Deep down I knew it was gonna be OK."
>
> Quintanilla: "Back on the bus, when Chris told you he loved you, I believed him."
>
> Selena: "He does love me."
>
> Quintanilla: "But it scared me. I don't know how to let you go."

Both father and daughter break down, crying in each other's arms. Subsequently we see Selena invite Chris into her father's home, and he is embraced by her mother, sister, and brother. Everyone is nervous about how Quintanilla will react. He greets Chris: "Come here, son. You're a good man. Welcome to our family."

But has Quintanilla surrendered his daughter? Perhaps he has. He embraces his son-in-law and submits to his daughter's wish—to be married to the man who had been unacceptable to her father. There is almost a sublimated inversion of power dynamics. In other words, in each of these scenes Selena dictates her desires, but she must wrestle with her father's ultimate control. And indeed she does come out the winner. But does she? How do these scenes reveal the strength of the law of the father and a daughter's constant battle against that law for her own agency? There is a perpetual negotiation. And what is it about the power of the seduction fantasy within the heterosexual framework that creates a contradictory father-daughter bond where inevitable conflict between father and daughter feeds the contradictions? How she will lead her life is in question even when she is already displacing him from her decisions. In other words, she is still trapped within the confines of patriarchal conditions—and those are the conditions that condition her—but we cannot forget how she manipulates that control for her own benefit, for her own agency. And that is the power of the seduction fantasy. A woman can be a desiring subject; she is not just an object whose life is determined by a patriarch, as in the case of Delgadina.

The film does not address the lesbian controversy over the "obsessed" female fan, Yolanda Saldívar, who murdered Selena. Rumors about their friendship were rampant within days after the murder, but especially during the court trial held in Houston, Texas, in October 1995. On several occasions Yolanda Saldívar was accused of being a lesbian or of exhibiting sexual desire for Selena. If the film accomplishes anything, it seeks to confirm Selena's heterosexuality by stressing the love story between her and Chris. During the murder trial, the homophobia was apparent. The label "lesbian" was reintroduced when the Spanish station that carries the news magazine show *Primer Impacto* reported Saldívar's claim to police that Quintanilla had sent men to rape her, and that he himself had then raped her. When Quintanilla heard what Saldívar had accused him of, his response was, "Have you seen her?" implying that he would not touch a woman who looked like Saldívar. The charge of lesbianism was made by disgruntled fans, but also by Selena's father, to discredit Saldívar further, as if it were not enough that she stole, cheated, lied, and murdered—all these character flaws had to be conflated with lesbianism for many who wanted to believe that Saldívar was the perverse murderer. To his credit, director Gregory Nava ignored the lesbian rumors in his film, instead portraying Saldívar as a liar who betrayed her best friend.[40]

I prefer to address the narrative that is told within the heterosexual framework. A potentially lesbian relationship between Yolanda and Selena is its own conjecture and fantasy.[41] That will remain an interstitial silence for me. There is, instead, a rigid heterosexual economy in place here that demands critique. Up to now I have neglected the relevance of the lesbian component in de Lauretis's argument. She points out that "feminist psychoanalytic theory has reclaimed homosexuality as a prerogative or a component of female sexuality," because "the figure of the lesbian in contemporary feminist discourse represents the possibility of female subject and desire: she can seduce and be seduced, but without losing her status as subject."[42] I argue that within that heterosexual patriarchal structure, Selena was both seducing and being seduced. Her status as desiring subject was, however, a perpetual contest with her father precisely because she was living a heterosexual life. I tend to agree with de Lauretis, who argues that lesbians are not caged within a patriarchal regime of desire in the same way as heterosexual women who love and desire men. Lesbians, then, are both at once "desiring subject and desiring object" in ways not entirely possible for heterosexual women, who must battle for their subjecthood as desiring subject/object. And Selena was indeed fighting for her subjecthood.

I saw the Nava film on opening day in El Paso, Texas, a place where fans were familiar with Selena. From the first show until the late evening, the lines stretched outside the theater, with Mexican American and Mexican families towing little girls who were dressed like Selena. As the film began, I looked for Selena, but instead saw a story that seemed to be nothing more than hero worship for the father, a story that was more about Abraham Quintanilla than about Selena. He was portrayed as the exceptional father who may have been strict with his children, but only because he loved them and wanted success for them—success that he was still chasing. A year later I saw the Nava film again, and I was still disturbed. By the third year, I was grateful that Nava had provided Latina/o communities with a story that would help us remember something of a young woman still revered by so many. I tried to accept this man-made construction of Selena, but I could not forget how the lens of the father had controlled the story to interpret Quintanilla in a favorable light—the protective, loving father. And where was Selena? I did not see her until the end of the film, when Nava runs footage of crying fans holding up posters with the "real" Selena, not Jennifer López in the role of Selena. Not until then did I become aware once again of the loss.

To have lost Selena, especially all that she represented to the Chicano/a community as a tejana, I had to ask myself, Why am I still grieving after three years? Why, when I talk to other fans, do we still mourn? Who was this young woman who, as Nava wrote in the script, "crosses all barriers"? In many ways, the power of her seduction, her sensuality consciously performed, not only allowed my own lesbian gaze to be replenished, but, equally important, it allowed me to come home. I came home to Tex-Mex music when Selena reinscribed macho rancheras. Third space feminist perspective permitted me to hear a woman's agency in songs that are usually performed by men and in which women are only objects. When Selena sang, she was no victim. Moreover, she broke into an industry that did not welcome women.

Speaking to these complexities, José Limón argues that Selena was "negotiating and dancing through a contested site" of late capitalist Western pop culture; therefore, she was "not withdrawing into an alternative and essentialist project but rather constructing herself sexually under the hegemonic 'male gaze' even while marshaling all of her resources so as to be in effective performative command of it."[43] He further posits that Selena may not have been "a conscious autonomous agent," but her performed sexuality made her a "sexual revisionary" for her community.[44] Limón criticizes those whose own male gaze does not permit them to see her agency, but who rather are immersed in the "ample detail" of her curvaceous body, detail that Gaspar de Alba names as just plain "sexist."[45] It is the heterosexual male gaze that cannot see through to Selena's agency, but often the female gaze within a heterosexual regime is also blind to Selena as subject. Here is a woman who is "an agent, a sexed and desiring subject, even a protagonist" in her "symbolic exchange" with her audiences, both men and women.[46] Selena as "sexed and desiring subject" enacted decolonial desire, that interstitial space that cannot be seen within modernist trappings, reducing woman to an object of the male gaze, woman seduced and disempowered by a patriarchal scheme.

Selena, however, seemed to play with racialized and sexualized categories, inverting them for her own benefit. She proudly performed a working-class sexuality, a sexuality with a complex history for Chicanas.[47] From the sixteenth century, Chicanas, Mexicanas, and Indias were indeed victimized by colonizers who raped women and used them as objects, but their subjecthood cannot be negated. Antonia Castañeda successfully argues that the sexual politics of the frontier enforced the rape of Indian women, helping the Spanish colonizers win the frontier. Indian women such as Toypurina resisted their colonizers.[48] In other words, because women have had to negotiate gendered relations that victimized them did not mean that they were necessarily only objects of that abuse. Through the centuries, Mexican women have been objectified in male travel journals, songs, stories, and now film. At every turn, their cultural expression of sexuality has been misread.[49] Selena reified and reaffirmed that cultural expression and made money for herself and, yes, for the men who could cash in. But let us not forget what she meant to so many, and what she represented. Selena as cultural icon, even more so now in death, symbolizes a particular Chicana feminist agency that her audiences embraced. She offered working-class Chicanas/Mexicanas public affirmation. Not only did it become acceptable to dress, walk, dance, act, and talk sensuously, and to wear thick makeup, scant clothes, and long hair, because Selena did it; but Selena made it acceptable to do so and not be labeled a whore, by affirming a cultural sexuality with historical roots. If Selena could break these barriers with her father, then other young Chicanas/ Mexicanas could do the same and not be alienated from their families. For the heterosexual female gaze, Selena provided an option—the affirmation of Chicana/Latina sexuality.[50]

MALINCHE, THE PHALLIC MOTHER: THE CASTRATION FANTASY

In "Sexuality and Discourse: Notes from a Chicana Survivor," I probed the Oedipal arrangement as a metaphor for colonial sexual relations. Freud's Oedipus is generated by repressed desire, produced by a prohibition that can be reduced to the following dictum: "you will not marry your mother, and you will not kill your father."[51] These repressed desires are retained within the unconscious mind and body; the desiring mind and body are therefore sculpted by repression. What would it mean to defy Oedipus in colonial/neo-colonial regions such as the Southwest, where sexualities are dictated and encoded upon the body by the law everywhere, but in specific ways, depending upon regional laws and morals? In *Anti-Oedipus,* Deleuze and Guattari claim that we have been fooled by the Oedipal triangle. Instead, desire and its machines may offer an alternative. They suggest that "desire is revolutionary," while the Oedipal triangle is the entanglement that entraps us. I argued that Oedipus is the Western colonial-sexual prototype imprinted upon the colonial subject who has to enter new psychic terrain in order to resist Oedipus. That new terrain is "desire," with all its potential to disrupt repressive social machines. But can we move beyond Oedipus? Has it been so encoded upon our bodies, their desires, that we are doomed to repetition, a repetition which, I think, recycles a specific Chicano nationalism rooted in patriarchal discourse and activism? Again I contend that sexuality and its discourse is precisely the problem we face in Chicana/o nationalisms and feminisms. The Oedipal triangle reemerges, like the "return of the repressed," to haunt relationships. *Anti-Oedipus* may attempt liberatory relationships and freedom from the Oedipal arrangement, but even they are already inscribed by the past.

That which I attempted in "Sexuality and Discourse" was a prescribed method for deconstructing Chicano/a ideologies and dominant thoughts that have sculpted our histories. Chicano/a history, I claimed in chapter 1 of this book, excluded voices that did not conform to a dominant intellectual paradigm being constructed and written. "Sexuality and Discourse" challenged the way "sex" and its language, often silenced, implicitly guide the minds of those writing our histories. By focusing upon Octavio Paz and his denigrations of La Malinche, I devised what I called the Oedipus Conquest Complex to interrogate preconceptions about Indias/mestizas/ Chicanas. The corrido, or ballad, about Delgadina also critiques a dominant, all-encompassing patriarchal "order of things" that demands disclosure. In other words, even when unnamed, sexual power relations are present, often hidden and unspoken yet performed between and among people.

But whose desire is enacted? Whose Oedipal moment is privileged? The "nation" becomes the family. Nationalism becomes the "return to the mother," the original place or space. Aztlán is that symbolic original place where the nation will survive again in pre-Oedipal bliss. Women are not allowed to be sexed or to have sex; therefore sexual difference is not possible for Chicanas. They can be only pre-Oedipal, hence pre-sexual, in this scenario of nationalism. Only men may have their Oedipal moment, their castration fantasy, hence their sex. Feminism disrupts this pre-Oedipal space in which the womb symbolizes Aztlán. The nationalist imperative is to move back in time, a regression, a return to the mother, but the mother cannot be Malinche. She must be La Virgen de Guadalupe; she cannot be sexual. She must be pure for the nationalist dream. In this way, Aztlán is not an empirical, internal colony, but an imaginary, a maternal imaginary, while the father's significance is something else. He has many possibilities under patriarchal nationalism; he is many heroes—from Emiliano Zapata to Ruben Salazar. He is not an object; nor is he represented through the "land"; nor is he judged for being whore or virgin. He is always already a hero, a leader—a leader who must lead his people to a land. And the land is maternal; it is pure, virginal; it is where the family will all be safe in the womb. Hence, nationalism becomes a return to the mother—Aztlán—where woman can be only metaphor and object. When she has agency like La Malinche, she is repudiated by the nation as the betrayer, the whore, la chingada. Just as Oedipus is everywhere, always, reinscribing sociosexual and cultural relations, for Indias/mestizas/Chicanas La Malinche is always everywhere, reinscribing women's agency. In Chicano/a myths, histories, tropes, taxonomies, and so on, La Malinche cannot be avoided. La Malinche encodes all sociosexual relations and there is no way out. Well, maybe there has been a way out. Feminists have reinscribed Malinche with new "flesh," with a new imagined history.[52] For Chicana feminists, Malinche has become the powerful mother—not the phallic mother feared by modernist, patriarchal nationalists, but an enduring mother, a cultural survivor who bore a mestizo race.

POWER/DESIRE

To discuss power and desire, I call upon Foucault, who continues to incite and inspire poststructural and postcolonial theorists. His work, encoded with desire, has contested our contemporary society with insights on power/knowledge. His *Technologies of the Self* has guided many, including feminist theorist Teresa de Lauretis, who scrutinizes social construction and its "technologies of gender." In *The Practice of Love*, de Lauretis rereads Freud's theory, a "negative theory of sexuality [in which] perversion appears as the negative or nether side of . . . so-called sexual normality."[53] She elaborates upon "a model of desire that goes beyond the Oedipus complex and in its own way resolves it" for the perverse, intimating lesbians.[54] De Lauretis reads Freud with Foucault's "self-analysis," or technology of the self, to conclude finally how society designs the body, its desires, and more specifically lesbian desire. Foucault began to theorize the inscription of history upon the body, and how the material body itself was engraved with psychic desires that could be realized in any number of ways. That he was so intrigued with sadomasochism as a form of queer liberation also demonstrates how he thought desire moved beyond the moralism and ethics of contemporary Eurowestern "family values." The normal or normative was and has been considered heterosexuality in Europe and in the Americas since the sixteenth century. Any deviation from the "law," from so-called "normal" heterosexuality, was deemed "criminal," and therefore had to be punished or disciplined. Criminals and deviants became one and the same. Both had to be disciplined by "moral engineering," which reconstructed bodies and pleasures to fit society's "natural laws."[55] Lodged in this repressive society is power—power *over* desire, a power to police desire, to remake the deviant into the "normal." In *History of Sexuality*, Foucault aims his discourse at the conflict between power and desire. The question for Foucault, then, is what do we do when the desire for power overwhelms and polices the power of desire?

How do we reinscribe our bodies with the passions of desire when power and desire are so enmeshed? In his preface to *Anti-Oedipus*, Foucault asked,

> How does one keep from being fascist, even (especially) when one believes oneself to be a revolutionary militant? How do we rid our speech and our acts, our hearts and our pleasures, of fascism? How do we ferret out the fascism that is ingrained in our behavior?[56]

A dangerous, fascist militancy is tantamount to a nationalism that repudiates women's voices, intolerant of any differences. That is the space where power polices desire. We are threatened once again by a reemergence of uncompromising nationalist movements in which feminisms are dismissed as bourgeois, in which queer voices are scoffed at as a white thing, in which anyone who does not sustain the "family values" of modernist, patriarchal nationalism is not tolerated and is often silenced. This reemergence *is* the return of the repressed, where a community becomes fascist, staging a revolution that trivializes sexualities, differences, and technologies of desire.

The Mexican Revolution and its nationalism has served as a history lesson for the Chicano/a movement. I attempted to speak to this in part two of this book. But the women of the revolution have been so idealized and romanticized that they have come to represent for contemporary Chicano nationalists imagined values and morals to fit a nationalist paradigm. Chicanas are expected to mimic the Adelitas, camp followers who serviced the male soldiers, cooking tortillas and mating with the men. Early-twentieth-century journalist John Reed chronicled the Mexican Revolution and wrote a popular account of soldaderas epitomizing the passive, willing Mexicana eager to be protected by a male soldier, any male soldier. When one partner died, she simply took up with another.[57] Reed interpreted this as passive acceptance, not agency. What Reed also overlooks are the soldaderas who were tortilleras—marimachas, mariconas, and jotas; but of course, historical erasure has not permitted those queer voices to be heard. Elizabeth Salas, in her study *Soldaderas in the Mexican Military,* hints at some of the women who cross-dressed in male uniforms, not only to survive the revolution, but to engineer their own revolution.[58] But women's activism often disappears even when they are weaving their politics differentially in historical movements such as the Mexican Revolution. In chapters 2 and 3, I argued that Mexican feminists during the Revolution of 1910 spoke and acted a feminism-in-nationalism, moving within dominant discourses of nationalism that wanted to relegate them to gender-specific duties. Contemporary nationalist discourses imitate similar demands.

DESIRE AND HISTORY

Will history, its memory, its desire, free us, navigate us through passion where the unthought, the unspoken, shuffle through unidentifiable spaces, moving us out of Oedipus, from the colonial imaginary into identities where power relations that police, whether from above or below, are disrupted by a decolonial imaginary? I have suggested that some answers lie in a psychic terrain, that unseen region where our only hope is a new consciousness, a healing consciousness, where desiring devices can serve to free us and not obstruct, stifle, and limit our identities.

Desire, its historical construction, its discourse, has been repressive, even fascist, in its colonial forms. Silent Tongue and her mestiza daughters, Delgadina, and La Malinche—all had to negotiate colonial desire practiced upon their physical, psychic bodies. Selena, however, represents the move toward decolonial desire. Women's desires have been like archaeological silences. How do we name and theorize the new machines of this revolutionary desire, whether using metaphors of the third space or metaphors as yet unspoken? Desire nonetheless stubbornly occupies the colonial imaginary, where its passion is often caged in political-social institutions where power in its doubling effect works for us and against us. The challenge is to redefine the rules of formation, as I have argued, in historical studies to voice our many differences, to sift out the technologies of decolonial desire, where the colonial object may fantasize her desires to become decolonial subject. Ultimately, the point is to move beyond colonialist history by implementing the decolonial imaginary with a third space feminist critique to arrive finally at postcoloniality, where postnational identities may surface.

Throughout this chapter, I have specified how "Sexuality and Discourse" are relevant to history and its historiographic construction. I recapitulated how history—its stories, narration, studies—is devised through power, through knowledge, through sexuality erased, empowered, silenced, or imposed upon historical bodies. In other words, sexuality and its discourse can be a methodological instrument for historiography, a historiography that witnesses power relations that cannot be avoided—power relations established through sexualities that remain unspoken, unsaid, even avoided, yet always already present. Somewhere between Foucault's archaeology and genealogy, supplemented with a perverse reading of psychoanalysis, may lie new perspectives for understanding the making, or the poetics, of history and its study.

Conclusion

THIRD SPACE FEMINIST (RE)VISION

"Forget the Alamo."
—Pilar in *Lone Star*

When Pilar, the mixed-race Chicana in the John Sayles film *Lone Star*, ends the film with a resolute, quiet, matter-of-fact "forget the Alamo," she is reinscribing a colonial imaginary with a decolonial one.[1] At that liberatory moment, the decolonial imaginary is enacted as hope, as love, transcending all that has come before, all that has been inherited only to damage daughters and sons who have fallen heir to a history of conquest, of colonization, of hatred between brown and white. "Let's start from scratch," she pleads to the man she loves, despite just having learned from him that they are half-brother and half-sister, a secret kept from them by Pilar's Mexican mother and Sam's Anglo father, who were clandestine lovers in the small, generically named border town of Frontera, Texas. Sam, Pilar's lover, her half-brother, the postmodern Euroamerican, fragmented in his responsibilities as sheriff in a racist town, nods his head faintly, agreeing. We know by now that his love for Pilar is immutable. For the lovers, to "forget the Alamo" and "start from scratch," as they sit in front of a blank white drive-in movie screen in the light of day, means they have agreed to remake their story, to transcend an inhibiting, treacherous past. The blank screen in front of them represents newness. But Pilar speaks the words, not Sam. If Sam had spoken them, I would have walked away from the theater a cynic, disappointed and angry because one more time, a white man was trying to persuade me to forget a history of brutality and move on. John Sayles, perhaps himself the postmodern man, wrote the script and directed the actors, and he is indeed the white man who once again will attempt to persuade me to erase a history that still brutalizes. But somehow, by placing the words in Pilar's mouth, he has unwittingly compelled me to listen and wonder why I have been so jolted.

I, a tejana by cultural construction, have been trying all my life to forget the Alamo, but ironically I chose history as my profession. As a historian, I cannot forget the Alamo; as a tejana, I am not allowed to forget the Alamo. It is imprinted upon my body, my memories, my childhood. But to hear the words "Forget the Alamo" from a Chicana is, for me, a freeing, a freedom from a history that nags me for re-vision. I'm anxious to move to another site of remembrance. I am anxious to remake and reclaim another story—stories of love, of compassion, of hope.

I am, however, caught in the time lag between the colonial and the postcolonial, in a decolonial imaginary reinscribing the old with the new. My history of Chicanas, a feminist history, has been written inside a decolonial time lag, with a third space feminist critique, between what has been, what is, and what many of us hope will be. All at once we live the past, present, and future. History itself has encoded upon it a tool for a liberatory consciousness. Marx was probably the first theorist-philosopher to teach this lesson to Chicana/o historians. It has taken Foucault, however, to warn us that power/knowledge disrupts the classic terrain of binaries. We can no longer resort to simple binaries that determine enemies or friends according to their color, class status, gender, sexualities, and any other differences that become our historical bodies. If we choose to enact the tool of history and call it third space feminist consciousness, as I have done throughout this book, then we begin to build another story, uncovering the untold to consciously remake the narrative. Third space feminism allows a look to the past through the present always already marked by the coming of that which is still left unsaid, unthought. Moreover, it is in the maneuvering through time to retool and remake subjectivities neglected and ignored that third space feminism claims new histories, Chicana feminist histories that may one day—finally—"forget the Alamo."

NOTES

INTRODUCTION

1. Foucault, *The Archaeology of Knowledge* (New York: Pantheon Books, 1972), 17.

2. Joan Wallach Scott, *Gender and the Politics of History* (New York: Columbia University Press, 1988).

3. Mary Austin Holley Papers, Barker Library, University of Texas, Austin.

4. Bernardino de Sahagún, *Historia general de las cosas de Nueva Espana* (Mexico, D.F.: Editorial Porrúa, 1982); Diego de Landa, *Relación de las cosas de Yucatán* (Mexico, D.F.: Editorial Porrúa, 1959).

5. Bartolomé de las Casas, *Historia de las indias,* 3 vols. (Mexico, D.F.: Fondo de Cultura Economica, 1951); Bernal Díaz, *The Conquest of New Spain* (New York: Penguin, 1963). Díaz's account is one of the more intriguing, simply because he believed that his was the only "true story" by an "honest eyewitness" to the conquest of Mexico.

6. Octavio Paz, *The Labyrinth of Solitude,* trans. Lysander Kemp (New York: Grove Press, 1961). Paz's reading of La Malinche is perhaps the most publicized and the most abhorrent to most Chicanas. "Chingando" is the slang for "fucking." Like its counterpart in English, it has many meanings.

7. Scott, *Gender and the Politics of History,* 4–5. In the introductory essay, Scott argues, "I think post-structuralism (or at least some of the approaches generally associated with Michel Foucault and Jacques Derrida) can offer feminism a powerful analytic perspective. I am not suggesting the dogmatic application of any particular philosopher's teachings and I am aware of feminist critiques of them. Still I want to indicate the places where and the ways in which, for me, the openings they provide to new intellectual directions have proved not only promising but fruitful." Like Scott, I too am aware of feminist critiques launched against Foucault in particular. I think, however, that I am seeking in his methods of archaeology and genealogy "openings" for different ways of seeing and conceptualizing Chicana histories by examining, as Scott suggests, the politics of meaning.

8. Charles C. Lemert and Garth Gillian, *Michel Foucault: Social Theory and Transgression* (New York: Columbia University Press, 1982), 55–56.

9. I am grateful to Homi Bhabha for this observation, which he made in the summer of 1993 at the School of Criticism and Theory.

10. Chéla Sandoval, "U.S. Third World Feminism: The Theory and Method of Oppositional Consciousness in the Postmodern World," *Genders* 10 (Spring 1991): 1–24. See also a more recent essay in which Sandoval discusses her methodology as a form of resistance at the same time that it bridges differences. Chéla Sandoval, "Re-entering Cyberspace: Sciences and Resistance," *Dispositio/n* 19, no. 46 (1994): 75–93.

11. Sandoval, "U.S. Third World Feminism," 23, n. 58.

12. Ibid., 1.

13. Foucault, *The Order of Things: An Archaeology of the Human Sciences* (New York: Vintage Books, 1970), 386–87.

14. Hayden White, *The Content of the Form: Narrative Discourse and Historical Representation* (Baltimore: Johns Hopkins Universty Press, 1987).

15. Hayden White, "'Figuring the Nature of the Times Deceased': Literary Theory and Historical Writing," in *The Future of Literary Theory*, ed. Ralph Cohen (New York: Routledge, 1989), 19–43. See p. 39.

16. Hayden White, *Metahistory: The Historical Imagination in Nineteenth-Century Europe* (Baltimore: Johns Hopkins University Press, 1973). See p. 3, n. 4.

17. Foucault, *The Archaeology of Knowledge*, 25.

18. Homi K. Bhabha, *The Location of Culture* (New York: Routledge, 1994); Foucault, *The Archaeology of Knowledge*; Juan Gómez-Quiñones and Luis Arroyo, "On the State of Chicano History: Observations on Its Development, Interpretations, and Theory, 1970–1974," *Western Historical Quarterly* 7, no. 2 (April 1976): 155–85; Scott, *Gender and the Politics of History*; Gayatri Chakravorty Spivak, *In Other Worlds: Essays in Cultural Politics* (New York: Routledge, 1988); White, *Metahistory*; Gloria Anzaldúa, *Borderlands/La Frontera: The New Mestiza* (San Francisco: Spinsters/Aunt Lute, 1987); Teresa de Lauretis, *Technologies of Gender: Essays on Theory, Film, and Fiction* (Bloomington: Indiana University Press, 1987); Sandoval, "U.S. Third World Feminism"; Antonia I. Castañeda, "Women of Color and the Rewriting of Western Women's History: The Discourse, Politics, and Decolonization of History," *Pacific Historical Review* 61 (November 1992): 501–33; Deena González, "Chicana Identity Matters," in *Culture and Difference: Critical Perspectives on the Bicultural Experience in the United States*, ed. Antonia Darder (Westport, Conn.: Bergin and Garvey, 1995), 41–53; Vicki L. Ruiz, *Cannery Women, Cannery Lives: Mexican Women, Unionization, and the California Food Processing Industry, 1930–1950* (Albuquerque: University of New Mexico Press, 1987).

19. See my essay "Sexuality and Discourse: Notes from a Chicana Survivor," in *Chicana Lesbians: The Girls Our Mothers Warned Us About*, ed. Carla Trujillo (Berkeley: Third Woman Press, 1991), 159–84. I conceptualized "sitio y lengua," site and discourse, to argue for Chicana language and the space for the ongoing construction of that language and its theory. I posit and still believe that for the exploited, the colonized, the marginalized, etc., oppression is "that intimate place where theory is born" (166). I was also speaking to the contributions made by Chicana lesbians, contributions that seem to be consistently negated by many Chicana feminists. The recent anthology by Alma García, for example, acknowledges Chicana lesbians only as entering feminist discourse as late as 1991. My point is that Chicana lesbian voices, like Chicana history, like Chicano history, all have undergone the peril of being silenced by those who have not heard the voices on the margins always already speaking, writing, and reconstructing the past. See Alma M. García, *Chicana Feminist Thought: The Basic Historical Writings* (New York: Routledge, 1997).

I. SEXING THE COLONIAL IMAGINARY

1. Linda Hutcheon, *The Poetics of Postmodernism: History, Theory, Fiction* (New York: Routledge, 1988), 3. My study is in dialogue with the writings of current historians who philosophize history and its historiography. They are Juan Gómez-Quiñones, Michel Foucault, Joan Wallach Scott, Gayatri Chakravorty Spivak, and Hayden White, discussed in the preface to this book. The following historical studies engage critiques of history that are pertinent to its theorizing within a postmodern realm: Dominick LaCapra, *History and Criticism* (Ithaca, N.Y.: Cornell

University Press, 1985); Michel de Certeau, *The Writing of History*, trans. Tom Conley (New York: Columbia University Press, 1988); Emmanuel Le Roy Ladurie, *Carnival in Romans*, trans. Mary Feeney (New York: Braziller, 1979); Peter Novick, *That Noble Dream: The "Objectivity Question" and the American Historical Profession* (Cambridge: Cambridge University Press, 1988); Jacques Derrida, *Of Grammatology*, trans. Gayatri Spivak (Baltimore: Johns Hopkins University Press, 1976); and Paul Ricoeur, *Time and Narrative: Volume I*, trans. Kathleen McLaughlin and David Pellauer (Chicago: University of Chicago Press, 1984).

2. Hutcheon, *The Poetics of Postmodernism*, xiii.

3. Ibid., 92.

4. Gayatri Chakravorty Spivak, "Subaltern Studies: Decontructing Historiography," in *Selected Subaltern Studies*, ed. Ranajit Guha and Gayatri Chakravorty Spivak (New York: Oxford University Press, 1988), 13.

5. Hutcheon, *The Poetics of Postmodernism*, 223.

6. Hubert L. Dreyfus and Paul Rabinow, *Michel Foucault: Beyond Structuralism and Hermeneutics* (Chicago: University of Chicago Press, 1982), 61.

7. Ibid., 65.

8. Foucault, *The Archaeology of Knowledge*, 3.

9. Homi Bhabha, *The Location of Culture*, 195–96. "I suggest that the postcolonial perspective is subversively working in his text in that moment of contingency that allows the contiguity of his argument—thought following thought—to progress."

10. Ibid., 38.

11. Ibid.

12. Sandoval, "U.S. Third World Feminism," 14. Sandoval refers to "this in-between space, this third gender category" to cite U.S. third world feminists who have been articulating from that third space. See p. 5.

13. Edward Said, *Orientalism* (New York: Vintage Books, 1978). In his introduction, Said adopts Foucault's method, his "notion of discourse," to argue that Western culture and ideology produced the Orient through discourse (3). Todorov, in a sense, argues like Said that the Spanish Conquest produced the Americas through the limitations of sign systems. See Tzvetan Todorov, *The Conquest of America: The Question of the Other*, trans. Richard Howard (New York: Harper and Row, 1984).

14. For an in-depth discussion of objectivity in the human sciences, refer to Renato Rosaldo, *Culture and Truth: The Remaking of Social Analysis* (Boston: Beacon Press, 1989), 168–73.

15. See, for example, Patricia Nelson Limerick, *The Legacy of Conquest: The Unbroken Past of the American West* (New York: W. W. Norton, 1987).

16. See Tomás Almaguer, "Ideological Distortions in Recent Chicano Historiography: The Internal Model and Chicano Historical Interpretation," *Aztlán* 18, no. 1 (Spring 1989): 7–28. The essay is a critical revision of Almaguer's earlier treatise "Toward the Study of Chicano Colonialism," *Aztlán* 2 (Spring 1971): 7–21. As a social scientist, Almaguer takes quite seriously the materialist improbabilities of the internal colonial model. I propose to engage coloniality's imaginary and the psychic implications with respect to material, tangible conditions. The intangible, psychic imaginary is what interests me. Of course, Rodolfo Acuña is credited for popularizing the paradigm in his textbook *Occupied America: The Chicano's Struggle toward Liberation* (New York: Harper and Row, 1972). In the second and third editions, the subtitle was changed to *A History of Chicanos*. Other Chicano scholars in the 1970s were theorizing the utility of the internal colonial model. For early essays, see Octavio Ignacio V. Romano, "The Anthropology and Sociology of the Mexican Americans: The Distortion of Mexican American History," *El Grito* 2 (Fall 1968): 13–26; Mario Barrera, Carlos Muñoz, and Charles Ornelas, "The Barrio as

Internal Colony," *Urban Affairs Annual Review,* ed. Harlan Hahn, 6 (1972): 465–98; and Guillermo V. Flores, "Race and Culture in the Internal Colony: Keeping the Chicano in His Place," in *Structures of Dependency,* ed. Frank Bonilla and Robert Girling (Stanford, 1973).

17. Almaguer's revision in 1987 is an example.

18. Bhabha, *The Location of Culture,* 238.

19. I am not claiming to be the first to call attention to this interstitial space in which silences can be located. Certainly, feminists have been addressing these issues. See, for example, Teresa de Lauretis, who refers to "the space-off, the elsewhere, of those discourses: those other spaces both discursive and social that exist, since feminist practices have (re)constructed them, in the margins (or 'between the lines,' or 'against the grain') of hegemonic discourses and in the interstices of institutions, in counter-practices and new forms of community." De Lauretis, *Technologies of Gender,* 26.

20. Bhaba, *The Location of Culture,* 45. Here Bhabha refers specifically to Frantz Fanon and the problem of colonial identity.

21. Jacques Lacan, *Ecrits: A Selection* (New York: W. W. Norton and Co., 1977), 1–7.

22. White, *Metahistory,* 31–38 and passim. He relies on the four basic tropes of modern language theory: Metaphor, Metonymy, Synecdoche, and Irony. As a historian, White resurrected "The Four Master Tropes" from Edmund Burke's *A Grammar of Motives* to question the "artistic" elements of "realistic" historiography. See *Metahistory,* 3, n. 4. This is precisely why I find White's philosophy of history so meaningful. For the explication of the master tropes, refer to Edmund Burke, *A Grammar of Motives* (Berkeley: University of California Press, 1969), 503–17. After the publication of *Metahistory,* White was challenged by historians, both traditionalists and Marxists, for his relativist approach. Postmodern theorists and historians have begun to appreciate White's postmodern historiography. For a more current critique of White's work, see Wulf Kansteiner, "Hayden White's Critique of the Writing of History," *History and Theory* 32 (1993): 273–95.

23. White, *Metahistory,* ix and passim.

24. Ibid., 3, n. 4. In this lengthy footnote, White refers to poststructuralists such as Foucault—upon whom I rely heavily—and Jacques Derrida to point out how they are also "captives of tropological interpretation," yet unaware.

25. I use "Chicano" and not "Chicano/a" or "Chicana/o," because I think that during the early years of conceptualizing Chicano history, the "a" was still so peripheral that I would prefer to accentuate the "o" of Chicano.

26. The Great Events of U.S. history are marked by dates such as 1776, the signing of the Declaration of Independence; 1861–65, the Civil War; 1942–45, World War II, etc. Chicano history is outside these great events. U.S. history textbooks reflect the demarcation, which has to do more with the regional history of the eastern seaboard than with the Southwest. The Civil War is privileged as the historical moment that changed the face of the Union. The Southwest, however, had already been changed drastically by the U.S.–Mexican War of 1846–48, but this split is not recognized in U.S. history. A U.S. East Coast–centrism dictates how U.S. history is taught and written, leaving Chicano history outside affected by its own great events.

27. The historiographic essay by Juan Gómez-Quiñones and Luis L. Arroyo published in 1976 locates similar themes and argues for their development through historical investigation. See Gómez-Quiñones and Arroyo, "On the State of Chicano History." This essay set the stage for the forthcoming studies in Chicano/a history. Gómez-Quiñones had published another historiography five years earlier, in which he had already begun to conceptualize how Chicano history

could be written. In that essay his periodization of Chicano history was a recommendation for future studies as much as it was an acknowledgment of how studies had been categorized within particular eras. See Juan Gómez-Quiñones, "Toward a Perspective on Chicano History," *Aztlán* 2, no. 1 (Fall 1971): 1–49.

28. In his pathbreaking study on Chicano culture and legal discourse, literary critic Carl Gutiérrez-Jones employs three of the Great Events, excluding the Spanish conquest, as critical periods for writing a genealogy of Chicana activists. See Carl Gutiérrez-Jones, *Rethinking the Borderlands: Between Chicano Culture and Legal Discourse* (Berkeley: University of California Press, 1995).

29. Even "pre-Colombian" is a category tarnished with a European perspective.

30. Foucault's take on origins is elucidating for historians. He says, "It is no longer origin that gives rise to historicity; it is historicity that, in its very fabric, makes possible the necessity of an origin which must be both internal and foreign to it; like the virtual tip of a cone in which all differences, all dispersions, all discontinuities would be knitted together so as to form no more than a single point of identity"; *The Order of Things*, 329.

31. There are many events and political circumstances that have affected Mexican immigration throughout the twentieth century. Each of those is pertinent. I argue, however, that because the first massive migration occurred during and after the Mexican Revolution, this event set the stage for the next decades. I am arguing that the four Great Events of Chicana/o history mark the moments when newness entered the world of the Chicana/o population.

32. Ernesto Chavez has probed the ideology of members of the Chicano movement in Los Angeles during the 1960s and 1970s. See his dissertation: Ernesto Chávez, "Creating Aztlán: The Chicano Movement in Los Angeles, 1966–1978" (Ph.D. diss., University of California, Los Angeles, 1993).

33. Manuel Gamio, *The Mexican Immigrant: His Life Story* (Chicago: University of Chicago Press, 1930); Paul S. Taylor, *An American-Mexican Frontier: Nueces County, Texas* (Chapel Hill: University of North Carolina Press, 1934); Ernesto Galarza, *Merchants of Labor: The Mexican Bracero Story—An Account of the Managed Migration of Mexican Farm Workers in California, 1942–1960* (Charlotte and Santa Barbara: McNally and Loftin, 1964); and Carey McWilliams, *North from Mexico: The Spanish-Speaking People of the United States* (Boston: J. B. Lippincott Co., 1949).

34. Carlos E. Castañeda, *Our Catholic Heritage in Texas, 1519–1936*, 15 vols. (Austin: University of Texas Press, 1936–58).

35. George I. Sánchez, *Forgotten People: A Study of New Mexicans* (Albuquerque: University of New Mexico Press, 1940); Jovita González, "Social Life in Cameron, Starr, and Zapata Counties" (M.A. thesis, University of Texas at Austin, 1930); Jovita González, "Tales and Songs of the Texas Mexicans," *Publications of the Texas Folklore Society* 8 (1930): 86–116; and Américo Paredes, *With His Pistol in His Hand: A Border Ballad and Its Hero* (Austin: University of Texas Press, 1971).

36. David Gutiérrez, "Significant to Whom? Mexican Americans and the History of the West," *Western Historical Quarterly* 24, no. 4 (November 1993): 524–25.

37. Ibid., 525.

38. See Edward P. Thompson, *The Making of the English Working Class* (New York: Vintage Books, 1966). This monograph had a stunning impact on Chicano historians. Thompson's erudite study links class to culture in the same way Chicanos such as Gómez-Quiñones and Arroyo postulated.

39. Foucault, *The Archaeology of Knowledge*, 200. Foucault does not negate the prominence of social change; in fact, his books, especially *Discipline and Punish*, show how social change is related to political action. He says, "Social historians are supposed to describe how people act without thinking, and historians of ideas are supposed to describe how people think without acting. Everybody both acts

and thinks. The way people act or react is linked to a way of thinking, and of course thinking is related to tradition." See Foucault, "Technologies of the Self," in *Technologies of the Self: A Seminar with Michel Foucault*, ed. Luther H. Martin, Huck Gutman, and Patrick H. Hutton (Amherst: University of Massachusetts Press, 1988), 14; Foucault, *Discipline and Punish: The Birth of the Prison* (New York: Vintage Books, 1977).

40. Lemert and Gillan, *Michel Foucault*, 55–56.

41. Foucault, *The Archaeology of Knowledge*, 13. White, *The Content of the Form*, 120. Here White makes reference to Foucault's vertical, not horizontal, history.

42. Ibid.

43. Foucault, *The Archaeology of Knowledge*, 200. Emphasis mine.

44. Dreyfus and Rabinow, *Michel Foucault*, 102.

45. Ibid., xxv.

46. Alex M. Saragoza, "The Significance of Recent Chicano-Related Historical Writings: An Appraisal," *Ethnic Affairs* 1 (Fall 1987): 24–62. Even as late as 1987, Saragoza cites only one study by a Chicana in his essay. To read Chicano historiography through this essay would lead one to believe erroneously that Chicanas had not made a contribution to Chicano/a studies by 1987.

47. Thomas Sheridan, *Los Tucsonenses* (Tucson: University of Arizona Press, 1988); Richard Griswold del Castillo, *The Los Angeles Barrio* (Berkeley: University of California Press, 1980). These are only two examples.

48. Emilio Zamora and Roberto Calderón, "Manuela Solis Sager and Emma Tenayuca: A Tribute," in *Chicana Voices: Intersections of Class, Race, and Gender*, ed. Teresa Córdova et al. (Albuquerque: University of New Mexico Press, 1993), 30–41.

49. Gutiérrez, "Significant to Whom?" 519–39.

50. Ibid., 534–35 and nn. 24, 25, 26.

51. Ibid., 520.

52. Cynthia Orozco, "Chicana Labor History: A Critique of Male Consciousness in Historical Writing," *La Red/The Net* 77 (January 1984): 2–5. Orozco bravely critiqued Rodolfo Acuña's "men's" labor history at a time when a feminist critique of Chicano male scholars was interpreted as divisive, anti-nationalist, and, in essence, anti-Chicano.

53. Vicki L. Ruiz, "Texture, Text, and Context: New Approaches in Chicano Historiography," *Mexican Studies/Estudios Mexicanos* 2 (Winter 1986): 145–52.

54. Ruiz's essay, published in 1986, refers to books published in 1982 and 1984. They are Francisco E. Balderrama, *In Defense of La Raza: The Los Angeles Mexican Consulate and the Mexican Community, 1929–1936* (Tucson: University of Arizona Press, 1982); Albert Camarillo, *Chicanos in California: A History of Mexican Americans in California* (San Francisco: Boyd and Fraser Publishing Co., 1984); John R. Chávez, *The Lost Land: The Chicano Image of the Southwest* (Albuquerque: University of New Mexico Press, 1984); Richard Griswold del Castillo, *La Familia: Chicano Families in the Urban Southwest, 1848 to the Present* (Notre Dame: University of Notre Dame Press, 1984); Mauricio Mazón, *The Zoot Suit Riots: The Psychology of Symbolic Annihilation* (Austin: University of Texas Press, 1984).

55. Francsico Balderrama has since co-authored another study on repatriation, in which women are integrated into the narrative. See Francisco E. Balderrama and Raymond Rodríguez, *Decade of Betrayal: Mexican Repatriation in the 1930s* (Albuquerque: University of New Mexico Press, 1995).

56. Antonia I. Castañeda, "Gender, Race, and Culture: Spanish-Mexican Women in the Historiography of Frontier California," *Frontiers* 11, no. 1 (1990): 8–20. An earlier historiography of the Spanish Borderlands was published in 1988, but gender was merely an afterthought in Gerald E. Poyo and Gilberto M. Hinojosa,

"Spanish Texas and Borderlands Historiography in Transition: Implications for United States History," *Journal of American History* 75 (September 1988): 393–416.

57. Castañeda, "Gender, Race, and Culture," 8. For a discussion of gender ideology and a critique of its apparent location in a Mexican social movement, see my essay "A La Mujer: A Critique of the Partido Liberal Mexicano's Gender Ideology on Women," in *Between Borders*, ed. Adelaida del Castillo (Los Angeles: Floricanto Press, 1990), 459–82.

58. See her detailed examination of the Anglo male travel literature for the mid-nineteenth century. These men wrote blatant stereotypical passages about Mexican women. Antonia I. Castañeda, "Anglo Images of Nineteenth Century Californianas," in Del Castillo, *Between Borders*, 213–36. See also Deena González, "La Tules of Image and Reality: Euro-American Attitudes and Legend Formation on a Spanish-Mexican Frontier," in *Building with Our Hands: New Directions in Chicana Studies*, ed. Adela de la Torre and Beatríz M. Pesquera (Berkeley: University of California Press, 1993), 75–90; and David Langum, "California Women and the Image of Virtue," *Southern California Quarterly* 59 (Fall 1977): 245–50.

59. Antonia I. Castañeda, "Sexual Violence in the Politics and Policies of Conquest: Amerindian Women and the Spanish Conquest of Alta California," in de la Torre and Pesquera, *Building with Our Hands*, 15–33. Similarly, Deena González is sexing the colonial imaginary of the nineteenth century in her essays. For example, see Deena González, "Chicana Identity Matters," in *Culture and Difference: Critical Perspectives on the Bicultural Experience in the United States*, ed. Antonia Darder (Westport, Conn.: Bergin and Garvey, 1995), 41–53.

60. For a fresh perspective that utilizes cultural critique in his analysis of recent publications in Chicano/a history, see the review essay by Ernesto Chávez, "Culture, Identity, and Community: Musings on Chicano Historiography at the End of the Millennium," *Estudios Mexicanos/Mexican Studies* 14, no. 1 (Winter 1998): 213–35.

61. Walter Prescott Webb, *The Texas Rangers: A Century of Frontier Defense* (Cambridge: Houghton-Mifflin Co., 1935); Paredes, *With His Pistol in His Hand*; Julian Samora et al., *Gunpowder Justice: A Reassessment of the Texas Rangers* (Notre Dame: University of Notre Dame Press, 1979).

62. The film *The Ballad of Gregorio Cortez*, with Edward James Olmos as Cortez, is an excellent depiction of cultural collision on the U.S.–Mexico border in the early twentieth century. The script was based on Paredes's book *With His Pistol in His Hand*. For an enlightening analysis of the film, see Rosalinda Fregoso, *The Bronze Screen: Chicana and Chicano Film Culture* (Minneapolis: University of Minnesota Press, 1993).

63. Marta P. Cotera, *Diosa y Hembra: The History and Heritage of Chicanas in the U.S.* (Austin: Information Systems Development, 1976); Adelaida R. Del Castillo, "Malintzin Tenepal: A Preliminary Look into a New Perspective," in *Essays on La Mujer*, ed. Rosaura Sánchez and Rosa Martínez Cruz (Los Angeles: Chicano Studies Research Center Publications, University of California, 1977), 129–49; Alfredo Mirandé and Evangelina Enríquez, *La Chicana: The Mexican-American Woman* (Chicago: University of Chicago Press, 1979).

64. Louis Althusser, "Ideology and Ideological State Apparatuses (Notes toward an Investigation)," in *Lenin and Philosophy and Other Essays* (London: New Left Books, 1970).

65. Juan Gómez-Quiñones, *Sembradores: Ricardo Flores Magón y El Partido Liberal Mexicano* (Los Angeles: Chicano Studies Research Center Publications, University of California, 1973).

66. Juan Gómez Quiñones, "On Culture," *Revista Chicano-Riqueña* 5, no. 2 (1977): 29–47. Gómez-Quiñones, like Gayatri Spivak, grasps the importance of culture

and its relationship to socioeconomic conditions. Unlike Spivak's, however, his contributions are often overlooked.

67. Juan Gómez-Quiñones, *Roots of Chicano Politics, 1600–1940* (Albuquerque: University of New Mexico Press, 1994), 1–87.

68. Albert Memmi, *The Colonizer and the Colonized* (Boston: Beacon Press, 1967), 70.

69. Novick, *That Noble Dream.*

70. Castañeda, *Our Catholic Heritage;* Sánchez, *Forgotten People.* I discuss this more thoroughly in the earlier part of this chapter.

71. Ranajit Guha, "Dominance without Hegemony and Its Historiography," *Subaltern Studies* 6 (1987): 211. Guha's essay, despite its binary oppositions, is worthwhile to those who are theorizing colonialist historiography.

72. If we turn to the written past, we find that Mexico and the current Southwest had already endured three hundred years of Spain's colonial rule, and that Mexico stood between a colonial and postcolonial moment. Liberated from Spain, yet controlled by criollos—the children of Spanish parents—Latin America, Mexico, Central America, and more than half of the continent that would become the United States were engraved with all things Spanish. Three centuries after Spain had inscribed Mexico and the region called the Spanish Borderlands, independence wars from 1810 to 1821 finally won self-rule for Mexico. But the Spanish Borderlands were too far north, too distant from the center of rule in Mexico City.

73. Guha, "Dominance without Hegemony," 212.

74. Mainstream U.S. historiography dismisses the book for its non-scholarly presentation, which jettisons a balanced, objective depiction of the facts in favor of polemics. I think the value of the text is that it could take the objective "facts" of the Mexican War of 1846–48, for example, to show how the interpretation of those facts served a Pulitzer Prize–winning historian such as Justin H. Smith, who studied volumes of documents to conclude finally that Mexico was at fault for the war, and the United States could therefore be vindicated. The historian's imaginary interprets events to create a narrative. How, then, is Smith's project not polemical? Justin H. Smith, *The War with Mexico* (Gloucester, Mass.: Peter Smith, 1963).

75. McWilliams, *North from Mexico.*

76. Acuña, *Occupied America.* The text has been reissued in second and third editions since its initial appearance.

77. Mario Barrera, *Race and Class in the Southwest: A Theory of Racial Inequality* (Notre Dame: University of Notre Dame Press, 1979). Tomás Almaguer, Carlos Muñoz, Charles Ornelas, Guillermo Flores, and other Chicano scholars were circulating the notion of "internal colony" in the early seventies. Acuña popularized it by deploying the model in his history text.

78. This phrase is taken from Limerick, *The Legacy of Conquest.* Limerick's book is an excellent synthesis of east-to-west migration and the ideology of the frontier. It is important to note, however, that the Spanish-Mexicans historically—during the sixteenth, seventeenth, and eighteenth centuries—were their own kind of colonizers of Native American, or Indian, land in the Americas.

79. Mark Reisler, *By the Sweat of Their Brow: Mexican Immigrant Labor in the U.S., 1900–1940* (Westport: Greenwood Press, 1976); Laura Arroyo, "Industrial and Occupational Distribution of Chicana Workers," *Aztlán* 4 (Fall 1973); Rosaura Sánchez, "The Chicana Labor Force," in *Essays on La Mujer,* ed. Rosaura Sánchez and Rosa Martínez Cruz (Los Angeles: Chicano Studies Research Center Publications, University of California, 1977); Lawrence Cardoso, *Mexican Immigration to the U.S., 1897–1931* (Tucson: University of Arizona Press, 1980); David Montejano, *Anglos and Mexicans in the Making of Texas, 1836–1986* (Austin: University of Texas

Press, 1987); Emilio Zamora, "Mexican Labor Activity in South Texas, 1900–1920" (Ph.D. diss., University of Texas at Austin, 1983).

80. Anna Nieto-Gómez, "Chicanas in the Labor Force," *Encuentro Femenil* 1, no. 2 (1974): 28–33.

81. Contemporary publications on labor and immigration make a push toward an integrationist approach in which women are an important part of the story as workers and immigrants. The difference from the earlier work is that women are not peripheral to the study, but rather an integral part. Sex-gender ideology is not necessarily challenged in recent publications, however, in the way that Ruiz begins to do. See Ruiz, *Cannery Women*, and Camille Guerin-González, *Mexican Workers and American Dreams: Immigration, Repatriation, and California Farm Labor, 1900–1939* (New Brunswick, N.J.: Rutgers University Press, 1994).

82. James Clifford, "Diasporas," *Cultural Anthropology* 9, no. 3 (1994): 304. For a review of diaspora studies, consult this essay. Clifford raises the point that "border and diasporas bleed into one another."

83. Historians of immigration studies might be able to respond to the utility of diaspora studies. Tomás Almaguer's monograph on Chicanos, African Americans, Native Americans, and Asians in California, unfortunately, does not venture into new theoretical ground, although its comparative approach is appealing to many. David Gutiérrez's work on Mexican immigration offers insights into the complexity of immigration politics and culture; a consciously gendered interpretation, however, remains unmarked. See Tomás Almaguer, *Racial Fault Lines: The Historical Origins of White Supremacy in California* (Berkeley: University of California Press, 1994); David G. Gutiérrez, *Walls and Mirrors: Mexican Americans, Mexican Immigrants, and the Politics of Ethnicity* (Berkeley: University of California Press, 1995). Current anthologies probe some of the current debates on immigration. See David G. Gutiérrez, ed., *Between Two Worlds: Mexican Immigrants in the United States* (Wilmington, Del.: Scholarly Resources, 1996). The essay by Roger Rouse titled "Mexican Migration and the Social Space of Postmodernism," a reprint from the journal *Diaspora*, addresses original questions. See also Camille Guerin-González and Carl Strikwerda, eds., *The Politics of Immigrant Workers: Labor Activism and Migration in the World Economy since 1830* (New York: Holmes and Meier, 1993).

84. Albert M. Camarillo, "The 'New' Chicano History: Historiography of Chicanos of the 1970s," in *Chicanos and the Social Sciences: A Decade of Research and Development, 1970–1980*, ed. Isidro D. Ortiz (Santa Barbara: Center for Chicano Studies, University of California, 1983), 9–17.

85. Foucault summarizes in his introduction to *The Order of Things*, "The history of madness would be the history of the Other—of that which, for a given culture, is at once interior and foreign, . . . whereas, the history of the order imposed on things would be the history of the Same—of that which, for a given culture, is both dispersed and related, therefore to be distinguished by kinds and to be collected together into identities." See *The Order of Things*, xxiv.

86. Bhabha, *The Location of Culture*, 241. I think the assimilationist imperative is best exemplified in the book by George J. Sánchez whose title, perhaps unwittingly, makes the argument that Mexicans are immigrants who have been in the process of "becoming" Americans. See Sánchez, *Becoming Mexican American: Ethnicity, Culture and Identity in Chicano Los Angeles, 1900–1945* (New York: Oxford University Press, 1993). A recent work by Neil Foley challenges the assimilationist imperative and instead targets the racialization of Mexicans; see Neil Foley, *The White Scourge: Mexicans, Blacks, and Poor Whites in Texas Cotton Culture* (Berkeley: University of California Press, 1998). A close examination of Foley's book shows how he universalizes the male experience or story. Not only is gender unmarked,

but women are peripheral and inconsequential to his conclusions. To his credit, Sánchez places women's stories at the center of his work. Foley's book, although a more recent publication, falls into my immigrant/labor category, in which women are shoved against the backdrop of history and their unique differences are erased. That erasure occurs precisely because the male experience remains unchallenged and accepted as universal. Sánchez, on the other hand, shows movement into a historical domain that complicates women's experiences.

87. Lemert and Gillan, *Michel Foucault*, 11.

88. See, for example, Fernand Braudel, *The Mediterranean*, 2 vols. (New York: Harper and Row, 1972). Braudel's work greatly influenced historians in the United States who discovered the usefulness of quantitative methods for uncovering those who had been neglected.

89. Stephan Thernstrom, *The Other Bostonians: Poverty and Progress in the American Metropolis, 1880–1970* (Cambridge, Mass.: Harvard University Press, 1973). Thernstrom investigated only men in the city directories, claiming that because women married and changed names, they could not be traced over the decades as easily as men could.

90. Camarillo argued that to examine the Mexican American population, it is imperative to focus on occupational structure rather than occupational mobility as Thernstrom does. Upward mobility patterns can be determined from "data on wealth, value of property holdings, and wages." Such data is not consistently available for the nineteenth and early twentieth centuries, and it is even less available for Chicanos and Chicanas (243). Occupational structure, on the other hand, tells us about the occupational universe of a specific population group. Camarillo also points out that occupational structure "profiles the changes in the region's economy" (242). As agricultural work declined, workers moved into semiskilled and skilled service work in an urban economy. See Albert Camarillo, *Chicanos in a Changing Society: From Mexican Pueblos to American Barrios in Santa Barbara and Southern California, 1848–1930* (Cambridge: Harvard University Press, 1979).

91. David Montejano, *Anglos and Mexicans in the Making of Texas, 1836–1986* (Austin: University of Texas Press, 1987). Montejano's prize-winning monograph provides an excellent overview of colonization and its consequences in Texas. One is left to wonder, however, if a conscious gendered analysis would have transformed his interpretation of "the making of Texas."

92. Ramon Gutiérrez, *When Jesus Came, the Corn Mothers Went Away: Marriage, Sexuality, and Power in New Mexico, 1500–1846* (Stanford: Stanford University Press, 1991); Lisbeth Haas, *Conquests and Historical Identities in California, 1769–1936* (Berkeley: University of California Press, 1995); George J. Sánchez, *Becoming Mexican American*; Antonia I. Castañeda, "Presidarias y Pobladoras: Spanish-Mexican Women in Frontier Monterey, Alta California, 1770–1821" (Ph.D. diss., Stanford University, 1990); Deena González, *Refusing the Favor: The Spanish-Mexican Women of Santa Fe, 1820–1880* (New York: Oxford University Press, in press); Vicki L. Ruiz, *From out of the Shadows: Mexican Women in Twentieth-Century America* (New York: Oxford University Press, 1998). I would, however, place the work of Castañeda, González, Gutiérrez, Haas, and Ruiz in the Gendered History category moving outside and into Technologies of Desire/Sexualities/Gender.

93. I believe that the national trend toward diversity and multiculturalism has foundations in social history of the other as the same in difference. The multicultural imperative becomes a political project with its own values. Again, it would seem that Albert Camarillo foresaw the links. See Albert Camarillo, "Mexicans and Europeans in American Cities: Some Comparative Perspectives, 1900–1940," in *From "Melting Pot" to Multiculturalism: The Evolution of Ethnic Relations in*

the United States and Canada, ed. Valeria Gennaro Lerda (Rome, Italy: Bulzoni Editore, 1990), 237–62.

94. Adelaida R. del Castillo and Magdalena Mora, eds., *Mexican Women in the United States* (Los Angeles: Chicano Studies Research Center Publications, University of California, 1980); Adelaida R. del Castillo, *Between Borders: Essays on Mexicana/Chicana History* (Encino, Calif.: Floricanto Press, 1990). Although the latter was published in 1990, the conference from which the essays were taken was held in 1982. Both books exhibited a strong Marxist analysis, but the writing in *Between Borders* makes a socialist-feminist move.

95. Teresa Córdova et al., eds. *Chicana Voices: Intersections of Class, Race, and Gender* (Albuquerque: University of New Mexico Press, 1993).

96. The subtitle to the edited volume by Córdova.

97. De la Torre and Pesquera, *Building with Our Hands.*

98. Norma Alarcón, "Chicana Feminism: In the Tracks of 'the' Native Woman," *Cultural Studies* 4, no. 3 (October 1990): 248–56; Martha P. Cotera, *The Chicana Feminist* (Austin: Information Systems Development, ca. 1977); Yolanda Broyles, "Women in El Teatro Campesino: ¿Apoco Estaba Molacha La Virgen de Guadalupe?" in Córdova, *Chicana Voices;* Angie C. Chabran, "Chicana/o Studies as Oppositional Ethnography," *Cultural Studies* 4, no. 3 (October 1990): 228–47; Alma M. García, "The Development of Chicana Feminist Discourse, 1970–1980," *Gender and Society* 3, no. 2 (June 1989): 217–38; Sonia Saldívar-Hull, "Feminism on the Border: From Gender Politics to Geopolitics," in *Criticism in the Borderlands: Studies in Chicano Literature, Culture, and Ideology,* ed. Hector Calderón and José David Saldívar (Durham, N.C.: Duke University Press, 1991), 203–20; Ada Sosa-Riddell, "Chicanas and El Movimiento," *Aztlán* 5, nos. 1–2 (1974): 155–65; Denise A. Segura and Beatríz M. Pesquera, "Beyond Indifference and Antipathy: The Chicana Movement and Chicana Feminist Discourse," *Aztlán* 19, no. 2 (Fall 1989–90): 69–92.

99. Anna Nieto-Gómez, "La Feminista," *Encuentro Femenil* 1, no. 2 (1974): 34–37. Maylei Blackwell acknowledges Anna Nieto-Gómez and her contributions to Chicana feminism during the harshly sexist, nationalist Chicano movement of the 1960s and 1970s. Blackwell conducted valuable oral interviews with Nieto-Gómez in 1991 to write about her organization, the Hijas de Cuauhtémoc. See Blackwell, "Contested Histories and Retrofitted Memory: Chicana Feminist Subjectivities between and beyond Nationalist Imaginaries—An Oral History of the Hijas de Cuauhtémoc" (Qualifying Essay, History of Consciousness, University of California at Santa Cruz, May 1997). Her essay offers a useful critique of historiography. She argues, "If historiography can be seen as a political practice which is politically charged, then I, along with the subjects of this history, can build a narrative and discursive practice which allows for the kind of writing which can speak silences in a multi-sited way" (3).

100. Teresa Córdova, "Roots and Resistance: The Emergent Writings of Twenty Years of Chicana Feminist Stuggle," in *Handbook of Hispanic Cultures in the United States: Sociology,* ed. Félix Padilla (Houston: Arte Público Press, 1994), 175–202.

101. On a panel at the National Association of Chicano Studies held at the University of California, Riverside, in 1981, González and three other openly gay panelists bravely brought Chicana lesbians and Chicano gay men to the forefront. The homophobia was so severe that not for another decade was lesbianism discussed at NACS. In 1983, at another NACS conference, in Ypsilanti, Michigan, Gloria Anzaldúa was confronted with homophobic remarks by the majority of participants. It is interesting that these instances have been so negated that when many Chicana heterosexual feminists decide to conduct a genealogy of Chicana feminism, they conveniently forget the early efforts by Chicana lesbians whose

work was silenced, repressed, and rejected for publication. Cherríe Moraga, one of the first Chicana lesbians writing about feminism, did not deliberately address Chicano studies, but her anthology, co-edited with Gloria Anzaldúa, was a significant intervention in Chicano/a studies. See Gloria Anzaldúa and Cherríe Moraga, *This Bridge Called My Back: A Collection of Writings by Radical Women of Color* (Watertown, Mass.: Persephone Press, 1981). For a critique of Chicana lesbian erasure in the academy, see Deena González, "Speaking Secrets: Living Chicana Theory," in *Living Chicana Theory*, ed. Carla Trujillo (Berkeley: Third Woman Press, 1998), 46–77. See also the following articles: Alicia Gaspar de Alba, "Tortillerismo: Work by Chicana Lesbians," *Signs: Journal of Women in Culture and Society* 18, no. 4 (Summer 1993), 956–63; Yvonne Yarbro-Bejarano, "The Lesbian Body in Latina Cultural Production," *¿Entiendes? Queer Readings, Hispanic Writings*, ed. Emilie L. Bergman and Paul Julian Smith (Durham: Duke University Press, 1995), 181–97; and Carla Trujillo, "Chicana Lesbians: Fear and Loathing in the Chicano Community," in *Chicana Lesbians: The Girls Our Mothers Warned Us About*, ed. Carla Trujillo (Berkeley: Third Woman Press, 1991).

102. García, "Studying Chicanas: Bringing Women into the Frame of Chicano Studies," in Córdova, *Chicana Voices*, 19–29.

103. The history of women in the American West has its own resplendent historiography. Many scholars anchor the emerging field with the studies published in two anthologies: Susan Armitage and Elizabeth Jameson, eds., *The Women's West* (Norman: University of Oklahoma Press, 1987); Lillian Schlissel, Vicki Ruiz, and Janice Monk, eds., *Western Women: Their Land, Their Lives* (Albuquerque: University of New Mexico Press, 1988). The essay by Joan M. Jensen and Darlis A. Millar, however, is the first to broach new methods for the study of women in the American West; Jensen and Millar, "The Gentle Tamers Revisited: New Approaches to the History of Women in the American West," *Pacific Historical Review* 40 (1980): 173–214. In a comprehensive historiographic essay, Antonia I. Castañeda critiques how women of color have been conceptualized in the literature on women of the West; see Castañeda, "Women of Color." See also Deena González, "La Tules of Image and Reality," and Sarah Deutsch, *No Separate Refuge: Culture, Class, and Gender on an Anglo-Hispanic Frontier in the American Southwest, 1880–1940* (New York: Oxford University Press, 1987).

104. Joan Kelly Gadol, "Did Women Have a Renaissance?" in *Becoming Visible: Women in European History*, 2nd ed., ed. Renate Bridenthal, Claudia Koonz, and Susan Mosher Stuard (Boston: Houghton Mifflin, 1987). I would like to thank my colleague Sandra McGee Deutsch for her insights and conversations with me about how Latin American women's history is often neglected by specialists in European women's history. For an excellent example of women's political agendas on the "right" in Latin America, see Sandra McGee Deutsch, "The Right under Radicalism, 1916–1930," in *The Argentine Right: Its History and Intellectual Origins, 1910 to Present*, ed. Sandra McGee Deutsch and Ronald H. Dolkhart (Wilmington, Del.: Scholarly Resources, 1993), 34–63.

105. Anna Macías, "The Mexican Revolution Was No Revolution for Women," in *Is the Mexican Revolution Dead?*, ed. Stanley R. Ross, 2nd ed. (Philadelphia: Temple University Press, 1975).

106. Anzaldúa, *Borderlands/La Frontera*.

107. José Vasconcelos, *La raza cósmica: Misión de la raza Ibero-Americana* (México, D.F.: Aguilar S.A. de Ediciones, 1961).

108. White, *The Content of the Form*, 121.

109. Anzaldúa, *Borderlands/La Frontera*, 77.

110. Ibid., 80.

111. I am thinking of the many publications by Chicana/o cultural critics who

consciously cross borders between literary criticism and historicized cultural events. Genaro Padilla and Rosaura Sánchez have most recently excavated historical documents to theorize the identity formation of elite Mexicans in nineteenth-century California and New Mexico. Their new historicism, however, privileges a history of the elite, while social history has attempted to write the unseen into Chicana/o history. See Padilla, *My History, Not Yours: The Formation of Mexican American Autobiography* (Madison: University of Wisconsin Press, 1993); Rosaura Sánchez, *Telling Identities: The California Testimonios* (Minneapolis: University of Minnesota Press, 1995).

112. Foucault, *The Archaeology of Knowledge*, 14.

113. Friedrich Nietzsche, *The Use and Abuse of History*, trans. Adrian Collins (Indianapolis and New York: Liberal Arts Press and Bobbs-Merrill, 1957).

114. See White, chap. 2 of *The Content of the Form*, 26–57.

115. Ashis Nandy, *The Intimate Enemy: Loss and Recovery of Self under Colonialism* (New Delhi: Oxford University Press, 1983), 62.

116. Foucault, *The Order of Things*, 372.

117. White, *Metahistory*, 7. White defines emplotment as "the way a sequence of events are fashioned into a story gradually revealed to be a story of a particular kind." He uses Northrop Frye's *Anatomy of Criticism* to identify "four different modes of emplotment: Romance, Tragedy, Comedy, and Satire." Frye, *Anatomy of Criticism: Four Essays* (Princeton: Princeton University Press, 1957).

118. I borrow from White, who argues that "the historian arranges the events in the chronicle into a hierarchy of significance by assigning events different functions as story elements in such a way as to disclose the formal coherence of a whole set of events considered as a comprehensible process with a discernable beginning, middle, and end." White, *Metahistory*, 7. My point is that Chicano/a historians have imposed a hierarchy of significance by choosing certain events, omitting others, and arranging the chosen events into their own notion of what is or is not important. I am simply arguing that I will consciously emplot my story and therefore arrange the events that I have found significant.

2. FEMINISM-IN-NATIONALISM

1. Ignacio Gamboa, *La Mujer Moderna* (Mérida, Yuc.: Imprenta "Gamboa Gúzman," 1906), 37; see also Anna Macías, *Against All Odds: The Feminist Movement in Mexico to 1940* (Westport, Conn.: Greenwood Press, 1982), 16, for the English translation.

2. Foucault, *The Archaeology of Knowledge*, 138.

3. Gayatri Chakravorty Spivak, "A Literary Representation of the Subaltern: A Woman's Text from the Third World," in *In Other Worlds: Essays in Cultural Politics* (New York: Routledge, 1988), 241.

4. Ibid.

5. Homi K. Bhabha lectured engagingly and extensively on the "dialectics of doubling" in his six-week course at the School of Criticism and Theory at Dartmouth College in the summer of 1993. I am grateful to him for his insightful analysis. For more on his theories, refer to his eloquent essays on the postcolonial in *The Location of Culture*. On pages 50, 52–57, 95, and 136–38, Bhabha' defines his notion of "doubling." I am using "doubling" to refer to the manner in which women "doubled" with men's agendas seeming to agree, yet in actuality articulating their own position.

6. See R. Radhakrishnan, "Nationalism, Gender, and the Narrative of Identity," in *Nationalisms and Sexualities*, ed. Andrew Parker, Mary Russo, Doris Sommer, and Patricia Yeager (New York: Routledge, 1992), 77–95.

7. Cultural critics continue to theorize the "third space" as intervention and political stance. The following are only a few examples of contemporary theorists who illustrate third space voices, politics, and feminisms. Gayatri Chakravorty Spivak, I believe, is avowing the third space in her essay "Can the Subaltern Speak?" in *Marxism and the Interpretation of Culture*, ed. Cary Nelson and Lawrence Grossberg (Chicago: University of Chicago Press, 1988), 271–313; Norma Alarcón affirms the third space in "Chicana Feminism"; see also Donna J. Haraway for acknowledgement of third space interventions in "Situated Knowledges: The Science Question and the Privilege of Partial Perspective," in *Simians, Cyborgs, and Women: The Reinvention of Nature* (New York: Routledge, 1991), 183–202; Hayden White elucidates the meaning of the third space in "Writing in the Middle Voice," *Stanford Literature Review* 9, no. 2 (Fall 1992): 179–87. The article by Chéla Sandoval on differential consciousness specifically traces the methodology of third space feminist politics; see Sandoval, "U.S Third World Feminism." I also rely on Foucault's archaeology, his precursor to his genealogical method, to examine where in discourse the gaps and the interstitial moments of history reappear to be seen or heard as that third space; see Foucault, *The Order of Things*, and especially *The Archaeology of Knowledge*. Roland Barthes also wrote about the "third meaning" "as both persistent and fugitive, apparent and evasive," hence an "obtuse meaning" and not the obvious. See his essay "The Third Meaning," in *The Responsibility of Forms: Critical Essays on Music, Art, and Representation*, trans. Richard Howard (Berkeley: University of California Press, 1991), 44.

8. For a comprehensive study on the Revolution in Yucatán, see Gilbert M. Joseph, *Revolution from Without: Yucatán, México and the United States, 1880–1924* (New York: Cambridge University Press, 1982).

9. Bhabha, *The Location of Culture*, 37.

10. Ibid.

11. Macías, *Against All Odds*, 152.

12. Evelyn Stevens, "Marianismo: The Other Face of Machismo in Latin America," in *Female and Male in Latin America: Essays*, ed. Ann Pescatello (Pittsburgh: University of Pittsburgh Press, 1973), 89–101; Barbara Welter, "The Cult of True Womanhood, 1820–1860," *American Quarterly* 18 (Summer 1966): 151–74. Welter, who coined the phrase "cult of true womanhood," argues that the domestic sphere robbed women of power and left them passive victims. Since then, many historians have disagreed with her. Silvia Arrom equates marianismo with the "cult of true womanhood," arguing that this Victorian idea from Europe and the United States greatly influenced Latin American women. Arrom, *The Women of Mexico City, 1790–1857* (Stanford: Stanford University Press, 1985), 259–68.

13. Fedelio Quintal Martín, *Yucatán, un periodo de Historia contemporanea, 1910–24* (México: Ediciones de la Universidad de Yucatán, 1974), 18, 20.

14. Ibid., 18–19.

15. Joseph, *Revolution from Without*, 129.

16. For more information on the origins of the Contagious Diseases Acts, refer to the female reformer credited with beginning the campaigns against the discriminatory legislation in England: Josephine E. Butler, *Personal Reminiscences of a Great Crusade* (1911; reprint, Westport, Conn.: Hyperion Press, 1976). The great crusader addressed the male double standard in her "Woman's Protest," where she declared, "it is unjust to punish the sex who are the victims of a vice, and leave unpunished the sex who are the main cause, both of the vice and its dreaded consequences" (9). The vice, of course, was prostitution, and the consequences were the sexually transmitted diseases.

17. *Reglamento del Artículo 222 del Código Sanitario para el Régimen de la Prostitución*, 22 December 1910, AGEY.

18. Ibid., articles 6 and 7.

19. Ibid., article 11.
20. Ibid., articles 11 and 12.
21. Ibid., article 14.
22. Ibid.
23. Ibid., article 9. He declared, "a radical social hygiene plan goes into effect."
24. Ibid.
25. Ibid.
26. Antonio Manero, *The Meaning of the Mexican Revolution* (Mexico, 1915), 100. In this chapter, Manero discussed "Public Education as a Cause of Revolution."
27. Ibid., 98.
28. Salvador Alvarado, *La reconstrucción de México: Un mensaje a los pueblos de America*, 2 vols. (México: Ediciones del Gobierno de Yucatán, 1980), 2:120.
29. Ibid., 2:115–16.
30. Ibid., 2:107–108.
31. Ibid., 2:109.
32. Ibid., 2:115–16.
33. Speech of General Salvador Alvarado, Governor of the State of Yucatán, at the Closing Session of the Second Pedagogic Congress, Held at Mérida (New York City, 1916) and *Carranza and Public Instruction in México: Sixty Mexican Teachers Are Commissioned to Study in Boston* (New York City, 1915).
34. Agustín Rivera y Sanroman, 1908. An untitled pamphlet by the author on the education of women in Mexico can be found in the Silvestre Terrazas Collection at the Bancroft Library, UC Berkeley.
35. Ibid.
36. Ibid.
37. Ibid.
38. Ibid.
39. Ibid.
40. Rivera refered to the sixteenth-century French essayist Michel de Montaigne.
41. My use of statistics may seem contradictory with my premises in chapter 1 about using quantitive methods to prove arguments, but in fact, I was not arguing against their usefulness in social history. I am merely pointing out that social history is its own political project, and that statistics are often the most convincing tools that can be employed to prove social inequities, especially where liberal politics are concerned. In other words, quantitative measures do serve a purpose; however, a conscious, self-reflexive approach can help to interrogate who is implementing statistics and for what purposes.
42. See the tables in *Estadística Escolar Primaria de la República Mexicana* (México, 1931).
43. Secretaría de Agricultura y Fomento, *Tercer censo de población de los Estados Unidos verificados el 27 de octubre de 1910*, 2 vols. (México: Oficina Impresora de la Secretaría de Hacienda, 1918).
44. *Estadística Escolar Primaria*, tables.
45. Ibid.
46. Alvarado discussed the advantages of coeducation at length at the Second Pedagogic Congress.
47. *Estadística Escolar Primaria*, tables.
48. *Tesorería General del Estado de Yucatán, Mérida*, 1913, 41–46.
49. Ibid., 13.
50. *Estadística Escolar Primaria*, tables.
51. *Speech of General Salvador Alvarado, . . . Second Pedagogic Congress*.
52. Roberto Reyes Barriere to Governor Salvador Alvarado, 22 October 1915, AGEY.
53. *Estadística Escolar Primaria*, tables.

54. Ibid.

55. *Speech of General Salvador Alvarado, . . . Second Pedagogic Congress.*

56. *La Mujer Moderna,* 31 October 1915. The only surviving copy of Galindo's magazine known to me is in the Benson Latin American Collection, housed at the University of Texas at Austin. I searched through archives in Mexico City and have not found any more copies. I am hoping that some may have survived in private collections.

57. Angeles Mendieta Alatorre, *La mujer en la revolución mexicana* (Mexico: Talleres Gráficos de la Nación, 1961), 78–79; Macías, *Against All Odds,* 33.

58. *La Mujer Moderna,* 31 October 1915, 14.

59. Centro de Estudios de Historia de México Condumex, Carranza Collection, carpetas 107, 120, December 1916. I discovered at least twenty letters from state governors to Carranza showing their support of the magazine.

60. *Carranza and Public Instruction in México,* 23.

61. Alvarado, *La reconstrucción de México* (Mexico, 1919); *Speech of General Salvador Alvarado, . . . Second Pedagogic Congress; La Voz de la Revolución,* January, November, and December 1916. These issues of the newspaper report the organizing of the congresses as well as the proceedings.

62. Hermila Galindo, *La mujer en el porvenir.*

63. Primer Congreso Feminista de Yucatán, *Anales de esa memorable asamblea* (Mérida: Talleres Tipográficos del "Ateneo Peninsular," 1916), 96.

64. Ibid.

65. Ibid.

66. Ibid.

67. Ibid.

68. Ibid., 97.

69. Ibid.

70. Ibid.

71. Ibid., 99.

72. Primer Congreso Feminista de Yucatán. García Ortiz's argument was one that had been popular in the United States when progressive reformers decided that women could help clean up society through their participation in social agencies which would do "housecleaning."

73. Macías, *Against All Odds.* In her chapter "Yucatán and the Women's Movement, 1870–1920," Macías argues that the congresses were split ideologically into three camps—the radical, moderate, and conservative. The proceedings do reflect this split. These categories should not be confused with contemporary notions of "radical" feminism, in which "radical" can often imply separatist lesbian of color politics.

74. Venustiano Carranza, *Ley sobre relaciones familiares* (México: Imprenta del Gobierno, 1917).

75. Primer Congreso Feminista de Yucatán, 108.

76. Ibid., 42–48.

77. *La Voz de la Revolución,* 10 January 1916, 1. Alvarado's newspaper kept the public informed about his activities in their state. The daily reported on the proceedings of both congresses. Unfortunately, the bound issues housed at the Hemeroteca Pino Suárez in Mérida are disintegrating because of humidity and age.

78. *Tercer censo de población de los Estados Unidos verificados el 27 de octubre de 1910,* 1266–1306. The census shows that only one woman was a dentist, twenty-nine were midwives (none were doctors), forty-two worked for the government in some capacity, and five were barbers. These were the non-traditional jobs, with the exception of midwives. Most other women worked in unskilled, ungainful employment.

79. Macías, *Against All Odds*, 75–76.
80. Primer Congreso Feminista de Yucatán, 127.
81. Salvador Alvarado, *La reconstrucción de México*. In these volumes, Alvarado addressed topics befitting a presidential candidate after he left Yucatán as its governor. In volume 2, pp. 107–19, he wrote that women's conditions in México needed improvement.
82. *La Voz de la Revolución*, 24 November 1916, 1.
83. Ibid., 30 November 1916, 4–5.
84. Hermila Galindo, *Estudio de la Señorita Hermila Galindo con motivo de los temas que han de absolverse en el Segundo Congreso Feminista de Yucatán* (Mérida, Yuc.: Imprenta del Gobierno Constitucionalista, 1916).
85. Ibid., 8.
86. Ibid., 7.
87. Anna Macías argues that attendance from primarily Yucatecan women made it a regional congress. She also points out that the Mexican feminist writer Artemisa Saénz Royo falsely claimed that the congresses were international, with women from Europe and Latin America. Macías, *Against All Odds*, 84, n. 79. See also Artemisa Saénz Royo's study, *Historia política-social-cultural del movimiento femenino en México* (México: M. León Sánchez, 1954). The proceedings from the congresses defend Macías's argument.
88. Salvador Alvarado, *Breves apuntes acerca de la administración del General Salvador Alvarado, como Gobernador de Yucatán, con simple expresión de hechos y sus consecuencias* (Mérida, Yuc.: Imprenta del Gobierno Constitucionalista, 1916), passim.
89. See my essay, "'She Has Served Others in More Intimate Ways': The Domestic Servant Reform in Yucatán, 1915–18," in *Las Obreras: The Politics of Work and Family*, ed. Vicki L. Ruiz, *Aztlán* 20, nos. 1–2 (1993): 11–33.
90. Hermila Galindo, *La doctrina Carranza y el acercamiento indolatino* (México, 1919).
91. Ibid., 19.
92. Ibid., 177.
93. Ibid., 171.
94. Hermila Galindo, *Un presidenciable: El General don Pablo González* (México: Imprenta Nacional S.A., 1919).
95. Macías, *Against All Odds*, 34.
96. She not only edited the journal *La Mujer Moderna*, she also served as an honored faculty member with a doctorate at the *Instituto Fiseotomológico Colombiano*. See title page of *La doctrina Carranza*.
97. Bhabha, *The Location of Culture*, 17. Gloria Anzaldúa theorizes how women of color speak in tongues among those who do not listen, or who do not hear the subtle interventions. Anzaldúa names this space "the Coatlicúe state," which is a liberatory, amorphous, transitory, translational, trans-identity state for anyone, not just women of color, who desires communication among differences. See Anzaldúa, *Borderlands/La Frontera*.
98. Ladino was referring to the mestizo population in Yucatán who identified as "white," meaning non-Indian, non-Maya.
99. Casimira Palma to the Department of Justice, 15 August 1915, AGEY.
100. Ibid.
101. Ibid.
102. Ibid.
103. The Department of Justice to Casimira Palma, 15 October 1915, AGEY.
104. Benigna Gám to the Governor, 5 August 1915. "Expediente relativo a la queja de la Señora Benigna Gám contra su esposo el Comandante Militar de Ticul C. Tomás F. Velasco," 1915, AGEY.

105. Gám to the Governor (1915).
106. The Governor regarding Benigna Gám, 10 August 1915, AGEY.
107. Cornelia Padrón to the Governor, 6 January 1916, AGEY.
108. Cornelia Padrón to the Governor, 2 December 1915, AGEY.
109. Silvero Santos to the Governor, 5 January 1916, AGEY.
110. Ibid.
111. Ibid.
112. Demetria Centeno, 22 December 1915, in *Apéndice 1916, No. 14*, Archivo Notarial del Estado de Yucatán (ANY).
113. Ibid.
114. Inez Manzanilla to the Governor, in "Decretos de General Alvarado," April 1915, AGEY.
115. Ibid.
116. Ibid.
117. Ramón Moguel Bolio to the Governor, in "Queja del Señor Ramón Moguel Bolio contra su hermana política Engracia Avila," 1915, AGEY.
118. Ibid.
119. Ibid.
120. Manuel González to the Governor, 4 August 1915, in "Oficio relativo a que ya le pagaron a la Sra Engracia Avila a representación a su madre María Nieves la cantidad de 2250 por el Ramón Moguel, 1915," AGEY.
121. The Governor regarding Sra María Nieves San Miguel, 7 August 1915, AGEY.
122. Galindo, *La doctrina Carranza*, 189–90.
123. Bhabha, *The Location of Culture*, 54.
124. Ibid.
125. Teresa de Lauretis, *Technologies of Gender*, 26.
126. Ibid.

3. THE POETICS OF AN (INTER)NATIONALIST REVOLUTION

1. The revolution occurred after Euoramerican conquest in 1848. It should qualify as Chicana/o history; however, many historians narrowly dictate Chicana/o history within United States perimeters and argue that a study of the Mexican Revolution must remain within those perimeters to be considered Chicana history. We run the risk of contributing to colonialist historiography when we narrow and bind Chicana/o history to the post-1848 continental United States.

2. The first issues of *Regeneración*, from 1900 to 1901, are housed at the Hemeroteca Nacional de México, the country's newspaper archive in Mexico City. Newspaper issues from 1914 to 1917 are also housed at the Hemeroteca. A complete collection of *Regeneración*, which was published in Los Angeles from 1910 to 1918, can be found in the Chicano Studies Research Center Library, University of California, Los Angeles.

3. Other monographs and articles which highlight the women of the Partido Liberal Mexicano are Ines Hernandez Tovar, "Sara Estela Ramirez: The Early Twentieth Century Texas-Mexican Poet" (Ph.D. diss., University of Houston, 1984); Emilio Zamora, "Sara Estela Ramírez: Una Rosa Roja en el Movimiento," in *Mexican Women in the United States*, ed. Adelaida Del Castillo and Magdalena Mora (Los Angeles: Chicano Studies Research Center Publications, University of California, 1980), 163–69; Emilio Zamora, *The World of the Mexican Worker in*

NOTES TO PAGES 57–61 / 147

Texas (College Station: Texas A&M University Press, 1993), chap. 6, "Socialists and Magonistas in the Cotton Belt, 1912–16."

4. Gómez-Quiñones, *Sembradores*. An issue of *Regeneración*, a contemporary newspaper that takes its name from the PLM's paper, was published in San Diego in 1993. The newspaper took a nationalist stance with a moralist pro-family, homophobic, anti-feminist agenda—in many ways conservative, compared to the anarchists of the PLM.

5. Bhabha, *The Location of Culture*.

6. The recent documentary *Chicano* uncovers the history of the Chicano movement as it emerged in the 1960s. Three male leaders are featured. Women narrate the men's stories, as if narration by women makes the history of the movement inclusive; in fact, women's feminist activities that paralleled the men's are not acknowledged in the documentary. The erasure is apparent to some.

7. Chávez, "Creating Aztlán."

8. Linda Hutcheon refers to Jacques Derrida's meditation on the "metaphysical foundations of historiography." I borrow loosely from a premise of "repetition and traces," which is quite useful to understanding how as historians we inevitably impose meanings upon the past; hence a chain of events is constructed across time through a repetition of rhetoric imposed upon the past from the present. See Hutcheon, *The Poetics of Postmodernism*, 97. See also Jacques Derrida, *Positions*, trans. Alan Bass (Chicago: University of Chicago Press, 1981).

9. For my purpose, the decolonial imaginary explains those in-between spaces that deconstruct the binaries of a colonialist history. Again, while I agree with the postcolonial as a perspective, as hope, as a utopian project, I propose that Chicana/o history is in the process of decolonizing otherness; hence the decolonial imaginary becomes the useful apparatus for critique. For a discussion of the "postcolonial perspective," see Bhabha, *The Location of Culture*, chap. 9, "The Postcolonial and the Postmodern." He argues that the postcolonial perspective attempts "to revise those nationalist or nativist pedagogies that set up the relation of Third World and First World in a binary structure of opposition. It forces a recognition of the more complex cultural and political boundaries that exist on the cusp of these often opposed political spheres" (173).

10. *Regeneración*, 24 September 1910.

11. Elizabeth Gurley Flynn, *I Speak My Own Piece: Autobiography of "The Rebel Girl"* (New York: International Publishers, 1955).

12. Eugene V. Debs, "Women," in *American Appeal*, 30 October 1926.

13. Ann Schofield, "Rebel Girls and Union Maids: The Woman Question in Journals of the AFL and IWW, 1905–1920," *Feminist Studies* 9 (Summer 1983): 335–55.

14. Michael Miller Topp, "Immigrant Culture and the Politics of Identity: Italian-American Syndicalists in the U.S., 1911–1927" (Ph.D. diss., Brown University, 1993). See esp. the chapter "The Intervention Debate: The Contested Definitions of Syndicalism and Masculinity in the Italian Socialist Federation," 106–52.

15. White, *Metahistory*.

16. Rafael Pérez-Torres, *Movements in Chicano Poetry: Against Myths, Against Margins* (New York: Cambridge University Press, 1995).

17. Ethel Duffy Turner, *Revolution in Baja California: Ricardo Flores Magón's High Noon* (Detroit: Blaine Etheridge Books, 1981), 109. Jesús Flores Magón became an agent for Francisco Madero, who by 1911 was no longer allied with the magonistas.

18. Ibid., 3, 103; see also Armando Bartra, *Regeneración, 1900–1918* (México, D.F.: ERA, 1977), for an excellent chronology of *Regeneración*'s publication.

19. *Los Angeles Times*, 2 October 1910; see Turner, *Revolution in Baja California*, 13,

for a discussion of Harrison Gray Otis's land grab in Mexico; the bombing of the *Times* building is discussed more fully in chapters 21 and 22 of Grace Stimson's *Rise of the Labor Movement in Los Angeles* (Los Angeles: University of California Press, 1955), 366–419.

20. Juan Gómez-Quiñones, "Social Change and Intellectual Discontent: The Growth of Mexican Nationalism, 1890–1911" (Ph.D. diss., University of California, Los Angeles, 1972), 149–50. Shirlene Soto, "The Mexican Woman: A Study of Her Participation in the Revolution, 1910–40" (Ph.D. diss., University of New Mexico, 1977), 28. In July of 1906, the PLM issued its reform program, in which were listed provisions for the protection of women. By 1910 the PLM's anarchist views were made known. Many studies have defined the PLM's anarchist ideology as a mixture of unorthodox anarchism, syndicalism, and communism. See Gómez-Quiñones, *Sembradores*; W. Dirk Raat, *Revoltosos: Mexico's Rebels in the United States, 1903–1923* (College Station: Texas A&M University Press, 1981); John Hart, *Anarchism and the Mexican Working Class, 1860–1913* (Austin: University of Texas Press, 1978). Hart argues that Mexican anarchism had a European influence, and he cites the intellectuals who migrated to Mexico, taking with them anarchist perspectives. See also David Poole, *Land and Liberty: Anarchist Influences in the Mexican Revolution—Ricardo Flores Magón* (Sanday, U.K.: Cienfuegos Press, 1977); James A. Sandos, *Rebellion in the Borderlands: Anarchism and the Plan of San Diego, 1904–1923* (Norman: University of Oklahoma Press, 1992).

21. *Regeneración*, 24 September 1910.

22. Ibid. This English translation is by Prensa Sembradora, from Del Castillo and Mora, eds., *Mexican Women in the United States*, 161.

23. *Regeneración*, 24 September 1910.

24. Ibid.

25. Margaret S. Marsh, *Anarchist Women, 1870–1920* (Philadelphia: Temple University Press, 1981), 19–20; Hart, *Anarchism and the Mexican Working Class*, 17; Ricardo Flores Magón, *Artículos Políticos, 1917* (México, D.F.: Ediciones Antorcha, 1981), 186–88; Gómez-Quiñones, *Sembradores*, 20.

26. E. V. Zenker, *Anarchism* (London: Methuen and Co., 1898), 9–11.

27. *Regeneración*, 24 September 1910.

28. John Kenneth Turner, *Barbarous Mexico*, 2nd ed., introduction by Sinclair Snow (1910; reprint, Austin: University of Texas Press, 1969); Ethel Duffy Turner, *Revolution in Baja California*, 2; Ethel Duffy Turner, "Writers and Revolutionists: An Interview Conducted by Ruth Teiser" (Berkeley: University of California, Bancroft Library, Regional History Office, 1967), 22; *Regeneración*, 24 December 1910.

29. *Regeneración*, 6 November 1910. "No pudiendo ser mujer, la mujer quiere ser hombre; se lanza con un entusiasmo digno de un feminismo más racional en pos de todas las cosas feas que un hombre puede ser y hacer. . . ."

30. Ibid.: "El 'feminismo' sirve de base a la oposición, de los enemigos de la emancipación de la mujer. Ciertamente no hay nada atractivo en una mujer alejada de la dulce misión de su sexo para empuñar el látigo de la opresión en una mujer huyendo de su graciosa individualidad femenina para vestir la hibridez del 'honbrunamiento.'"

31. Ibid.: "La igualdad libertaria no trata de hacer *hombre* de la mujer; de las mismas oportunidades a las fracciones de la especie humana para que ambas se desarrollen sin obstáculos . . . sin estorbarase en el lugar que cada uno tiene en una naturaleza. Mujeres y hombres hemos de luchar por esta igualdad racional . . . porque sin ella habrá perpetuamente en el hogar la simiente de la tirania, el retoño de la desdicha social."

32. 14 January 1911. "Revolucionarias: el día que nos veáis vacilar, escupidnos el rostro!" "Las Revolucionarias" was published in the same issue that announced

Guerrero's death, a blow to the PLM. In that issue Ricardo Flores Magón wrote an article in which he eulogized Guerrero and his importance to the PLM.

33. *Regeneración,* 11 September 1911: "He venido haciendo cargos concretos contra Antonio I. Villarreal. Le he llamado pederasta y asesino y otras cosas mas, y él, tan 'fresco.' Porque no contesta? El silencio no disculpa; antes, mejor, en el caso de Villarreal, acusa. Por todas partes se dice puesto que Villarreal se calla ante el tremendo cargo de que no es hombre, sino un ... pederasta.... Villarreal no tiene derecho a ver a ningún hombre de frente; Villarreal debe ser escupido por todos los hombres y por todas las mujeres."

34. Debs, "Women." Reprinted here by the Socialist Party, Debs's essays had initially appeared in the early twenties.

35. Flynn, *I Speak My Own Piece.*

36. Ibid., 9, 91, 103, 191–94.

37. Ibid., 4.

38. Ibid., 55–58.

39. *Regeneración,* 13 June 1914; Turner, *Revolution in Baja California,* 66–67. In an oral interview that I conducted on 17 April 1982 in Madera, California, *la magonista* Josephina Arancibia informed me that she had known Margarita Ortega. She confirmed Ortega's murder by the Huertistas in Mexicali.

40. Mendieta Alatorre, *La mujer en la revolución mexicana,* 39.

41. *Los Angeles Times,* 19 September 1907; Turner, "Writers and Revolutionists." Turner tells of Talavera's activities as a loyalist to the party. Her harassment by U.S. federal agents is cited in *Regeneración,* 14 October 1916.

42. *Los Angeles Times,* 19 September 1907.

43. Turner, "Writers and Revolutionists," 11.

44. In an interview on 17 April 1982, *magonista* Josephina Arancibia told me that she and her younger sister had visited the farm during summers. She remembered that while women helped to fold newspapers and worked in the fields planting and harvesting, they also did all the cooking and cleaning in the house. There are conflicting reports about the location of the communal farm; however, Señora Arancibia recalls that it was in the Silver Lake/Echo Park area of Los Angeles.

45. *Regeneración,* 6 December 1915.

46. Antonio de Pio, "La Mujer Obrera Bajo el Burgués" (The Working-Class Woman under the Bourgeoisie), *Regeneración,* 14 December 1912; René Chaughl, "La Mujer Esclava" (The Woman Slave), *Regeneración,* 20 January 1912; Paula Carmona de Flores Magón, "Que Luchen" (Let Them Fight), *Regeneración,* 8 October 1910; Antonio I. Villarreal, "La Mujer Pide Guerra" (Women Demand War), *Regeneración,* 1 October 1910; and Blanca de Moncaleano, "Para Ti, Mujer" (For You, Woman), *Regeneración,* 22 March 1913.

47. A. Graviota to Ricardo Flores Magón, Mexico, 16 May 1904, in the Silvestre Terrazas Collection, University of California, Berkeley, Bancroft Library. The letter from Graviota warns Flores Magón that he must stop the rumors scandalizing Juana Gutiérrez de Mendoza and Elisa Acuña y Rosetti. The letter reveals that the two women did not leave the *junta* in Laredo on congenial terms; the reasons why are uncertain. The Hemeroteca Nacional in Mexico City houses the only two surviving copies of *Vesper,* the newspaper edited by Juana Mendoza and Elisa Rosetti.

48. *Regeneración,* 8 October 1910. "Compañeras, madres mexicanas: empujad a vuestros maridos a la lucha. . . . Debemos luchar todos, hombres y mujeres. La mujer tiene muchas veces la culpa de que se abstenga el hombre de tomar parte en las grandes luchas por la libertad, sin pensar que con eso ho hace sino degradar al hombre y degradarse ella misma, porque la esclavitud no dignifica, la miseria no eleva el carácter."

49. *Regeneración,* 21 January 1911.

50. Ibid. "Mujeres somos; pero no hemos sentido flaguezas que nos empujen a abandonar la pelea.... Derecho tenemos a demandar entereza de los que vacilan."

51. The newspapers founded and edited by the Villarreal sisters were advertised as such in *Regeneración,* 3 September 1910, 10 September 1910, 17 September 1910, and many more issues. W. Dirk Raat offers a few paragraphs on the Villarreals in *Revoltosos.*

52. *El Paso Record,* 5 November 1909; see also the *San Antonio Light,* 18 August 1909, and *Woman's National Daily,* 2 November 1909, for more information on the Villarreals. These newspaper clippings can be located in the John Murray Papers, Bancroft Library, University of California, Berkeley.

53. Secretaría de Relaciones Exteriores, Archivo, México, D.F., Asunto Flores Magón, Colección L–E–918–954, sobre Juan Moncaleano. See also *Regeneración,* 12 October 1912 and 22 February 1913.

54. *Regeneración,* 22 February 1913. "No olvidéis que la mujer tiene derechos al igual que los hombres, que no habéis llegado al mundo tan sólo para multiplicar la humanidad, soplar el fagón, lavar ropa, y fregar platos. . . ."

55. *Regeneración,* 22 March 1913.

56. See *Luz,* 10 October and 21 November 1917, and 23 January 1918. I'm grateful to John Hart, professor of history at the University of Houston, for allowing me to copy his private collection of the newspaper *Luz.*

57. See *Regeneración,* 1, 8, 22, 29 March 1913 for news items on La Casa del Obrero Internacional, and 10 September, 8 October 1910, 14 December 1912, and 17 November 1917 for essays commending Ferrer Guardia and the workers' schools.

58. *Los Angeles Times,* March 1913; La Casa del Obrero Internacional in Los Angeles, California, no longer stands. See the Second Annual Report of the Municipal Charities Commission, City of Los Angeles, July 1914–July 1915, 64, for a brief report on the Los Angeles Orphans' Home, which was at Yale and Alpine in 1880. While the building remained, the Orphans' Home was moved in 1911; the PLM took over two years later.

59. City Hall Land Records, Los Angeles, Department of Buildings, Application to Alter, 10 March 1914.

60. R. G. Cox, *Regeneración,* 10 February 1917.

61. Turner, *Revolution in Baja California,* 82–83.

62. Unión del Barrio, *La Verdad,* "Concientización y Liberación," July–September 1993. "This writing emanated from attendance at the UCLA-based meeting June 14, 1993." Evidently the meeting was held to discuss the César Chávez Center, UCLA's new Chicano Studies Program.

63. Unión del Barrio, *La Verdad,* July–September 1993.

64. Ibid.

4. TEJANAS

1. Interviews with Estela Gómez (Reyes after her marriage), 8, 15, 22 June 1979, 5 February 1988, conducted by Thomas Kreneck, Houston Metropolitan Research Center, Houston Public Library. Kreneck and I conducted another interview on 18 May 1989. See also the Melesio Gómez Collection.

2. Bhabha, *The Location of Culture,* 169–70. Bhabha contends that "the migrants, the minorities, the diasporic come to change the history of the nation."

3. For an excellent synthesis of diaspora studies and its foremost proponents, see James Clifford, "Diasporas." His is one of the most comprehensive essays on diaspora, with an exhaustive bibliography. Other insightful works referring to gender and diaspora include Mary Louise Pratt, *Imperial Eyes: Travel Writing and*

Transculturation (London: Routledge, 1992); Janet Wolff, "On the Road Again: Metaphors of Travel in Cultural Criticism," *Cultural Studies* 7, no. 2 (1993): 224–39. For contemporary Mexican diaspora and postmodernity, see Roger Rouse, "Mexican Migration and the Social Space of Postmodernism," *Diaspora* 1, no. 1 (1991): 8–23.

4. Gómez-Quiñones, *Roots of Chicano Politics*, 42–49. According to Gómez-Quiñones, the "most complete discussion of the historical boundaries of Tejas" during its colonial years under Spain is José Antonio Pichardo, *Pichardo's Treatise on the Limits of Louisiana and Texas*, 2 vols., trans. Charles Wilson Hackett (Austin: University of Texas Press, 1931–32). For a cursory history of Indians in Texas, consult a foundational study: Elizabeth A. H. John, *Storms Brewed in Other Men's Worlds: The Confrontation of Indians, Spanish and French in the Southwest, 1540–1795* (College Station: Texas A&M University Press, 1975).

5. For an explanation of land shifting beneath people—that is, boundaries moving as a result of Euroamerican colonization—see González, *Refusing the Favor*.

6. Lisbeth Haas offers a creative argument about space and its effects on identities. Her work, influenced by Edward Soja, argues that "social meaning is derived largely through the organization of space." In her critique of linear history, Haas, like Soja and Michel Foucault, challenges how time, when conceptualized linearly to construct history, "peripheralizes the geographical or spatial imagination." Haas, *Conquests and Historical Identities in California*, 5. See also Edward W. Soja, *Postmodern Geographies: The Reassertion of Space in Critical Social Theory* (London: Verso, 1989).

7. Borderland studies initially emerged out of the Herbert Eugene Bolton school at the University of California, Berkeley, in the early twentieth century. It is interesting to see how "borderland" studies have evolved through the decades as both historians and more recently literary critics have adapted the imagination of borderlands. For examples of Spanish Borderland history, see Herbert E. Bolton, *Texas in the Middle Eighteenth Century* (Berkeley: University of California Press, 1915); Gerald E. Payo and Gilberto M. Hinojosa, "Spanish Texas and the Borderlands Historiography in Transition: Implications in United States History," *Journal of American History* 75 (September 1988). Antonia I. Castañeda challenged borderland historians who have neglected to historicize gender and the way in which the borderlands are transformed when gender politicizes the frontier. See Castañeda, "Gender, Race, and Culture." For examples of literary critics who have reinscribed the borderlands, refer to the anthology with an array of Chicana/o literary critics edited by Héctor Calderón and José David Saldívar, *Criticism in the Borderlands: Studies in Chicano Literature, Culture, and Ideology* (Durham, N.C.: Duke University Press, 1991).

8. Clifford, "Diasporas," 304.

9. For recent historical studies that accentuate the experience of Chicanos/as as an immigrant experience, see Gutiérrez, *Walls and Mirrors*, and George J. Sánchez, *Becoming Mexican American*. Both problematize "immigrant"; however, Gutiérrez tends to universalize the normative male immigrant experience by unmarking gender, therefore negating what is unique to women as immigrants. Historiography on immigrant women, I think, has shown how gender has marked the immigrant experience. As examples, see Rosalinda M. González, "Chicanas and Mexican Immigrant Families, 1920–40: Women's Subordination and Family Exploitation," in *Decades of Discontent: The Women's Movement, 1920–1940*, ed. Lois Scharf and Joan Jensen (Westport, Conn.: Greenwood Press, 1983), 59–83; Virginia Yans-McLaughlin, *Family and Community: Italian Immigrants in Buffalo, 1880–1930* (Ithaca, N.Y.: Cornell University Press, 1971). Both works measure how the conditions of the immigrant experience differ when women must contend with

their social and political lives in a new world. Gutiérrez does put forth the useful term "ethnic Mexican" to classify the Mexican origin population of the United States, whether citizens or not. For my purposes in this chapter, however, I resort to the women's self-naming in Texas during the 1920 and 1930s. Most of the women made distinctions between being tejanas, Mexicans, or Mexican Americans without a hyphen.

10. Clifford, "Diasporas," 308.

11. Ibid., 305. Clifford is summarizing William Safran's more strict definition of diaspora and interrogating its rigidity. See Safran, "Diasporas in Modern Societies: Myths of Homeland and Return," *Diaspora* 1, no. 1 (1991): 83–99.

12. Bhabha, *The Location of Culture*, 141.

13. Ibid., 139–70.

14. Pérez-Torres, *Movements in Chicano Poetry*. In chapter 3 Pérez-Torres theorizes "From the Homeland to the Borderlands, the Reformation of Aztlán," and in chapter 4 he discusses "Mythic Memory and Cultural Construction."

15. Bhabha, *The Location of Culture*, 149. Bhabha is, of course, making reference to Benedict Anderson, *Imagined Communities: Reflections on the Origin and Spread of Nationalism* (London: Verso, 1983). For Bhabha, "Anderson fails to locate the alienating time of the arbitrary sign in his naturalized, nationalized space of the imagined community" (161). In other words, while Anderson relies on historical memory for nationhood, Bhabha cuts through with the "syntax of forgetting." A people obliged to forget "in the construction of the national present is not a question of historical memory," but rather "the construction of a discourse on society that performs the problem of totalizing the people and unifying the national will" (160–61). This, for me, is precisely the gap in history where the forgotten voices, women's voices, exist as the nation is constructed—in this instance, the Chicano nation.

16. Stuart Hall, "Cultural Identity and Diaspora," in *Colonial Discourse and Post-Colonial Theory*, ed. Patrick Williams and Laura Chrisman (New York: Columbia University Press, 1994), 402.

17. See Paul Gilroy, *"There Ain't No Black in the Union Jack": The Cultural Politics of Race and Nation* (Chicago: University of Chicago Press, 1987). In chapter 5, "Diaspora, Utopia and the Critique of Capitalism," Gilroy points out that "As black styles, music, dress, dance, fashion and languages became a determining force shaping the style, music, dress, fashion and language of urban Britain as a whole, blacks have been structured into the mechanisms of this society in a number of different ways" (155).

18. Clifford, "Diasporas," 313.

19. Mario T. García, "Americans All: The Mexican American Generation and the Politics of Wartime Los Angeles, 1941–45," in *The Mexican American Experience: An Interdisciplinary Anthology*, ed. Rodolfo O. de la Garza et al. (Austin: University of Texas Press, 1985), 201–12. García's work was among the first to posit the argument regarding the transition from immigrant to Mexican American generation for the incoming Mexican population to the United States. See also the following essay by García, in which he alludes to his "generations" concept: "Americanization and the Mexican Immigrant, 1880–1930," *Journal of Ethnic Studies* 6 (1978): 19–34.

20. Bhabha, *The Location of Culture*, 175.

21. Clifford, "Diasporas," 311.

22. For example, see Milton M. Gordon, *Assimilation in American Life: The Role of Race, Religion, and National Origins* (Oxford: Oxford University Press, 1964), and Olivier Zunz, "American History and the Changing Meaning of Assimilation," *Journal of American Ethnic History* 4 (Spring 1985).

23. Arnoldo De León, *Ethnicity in the Sunbelt: A History of Mexican Americans in*

Houston (Houston: Mexican American Studies Program, University of Houston, 1989), xi.

24. Bhabha, *The Location of Culture*, 173; Sandoval, "U.S. Third World Feminism."

25. Camarillo, *Chicanos in a Changing Society*. Recently, George J. Sánchez provocatively suggested that the "Mexican American second generation was already shaped before the war"; see Sánchez, *Becoming Mexican American*, 256.

26. For more on how patriarchy remains constant for women whether in the old country or the new, see, for example, Patricia Zavella, *Women's Work and Chicano Families: Cannery Workers of the Santa Clara Valley* (Ithaca: Cornell University Press, 1987); Beatríz M. Pesquera, "'In the Beginning He Wouldn't Even Lift a Spoon': The Division of Household Labor," in de la Torre and Pesquera, *Building with Our Hands*, 181–95; Adela de la Torre, "Hard Choices and Changing Roles among Mexican Migrant *Campesinas*," in de la Torre and Pesquera, *Building with Our Hands*, 168–80.

27. De León, *Ethnicity in the Sunbelt*, x.

28. Vicki L. Ruiz, "'Star Struck': Acculturation, Adolescence, and the Mexican American Woman, 1920–1950," in de la Torre and Pesquera, *Building with Our Hands*, 109–29. Ruiz claims convincingly that acculturation was not simply a move from the old to the new, but rather a choice whereby weaving between the old and new constructed another identity.

29. Emma Pérez, "Oral Narratives as Chicana (His)story Text," Working Paper No. 32, Southwest Institute for Research on Women (Tucson: University of Arizona, 1994). This working paper is a preliminary look at Houston's working women from 1900 to 1940. In it I interrogate the meaning of conducting oral interviews and how one cannot predict, control, or fully interpret responses by interviewees. Something will always remain unsaid. I was introduced to the women from these social and cultural clubs by Thomas Kreneck, archivist at the Houston Metropolitan Research Center. Tom was generous with his time, and we often discussed the differences between us, our positionality with respect to the interviewees. We were both aware that the women sometimes looked to him as the authority, or they looked to me as a member of the tejana community, yet still separate from them. We were also acutely aware that oral history as a method poses its own questions. One's subject position must be consistently challenged.

30. De León, *Ethnicity in the Sunbelt*, 1–5.

31. David G. McComb, *Houston: A History* (Austin: University of Texas Press, 1969).

32. Mario T. García, *Desert Immigrants: The Mexicans of El Paso, 1880–1920* (New Haven: Yale University Press, 1981), 36.

33. Census Schedules, 1900, 1910, 1920, 1930.

34. *Directory of the City of Houston*, 1900, 1905, 1910, 1917, 1920, 1923, 1925, 1930, 1940.

35. Interview with Maria and Ralph Villagomez, 16 April 1979, conducted by Thomas Kreneck, Houston Metropolitan Research Center.

36. Ibid. Maria talked about going to the Azteca in the Second Ward, but she went only once, because that was the tejano side of town. See also *Gaceta Mexicana*, 15 February 1928, 15, and 1 May 1928, 26, for information on the theater.

37. Interviews with Estela Gómez, 8, 15, 22 June 1979, and Melesio Gómez Collection.

38. Interview with Carmen Cortez, 2 May 1989, conducted by Thomas Kreneck and Emma Pérez, Houston Metropolitan Research Center.

39. Melesio Gómez Collection, Chapultepec Minutes Book, 9 November 1931. The minutes indicate that women voted on the names Chapultepec and Azteca and favored Chapultepec.

40. Interview with Estela Gómez, 8 June 1979, conducted by Thomas Kreneck.

41. Interview with Estela Gómez, 18 May 1989, conducted by Thómas Kreneck and Emma Pérez.

42. Interview with Estela Gómez, 8 June 1979.

43. Interview with Estela Gómez, 8 February 1989.

44. Ibid.

45. Interview with Carmen Cortez, 16 December 1983 and 2 May 1989.

46. Gómez Collection, Chapultepec Club Minutes Book, November 1931 through April 1932.

47. Ibid.

48. Ibid.

49. Interview with Estela Gómez, 8 February 1989; Gómez Collection, Chapultepec Minutes Book, 1932; *El Tecolote,* scrapbook in Gómez Collection.

50. Interview with Carmen Cortez, 2 May 1989.

51. Interview with Estela Gómez, 8 February 1989.

52. Stella Quintenella was Estela Gómez, her family name. She initially married while still in the club and anglicized her name to Stella Quintenella. She was widowed, then married again, becoming Estela Reyes. I will refer to her as both Estela Gómez, her family name, and Estela Reyes.

53. Interview with Carmen Cortez, 2 May 1989.

54. The "Letter from Chapultepec" can be found in the Melesio Gómez Collection. An archival report on it was published in the *Houston Review* by Thomas Kreneck, who discovered the letter among Estela Gómez's papers. Thomas H. Kreneck, "The Letter from Chapultepec," *The Houston Review* 3, no. 2 (Summer 1981).

55. Gómez Collection, "Letter from Chapultepec."

56. Thomas H. Kreneck, "The Letter from Chapultepec," 269.

57. Ibid.

58. Interview with Estela Gómez, 8 February 1989.

59. Ibid.

60. Ibid.

61. Ibid.

62. De León, *Ethnicity in the Sunbelt,* 72.

63. Ibid., 71

64. Interview with Estela Gómez, 8 February 1989.

65. Houston *Chronicle,* 30 August 1940, 19B. See also De León, *Ethnicity in the Sunbelt,* 73.

66. Gómez Collection, Speech by Estela Gómez, 18 August 1941.

67. Ibid. Gómez concerned herself with workers' rights in Texas. Migration from Mexico had stripped her family of their status as landowners in the village of Piotillo in San Luis Potosí. In Houston, her father worked for the Southern Pacific Railroad by day to raise money to open his own businesses. He ultimately trained his daughters to have their own shops when they grew older. Melesio Gómez also facilitated the establishment of his daughters' businesses.

68. Gómez Collection, Speech, 18 August 1941.

69. Interview with Estela Gómez, 8 February 1989.

70. Interview with Catalina Sandoval, 3 February 1989, conducted by Thomas Kreneck and Emma Pérez, Houston Metropolitan Research Center.

71. Ibid. Sandoval was born in Aguascalientes, Mexico, on 21 April 1918. She was about nine years old when she entered school in the U.S.

72. Ibid.

73. Ibid. Sandoval said that the group agreed on thirteen members because they felt that thirteen was their lucky number. They decided to name the group after Terpsichore, the muse of dance, because they all liked to dance, and they planned to raise their money from dances.

74. Interview with Antoneta Rivas, 6 May 1989, conducted by Thomas Kreneck and Emma Pérez. *La Gaceta Mexicana*, 15 April 1928, reported news about a picnic sponsored by the Club Pan-Americano de la Y.W.C.A.

75. Interview with Antoneta Rivas, 6 May 1989.

76. Interview with Mrs. Fernando Salas, 4 October 1985, conducted by Thomas Kreneck; 20 May 1989, conducted by Thomas Kreneck and Emma Pérez.

77. Interview with Antoneta Rivas, 6 May 1989.

78. Interview with Mrs. Fernando Salas, 4 October 1985; Interview with Antoneta Rivas, 6 May 1989.

79. Interview with Antoneta Rivas, 6 May 1989.

80. Ibid.

81. Antoneta Rivas told me that her mother, Josefina Rosales Ypiña, had organized the theater club. Ibid.

82. At the 6 May 1989 interview with Mrs. Rivas, Mr. Rivas, who sat close by, remembered a club for young men in the 1930s called El Chorito de Agua, "Little Squirt of Water."

83. Interview with Antoneta Rivas, 6 May 1989.

84. Interview with Isidro García and Primitivo L. Niño, 9 April 1979, conducted by Thomas Kreneck.

85. Ibid.

86. Angie and Félix Morales Collection, Houston Metropolitan Research Center, Houston, Texas.

87. De León, *Ethnicity in the Sunbelt*, 81–82.

88. Ibid., 82.

89. Interview with Carmen Cortez, 16 December 1983 and 2 May 1989. See also the Carmen Cortez Collection.

90. Interview with Angie Morales, 5 February 1979, conducted by Thomas Kreneck. Kreneck and I returned to conduct another interview on 16 April 1989.

91. Angie and Félix Morales Collection, Box 10.

92. Interview with Angie Morales, 5 February 1979.

93. Ibid.

94. Ibid.

95. Ibid.

96. Camarillo, *Chicanos in a Changing Society*, 153.

97. Interview with Antoneta Rivas, 6 May 1989. Rivas recalled accompanying her mother, Josefina Rosales Ypiña, when she was a young girl of seven and eight years old.

98. For a thorough review of LULAC, its history, and its prominent female leaders, see Cynthia E. Orozco, "The Origins of the League of United Latin American Citizens (LULAC) and the Mexican American Civil Rights Movement in Texas with an Analysis of Women's Political Participation in a Gendered Context, 1910–1929" (Ph.D. diss., University of California, Los Angeles, 1993).

5. BEYOND THE NATION'S MATERNAL BODIES

1. Pérez, "Sexuality and Discourse."

2. In a review essay on Terri de la Peña's novel *The Latin Satins,* I attempted to make this argument about Selena and one of de la Peña's main characters, a lesbian Chicana singer who, for me, seemed quite femme in the description, although de la Peña may disagree with me about her own character. My point, however, was to argue that to use and flaunt femme sexuality is in itself empowering for those who choose to do so in such a conscious manner. In these instances, the performances are expressions of working-class Chicana feminist agency. Emma Pérez, "Selena's Sisters," *Lesbian Review of Books* 2 (Autumn 1995): 4.

3. Gilles Deleuze and Félix Guattari, *Anti-Oedipus: Capitalism and Schizophrenia* (Minneapolis: University of Minnesota Press, 1983).

4. De Lauretis, *The Practice of Love*, 83. De Lauretis is refering specifically to Jean Laplanche and Jean-Bertrand Pontalis, "Fantasy and the Origins of Sexuality," in *Formations of Fantasy*, ed. Victor Burgin, James Donald, and Cora Kaplan (London: Methuen, 1986), 5–34.

5. I use this psychoanalytic concept, "the phallic mother," to point out how Malinche is unconsciously perceived and feared by patriarchal "nationalists" who want so much to negate her agency. For feminists, Malinche is an originating feminist icon. For an explanation of the psychoanalytic concept, see Jean Laplanche and Jean-Bertrand Pontalis, *The Language of Psycho-Analysis*, trans. Donald Nicholson-Smith (New York: W. W. Norton, 1973), 311.

6. There are others, such as Homi Bhabha, whose work indirectly locates desire in the interstices of colonial-postcolonial cultures; Hayden White's tropes can be defined as desiring devices with the potential to reconstruct a new method for writing history, a method that privileges the historian's subject effects over a scientific objectivism; and certainly Donna Haraway's socialist-feminist work expresses desire for transformation, for a world safe for simians, cyborgs, and women. Works by lesbians of color Gloria Anzaldúa, Alicia Gaspar de Alba, Deena González, Paula Gunn-Allen, Audre Lorde, Cherríe Moraga, Sandy Soto, Yvonne Yarbro-Bejarano, and others consistently fuel my own work. They are but a few of the feminists whose theories and writings have been at the forefront of cultural and lesbian studies. Patrick Fuery's *Theories of Desire* (Carlton, Victoria: Melbourne University Press, 1995) is a brief overview of the mechanics of desire in more prominent poststructural theorists such as Jacques Lacan, Jacques Derrida, Roland Barthes, Michel Foucault, and French feminists Hélène Cixous, Luce Irigary, and Julia Kristeva. In his conclusion, he briefly discusses what he says is "inconclusive desire" in the writings by Deleuze and Guattari and Jean Baudrillard.

7. Michel Foucault, *History of Sexuality, Volume One: An Introduction*, trans. R. Hurley (New York: Vintage Books, 1980); Michel Foucault, *Technologies of the Self*, ed. Luther H. Martin, Huck Gutman, and Patrick H. Hutton (Amherst: University of Massachusetts Press, 1988), 16–49.

8. Ann Laura Stoler, *Race and the Education of Desire: Foucault's History of Sexuality and the Colonial Order of Things* (Durham, N.C.: Duke University Press, 1995). Stoler makes a quite convincing case for stretching Foucault's discursive analysis into the colonies to see how colonial/racialized bodies have been marked.

9. Ibid., 1–2.

10. Ibid., 2.

11. Ibid.

12. Michel Foucault, preface to Deleuze and Guattari, *Anti-Oedipus*, xiii.

13. Ibid., xii.

14. Gilles Deleuze and Félix Guattari, *A Thousand Plateaus: Capitalism and Schizophrenia*, vol. 2, trans. Brian Massumi (Minneapolis: University of Minnesota Press, 1987).

15. Deleuze and Guattari, *Anti-Oedipus*, 8.

16. Ibid., 9.

17. Ibid.

18. Ibid., 3.

19. Ibid., 114.

20. Ibid., 166.

21. Ibid., 167.

22. Ibid., 168–69.

23. Ibid., 169.

24. Ibid., 183.
25. Ibid.
26. De Lauretis, *The Practice of Love*, xx.
27. Elizabeth Grosz, "Refiguring Lesbian Desire," in *The Lesbian Postmodern*, ed. Laura Doan (New York: Columbia University Press, 1994), 78.
28. Ibid.
29. De Lauretis, *The Practice of Love*, 82–84.
30. A more severe critic of *Anti-Oedipus* is Gayatri Chakravorty Spivak; see "Can the Subaltern Speak?," 271–313. She argues, quite convincingly, that the "new hegemony of desire" (274) posed by Deleuze and Guattari is dangerous ground upon which to tread, because their "minimalist summary of Marx's project" (279) "dislocates classes and unwittingly secures a new balance of hegemonic relations" (280). Spivak's historical materialist rendering compels us to engage macrological issues such as "global capitalism" and "nation-state alliances," and micrological topics such as "theories of ideology and subject-formation" (279). Her effort to bring us back to a critique of capitalism in which worker exploitation is studied and interest becomes the privileged site for revolution remains a vital project. In the second part of my book, on the discursive events of Chicana history, I turned to historical materialism's impending trace. Spivak unequivocally states that to ask "whether revolution is desirable" is a foolish luxury of western wealth (291). While I am inclined to agree with Spivak, I nevertheless wonder, in her terms, if the subaltern could speak, would not desire be the subject of that discourse? Finally, I think that the question is not "whether revolution is desirable," but rather, Is desire revolutionary? How can desire make a revolution? How is desire already the part of revolution that is repressed?
   Perhaps, as Spivak argues, desire and power are only "totalizing concepts" (279); however, I am somewhere in between these notions of power and desire in that decolonial time lag, inching toward a postcolonial identity of liberation yet living in a neocolonial socioeconomic condition in which the colonial imaginary still marks desire and power.
31. I should explain that when I use "postcolonial," I borrow from Bhabha's notion of postcolonial perspectives that "emerge from the colonial testimony of Third World countries and the discourses of 'minorities' within the geopolitical divisions of East and West, North and South." I am imposing the postcolonial as hope, as the utopian project, but not as sociopolitical conditions that exist. For Chicanos/as, particularly, I have attempted throughout this book to show how the postcolonial remains utopian, and that Chicano/a historians are still caught in that time lag between the colonial and the postcolonial. I argue that only through the decolonial imaginary will the silent gain their agency. See Bhabha, *The Location of Culture*, 171. For more debates on postcoloniality, see the essays in Iain Chambers and Lidia Curti, eds., *The Post-colonial Question: Common Skies, Divided Horizons* (New York: Routledge, 1996). Iain Chambers's essay, "Signs of Silence, Lines of Listening," is the only article in the collection that alludes to Spanish colonialism in the the Southwest, specifically New Mexico. Chicanos/as, however, are usually not referenced in the postcolonial debates—and for good reason. For the most part, I think that there are still too many problems of crossing over to postcoloniality when the "post" of the colonial seems more like a perspective, that is, a desire to move beyond the colonial imaginary and into postcolonial hope. A more current work by Chicano literary critic José David Saldívar addresses his own perspective of decolonization; see José David Saldívar, *Border Matters: Remapping American Culture* (Berkeley: University of California Press, 1997).
32. Todd May, *Between Genealogy and Epistemology: Psychology, Politics and Knowledge in the Thought of Michel Foucault* (University Park: Pennsylvania State Univer-

sity Press, 1993), 5. May, speaking about Foucault's critique of Deleuze and Guattari, claims that Foucault rejected their transcendental concept of desire precisely because it was ahistorical.

33. When I speak of the "historical imagination," I am refering to Hayden White's *Metahistory*, where he discusses "the historical imagination in nineteenth century Europe" as the constructed consciousness of an era (ix).

34. I am indebted to Luz Calvo, graduate student in History of Consciousness at the University of California, Santa Cruz, who pointed out that the dream sequence in the film *Silent Tongue* was precisely the colonial primal scene.

35. I am interested in this film because the Indian women resist the white men and do not become their willing squaws. Hollywood almost always depicts a white male protaganist who has an Indian woman fall in love with him. This fantasy begins with La Malinche and Cortés and is reified in the romance between John Smith and Pocahontas, as recently depicted in an animated film by Disney. Films such as *Jeremiah Johnson* with Robert Redford and *Dances with Wolves* with Kevin Costner romanticize relationships between white men and Indian women. Although the woman in *Dances with Wolves* was white, she had become Sioux after being abducted as a child. Interestingly, Sam Shepard does not romanticize these forced affiliations, nor does he exoticize the frontier; instead he concentrates on brutal, harsh relationships. Everyone seems to be on a journey of death.

36. Teresa de Lauretis, *Alice Doesn't: Feminism, Semiotics, and Cinema* (Bloomington: Indiana University Press, 1984), 140.

37. De Lauretis, *The Practice of Love*, 155.

38. Alicia Gaspar de Alba argues that Selena was a man-made object—man-made, that is, by her father, Abraham Quintanilla, and "by the male-dominant industries that are now raking in the profits of the Selena phenomemon." Gaspar de Alba reviews the biography published only a year after Selena's death and takes issue with Joe Nick Patoski, the biographer, who is obsessed with Selena's "curvy" body. See "Selena Bio: Pura Homegirl," *San Antonio Express-News*, 24 March 1996, 4–5. For the biography, see Joe Nick Patoski, *Selena: Como la Flor* (New York: Little, Brown and Co., 1996). The review, by the way, was written before the film was released.

39. Rancheras are usually heart-rending ballads mourning the loss of a lover. Cumbias have a livelier rhythm and borrow from Caribbean beats.

40. After the murder, I too was curious about the possibility of a crime of passion committed by Yolanda Saldívar. A lengthy interview with her on Univisión in October 1995, in Spanish, raised serious doubts for me. I asked Teresa de Lauretis to watch the interview with me, and she provided a convincing argument that, I think, makes more sense. She pointed out that Saldívar could have been suffering from the same psychological condition experienced by obsessed fans who want to become the star with whom they are obsessed. The impending loss of Selena thus caused Saldívar to panic and subsequently murder her. When Selena's father forbade her to meet with Saldívar, Selena defied him and went to the Days Inn on 31 March 1995 to retrieve some lost documents from Yolanda. According to Saldívar, Selena broke off their friendship. Saldívar said that upon seeing Selena turn to leave, she panicked and fired her gun, shooting Selena in the back. Saldívar appeared to be someone who had never experienced Selena's popularity or adoration. This was the closest she would ever come to such fame. Moreover, by murdering Selena, Saldívar has linked herself in memory, in history, to Selena.

41. Cherríe Moraga has performed a monologue that she wrote called "My Name is Yolanda Saldívar." I have not seen the performance, but I think it is interesting that a Chicana lesbian is claiming Yolanda Saldívar, perhaps in an effort to address the homophobia during the trial, or maybe to tease out the

possibility of a lesbian relationship between Yolanda and Selena. What I prefer to draw upon is the way the Chicana/o lesbian, gay, queer communities adored Selena, her performance, her songs. In fact, her songs were reconceptualized by the queer community. "Amor Prohibido" (Prohibited Love) was one of the more popular songs among lesbians, gays, and particularly the "drag queens" who performed Selena's songs. The prohibition of love between two people from different classes is changed to mean prohibited love between same-sex partners. Deborah Vargas, in her own work, will address queer audiences, but especially the lesbian fans who revered Selena. Deborah Vargas, "Cruzando Fronteras: Selena, Tejano Public Culture and the Politics of Cross-Over," American Studies Association, Washington, D.C., 31 October 1997.

42. De Lauretis, *The Practice of Love*, 156.

43. José L. Limón, "Selena: Sexuality, Greater Mexico and the Song-and-Dance with Hegemony," *ETNOFOOR* 10 (1997): 105.

44. Ibid., 100.

45. Gaspar de Alba, "Selena Bio," 5.

46. De Lauretis, *The Practice of Love*, 155.

47. Limón, "Selena," 100. Limón also makes a convincing argument regarding her working-class sexuality and traces Mexican women's working-class sexuality to historical expressions in the nineteenth century.

48. Castañeda, "Sexual Violence in the Politics and Policies of Conquest," 21.

49. In a forthcoming publication, Deena González traces the historical hatred of Mexican women, a hatred reified in a fraternity song that is still sung during initiation ceremonies at fraternities at the University of California. Deena González, "Lupe's Song: On the Origins of Mexican Woman-Hating in the U.S.," American Historical Association, 11 January 1998.

50. For the lesbian gaze, there is something else altogether which is occurring. That is the subject of another essay.

51. Deleuze and Guattari, *Anti-Oedipus*, 114.

52. La Malinche has been represented in art, poetry, short stories, novels, films, and essays. I provide only a few examples. The following are literary and historical accounts: Norma Alarcón, "Chicana's Feminist Literature: A Re-vision through Malintzin/or, Malintzin: Putting Flesh Back on the Object," in Cherríe Moraga and Gloria Anzaldúa, eds., *This Bridge Called My Back: A Collection of Writings by Radical Women of Color* (Watertown, Mass.: Persephone Press, 1981), 182–90; Deena González, "Malinche as Lesbian: A Reconfiguration of 500 Years of Resistance," *California Sociologist*, Special Issue, 14 (Winter/Summer 1991): 90–97; Sandra Messinger Cypess, *La Malinche in Mexican Literature: From History to Myth* (Austin: University of Texas Press, 1991); Joanne Danaher Chaison, "Mysterious Malinche: A Case of Mistaken Identity," *The Americas* 32 (April 1976), 514–23; Federico Fernández de Castillejo, *El amor de la conquista: Malintzin* (Buenos Aires, 1943); Paz, *The Labyrinth of Solitude;* Gustavo A. Rodriquez, *Doña Marina* (México, 1935). For a poem by a Chicana writer, see Alicia Gaspar de Alba, "Malinchista, a Myth Revised," in *Three Times a Woman* (Tempe, Ariz.: Bilingual Review Press, 1989), 16. For a fascinating short story in which the author plays with time, moving from the conquest to a modern-day Mexico, see Mexican writer Elena Garro, "La culpa es de los tlaxcaltecos," in *La semana de colores* (México, 1987), 11–29.

53. De Lauretis, *The Practice of Love*, xi–xii.

54. Ibid., xix.

55. White, *The Content of the Form;* see pp. 128–29 for his discussion of "moral engineering." On p. 134 he refers to the "discipline of bodies and pleasures."

56. Deleuze and Guattari, *Anti-Oedipus*, xiii.

57. John Reed, *Insurgent Mexico* (New York: D. Appleton and Co., 1914), 99–109.

58. Elizabeth Salas, *Soldaderas in the Mexican Military: Myth and History* (Austin: University of Texas Press, 1990).

CONCLUSION

1. When I was growing up in Texas, I remember my father telling me how he would argue with co-workers about history and remind them to forget the Alamo.

BIBLIOGRAPHY

PRIMARY SOURCES

Archives

United States

Houston Metropolitan Research Center, Houston Public Library, Houston, Texas

Club "México Bello" Collection
Carmen Cortez Collection
Melesio Gómez Collection
LULAC Council #60 Collection
Mexican American Family History Collection
Mexican American Small Collection
Angie and Félix Morales Collection
Newspaper Microfilm Collection

Oral Interviews

Housed at the Houston Metropolitan Research Center, Houston Public Library, Houston, Texas

Cortez, Carmen. 16 December 1983, conducted by Thomas Kreneck. 2 May 1989, conducted by Thomas Kreneck and Emma Pérez
García, Isidro, and Primitivo L. Niño. 9 April 1979, conducted by Thomas Kreneck.
Gómez Reyes, Estela. 8, 15, 22 June 1979, 8 February 1989, conducted by Thomas Kreneck. 18 May 1989, conducted by Thomas Kreneck and Emma Pérez.
Morales, Angie. 5, 19 February 1979, conducted by Thomas Kreneck. 16 April 1989, conducted by Thomas Kreneck and Emma Pérez.
Rivas, Antoneta. 6 May 1989, conducted by Thomas Kreneck and Emma Pérez.
Salas, Mrs. Fernando (Elvira Luna). 4 October 1985, conducted by Thomas Kreneck. 20 May 1989, conducted by Thomas Kreneck and Emma Pérez.
Sandoval, Catalina. 3 February 1989, conducted by Thomas Kreneck and Emma Pérez.
Villagomez, Maria and Ralph. 16 April 1979, conducted by Thomas Kreneck.

Census Schedules

U.S. Bureau of the Census. *Manuscripts.* 1900.
U.S. Bureau of the Census. *Manuscripts.* 1910.

City Directories

Directory of the City of Houston, 1900.
Directory of the City of Houston, 1905.
Directory of the City of Houston, 1910.
Directory of the City of Houston, 1917.
Directory of the City of Houston, 1920.
Directory of the City of Houston, 1923.
Directory of the City of Houston, 1925.
Directory of the City of Houston, 1930.
Directory of the City of Houston, 1940.

University of California, Bancroft Library, Berkeley
John Murray Papers
Silvestre Terrazas Papers

University of California, Berkeley
Regional Oral History Office

University of California, Chicano Studies Research Center Library, Los Angeles

University of Texas, Benson Library, Austin
Latin American Collection

University of Texas, Barker Library, Austin
Mary Austin Holley Papers

Mexico City

Archivo de la Secretaría de Relaciones Exteriores
Ramo de la Revolución Mexicana, 1910–1920

Biblioteca Nacional
Biographical Collection

Hemeroteca Nacional de México
Periodical Collection

Centro de Estudios de Historia de México, CONDUMEX
Manuscript Collection
Archivo de Venustiano Carranza

Mérida

Archivo General del Estado de Yucatán (AGEY)
Ramo de Congreso
Ramo de Gobierno
Ramo de Justicia

Archivo Notarial de Estado de Yucatán (ANY)

Biblioteca General del Estado de Yucatán
Carrillo y Ancona Collection.

Hemeroteca Pino Suárez
Periodical Collection

Newspapers and Periodicals

United States

El Paso Record
Houston Chronicle
Houston Post
La Mujer Moderna
La Verdad
Los Angeles Times
Pan American Union Bulletin
Regeneración
San Antonio Light
Women's National Daily

Mérida, Yucatán

La Revista de Mérida
La Voz de la Revolución

Books, Pamphlets, Government Publications

Alvarado, Salvador. *Actuación revolucionaria del General Salvador Alvarado en Yucatán*. México: Costa-AmicEditor, 1965.

———. *Breves apuntes acerca de la administración del General Salvador Alvarado, como Gobernador de Yucatán, con simple expresión de hechos y sus consecuencias.* Mérida: Imprenta del Gobierno Constitucionalista, 1916.

———. *Carta al pueblo de Yucatán.* Mérida: La Voz de la Revolución, 1916.

———. "En légitima defensa." *El Demócrata*, 4 May 1922.

———. *Informe que de su Gestión como Gobernador Provisional del Estado de Yucatán.* Mérida: Imprenta Constitucional, 1918.

———. "Mi actuación revolucionaria." *El Universal*, 28 December 1918.

———. *Mi sueño: El primer dividendo de la Comisión Reguladora del Mercado de Henequén.* Mérida: Imprenta del Gobierno Constitucionalista, 1917.

———. *La reconstrucción de México: Un mensaje a los pueblos de América.* 2 vols. 1919. Reprint, México: Ediciones del Gobierno de Yucatán, 1980.

———. *Speech of General Salvador Alvarado, Governor of the State of Yucatán, at the Closing of the Second Pedagogic Congress, Held at Mérida.* New York, n.p., 1916.

Ayuso y O'Horibe, Dr. Hircano. *Campaña Anti-tuberculosa en las Escuelas: Conferencia organizada por la "Union de Profesores de Yucatán" el 20 de Julio de 1913.* Mérida, 1913.

Bulnes, Francisco. *Defensa y Ampliación de mi discurso pronunciado el 21 de junio de 1903 ante la Convención Nacional Liberal.* Mérida, 1903.

Butler, Josephine E. *Personal Reminiscences of a Great Crusade.* 1911. Reprint, Westport, Conn.: Hyperion Press, 1976.

Cámara Zavala, Gonzalo. "Paralelo entre las escuelas racionalistas de Barcelona y Mérida." *Boletín de la Liga de Acción Social* 2, no. 17 (May 1922): 66–69.

Carranza, Venustiano. *Ley sobre relaciones familiares.* México: Imprenta del Gobierno, 1917.

Carranza and Public Instruction in México: Sixty Mexican Teachers Are Commissioned to Study in Boston. New York City, 1915.

Código Sanitario del Estado de Yucatán. Reglamentos: Prostitución, Tuberculosis, Servicio Antirrábico. Mérida: Imprenta de la "Escuela Correccional de Artes y Oficios," 1911.

Colección de las Leyes y Reglamentos de Beneficencia Pública, 1906–1907. Mérida, 1907.

Colegio Femenil Yucateco. Mérida, 1920.

Colomé, Dr. Francisco. *Mortalidad infantil en Yucatán: Sus causas y su remedio.* Mérida, 1914.

Constitución política del estado libre y soberano de Yucatán: Decreto número 3. Yucatán, 1918.

Cortés, Gonzalo del Angel. *Feminismo en Acción.* Tabasco, México: Talleres tipográficos del gobierno constitucionalista, 1915.

Debs, Eugene V. "Women." *American Appeal,* 30 October 1926.

Escuela Normal de Profesores: Programa detallado de los estudios profesionales correspondientes el año de 1909–1910. Mérida, 1909.

Escuela Normal de Profesores del Estado: Cuestionarios correspondientes a las asignaturas del cuarto año de la enseñanza profesional. Mérida, 1912.

Estadística Escolar Primaria de la República Mexicana. México, 1931.

Flores Magón, Ricardo. *Artículos Políticos, 1917.* México, D.F.: Ediciones Antorcha, 1981.

Galindo, Hermila. *La doctrina Carranza y el acercamiento indolatino.* México: n.p., 1919.

———. *Estudio de la Señorita Hermila Galindo con motivo de los temas que han de absolverse en el Segundo Congreso Feminista de Yucatán.* Mérida: Imprenta del Gobierno Constitucionalista, 1916.

———. *La mujer en el porvenir.* Mérida: Imprenta y Litografía de "La Voz de la Revolución," 1915.

———. *Un presidenciable: El General don Pablo González.* México: Imprenta Nacional S.A., 1919.

Gamboa, Ignacio. *La Mujer Moderna.* Mérida: Imprenta "Gamboa Guzman," 1906.

Informe del Comisionado de Instrucción Pública a este Ramo de la Administración Municipal durante el período de 1908 a 1909. Mérida, 1910.

Instituto Literario de Niñas del Estado: Cuestiones aprobados por el H. Consejo de Instrucción Pública correspondientes a las asignaturas del primer año de la enseñanza profesional. Mérida: Imprenta de la "Escuela Correccional de Artes y Oficios," 1911.

Kuhne, Luis D. *Higiene y exposición científica de los sistemas de medicación alópata, homeópata, magnetismo y curación natural.* Mérida, 1908.

Lara y Prado, Luis. *La Prostitución en México.* México: Librería de la Vda. de Ch. Bouret, 1908.

Legislación Comprada: Dictamen sobre la ley aplicable al divorcio pronunciado en Yucatán por un matrimonio español. Mérida: Imprenta Constitucionalista, 1918.

Ley y reglamento sobre alcoholes y licores. Mérida, 1915.

López Z., Otilia. *Colegio de Niñas de Instrucción Primaria Interior y Superior dirigido por la Señorita Otilia López Z.* Mérida, 1905.

Manero, Antonio. *The Meaning of the Mexican Revolution.* Mexico, 1915.

Memorias de la Liga de Acción Social: Trabajos presentados en la sesión solemne efectuada el 10 de febrero de 1911. Mérida: Imprenta de Luis Rosado Vega, 1911.

Menéndez, Rodolfo. *Reseña histórica del Primer Congreso Pedagógico de Yucatán del 11 al 16 de septiembre de 1915: Lo decreto inauguró y clausuró del Estado.* Mérida: Imprenta del Gobierno Constitucionalista, 1916.

————. *Rita Cetina Gutiérrez.* Mérida, 1909.

México. Secretaría de Agricultura y Fomento. *Tercer censo de población de los Estados Unidos Mexicanos. Verificado el 27 de octubre de 1910.* 2 vols. México, 1918.

Partido Socialista de Yucatán. *Tierra y Libertad: Bases que se discutieron y aprobaron el Primer Congreso Obrero Socialista celebrado en Motul paras todas las Ligas de Resistencia.* Mérida, 1919.

Pérez Alcala, Felipe. *Ensayos biográphicos.* Mérida: Imprenta y linotipia de "La Revista de Yucatán," 1914.

Primer Congreso Feminista de Yucatán. *Anales de esa memorable asamblea.* Mérida: Talleres Tipográficos del "Ateneo Peninsular," 1916.

Programas detallados aprobados por el H. Consejo de Instrucción Pública para las Escuelas Primarias del Estado. Mérida, 1909.

Ramírez Garrido, José Domingo. *Al Margen del Feminismo.* Mérida: Talleres "Pluma y Lápiz," 1918.

Reed, John. *Insurgent Mexico.* New York: D. Appleton and Co., 1914.

Reglamento del Artículo 222 del Código Sanitario para el Régimen de la Prostitución. 22 December 1910. AGEY.

Rivera y Sanroman, Agustín. 1908. *Untitled.* Bancroft Library.

Secretaría de Agricultura y Fomento. *Tercer censo de población de los Estados Unidos verificados el 27 de octubre de 1910.* 2 vols. México: Oficina Impresora de la Secretaría de Hacienda, 1918.

Tesorería General del Estado de Yucatán, Mérida. 1913.

Trabajos de la "Liga de Acción Social" para el establecimiento de las escuelas rurales de Yucatán. Mérida: Imprenta Empresa Editora, 1913.

Turner, John Kenneth. *Barbarous Mexico.* 2nd ed. Introduction by Sinclair Snow. 1910. Reprint, Austin: University of Texas Press, 1969.

Zenker, E. V. *Anarchism.* London: Methuen and Co., 1898.

SECONDARY SOURCES

Books and Articles

Acuña, Rodolfo. *Occupied America: The Chicano's Struggle toward Liberation.* 1st ed. San Francisco: Canfield Press, 1972.

————. *Occupied America: A History of Chicanos.* 3rd ed. New York: Harper and Row, 1988.

Alarcón, Norma. "Chicana Feminism: In the Tracks of 'the' Native Woman." *Cultural Studies* 4, no. 3 (October 1990): 248–56.

————. "Chicana's Feminist Literature: A Re-vision through Malintzin/or, Malintzin: Putting Flesh Back on the Object." In *This Bridge Called My Back: Writings by Radical Women of Color,* edited by Cherríe Moraga and Gloria Anzaldúa, 182–90. Watertown, Mass.: Persephone Press, 1981.

Allen, Ruth Alice. *The Labor of Women in The Production of Cotton.* New York: Arno Press, 1975.

————. "Mexican Peon Women in Texas." *Sociology and Social Research,* November–December 1931, 131–42.

Almaguer, Tomás. "Ideological Distortions in Recent Chicano Historiography:

The Internal Model and Chicano Historical Interpretation." *Aztlán* 18, no. 1 (Spring 1989): 7–28.

———. *Racial Fault Lines: The Historical Origins of White Supremacy in California.* Berkeley: University of California Press, 1994.

———. "Toward the Study of Chicano Colonialism." *Aztlán* 2 (Spring 1971): 7–21.

Althusser, Louis. "Ideology and Ideological State Apparatuses (Notes toward an Investigation)." In *Lenin and Philosophy and Other Essays.* London: New Left Books, 1970.

Anderson, Benedict. *Imagined Communities: Reflections on the Origin and Spread of Nationalism.* London: Verso, 1983.

Anzaldúa, Gloria. *Borderlands/La Frontera: The New Mestiza.* San Francisco: Spinsters/Aunt Lute, 1987.

Anzaldúa, Gloria, and Cherríe Moraga. *This Bridge Called My Back: A Collection of Writings by Radical Women of Color.* Watertown, Mass.: Persephone Press, 1981.

Armitage, Susan, and Elizabeth Jameson, eds. *The Women's West.* Norman: University of Oklahoma Press, 1987.

Arrom, Silvia. *The Women of Mexico City, 1790–1857.* Stanford: Stanford University Press, 1985.

Arroyo, Laura. "Industrial and Occupational Distribution of Chicana Workers." *Aztlán* 4 (Fall 1973).

Balderrama, Francisco E. *In Defense of La Raza: The Los Angeles Mexican Consulate and the Mexican Community, 1929–1936.* Tucson: University of Arizona Press, 1982.

Balderrama, Francisco E., and Raymond Rodríguez. *Decade of Betrayal: Mexican Repatriation in the 1930s.* Albuquerque: University of New Mexico Press, 1995.

Barr, Chester Allwyn. "Occupational and Geographic Mobility in San Antonio, 1870–1900." *Social Science Quarterly* 51 (September 1970): 396–403.

Barrera, Mario. *Race and Class in the Southwest: A Theory of Racial Inequality.* Notre Dame: University of Notre Dame Press, 1979.

Barrera, Mario; Carlos Muñoz; and Charles Ornelas. "The Barrio as Internal Colony." *Urban Affairs Annual Review,* edited by Harlan Hahn, 6 (1972): 465–98.

Barthes, Roland. "The Third Meaning." In *The Responsibility of Forms: Critical Essays on Music, Art, and Representation,* translated by Richard Howard. Berkeley: University of California Press, 1991.

Bartra, Armando. *Regeneración, 1900–1918.* México, D.F.: Ediciones Era, 1977.

Bhabha, Homi K. *The Location of Culture.* New York: Routledge, 1994.

Bolton, Herbert E. *Texas in the Middle Eighteenth Century.* Berkeley: University of California Press, 1915.

Braudel, Fernand. *The Mediterranean.* 2 vols. New York: Harper and Row, 1972.

Broyles, Yolanda. "Women in El Teatro Campesino: ¿Apoco Estaba Molacha La Virgen de Guadalupe?" In *Chicana Voices: Intersections of Class, Race, and Gender,* edited by Teresa Córdova et al., 162–87. Albuquerque: University of New Mexico Press, 1990.

Buhle, Mari Jo. *Women and American Socialism, 1870–1920.* Chicago: University of Illinois, 1983.

Burke, Edmund. *A Grammar of Motives.* Berkeley: University of California Press, 1969.

Calderón, Héctor, and José David Saldívar. *Criticism in the Borderlands: Studies in*

Chicano Literature, Culture, and Ideology. Durham, N.C.: Duke University Press, 1991.

Camarillo, Albert. *Chicanos in California: A History of Mexican Americans in California.* San Francisco: Boyd and Fraser Publishing Co., 1984.

———. *Chicanos in a Changing Society: From Mexican Pueblos to American Barrios in Santa Barbara and Southern California, 1848–1930.* Cambridge: Harvard University Press, 1979.

———. "Mexicans and Europeans in American Cities: Some Comparative Perspectives, 1900–1940." In *From "Melting Pot" to Multiculturalism: The Evolution of Ethnic Relations in the United States and Canada,* edited by Valeria Gennaro Lerda, 237–62. Rome: Bulzoni Editore, 1990.

———. "The 'New' Chicano History: Historiography of Chicanos of the 1970s." In *Chicanos and the Social Sciences: A Decade of Research and Development, 1970–1980,* edited by Isidro D. Ortiz, 9–17. Santa Barbara: Center for Chicano Studies, University of California, 1983.

Cardoso, Lawrence. *Mexican Immigration to the U.S., 1897–1931.* Tucson: University of Arizona Press, 1980.

Castañeda, Antonia I. "Anglo Images of Nineteenth Century Californianas." In *Between Borders: Essays on Mexicana/Chicana History,* edited by Adelaida Del Castillo, 213–36. Los Angeles: Floricanto Press, 1990.

———. "Gender, Race, and Culture: Spanish-Mexican Women in the Historiography of Frontier California." *Frontiers* 11, no. 1 (1990): 8–20.

———. "Sexual Violence in the Politics and Policies of Conquest: Amerindian Women and the Spanish Conquest of Alta California." In *Building with Our Hands: New Directions in Chicana Studies,* edited by Adela de la Torre and Beatríz M. Pesquera, 15–33. Berkeley: University of California Press, 1993.

———. "Women of Color and the Rewriting of Western Women's History: The Discourse, Politics, and Decolonization of History." *Pacific Historical Review* 61 (November 1992): 501–33.

Castañeda, Carlos E. *Our Catholic Heritage in Texas, 1519–1936.* 15 vols. Austin: University of Texas Press, 1936–58.

Chabran, Angie C. "Chicana/o Studies as Oppositional Ethnography." *Cultural Studies* 4, no. 3 (1990): 228–47.

Chaison, Joanne Danaher. "Mysterious Malinche: A Case of Mistaken Identity." *The Americas* 32 (April 1976): 514–23.

Chambers, Iain, and Lidia Curti, eds. *The Post-colonial Question: Common Skies, Divided Horizons.* New York: Routledge, 1996.

Chávez, Ernesto. "Culture, Identity, and Community: Musings on Chicano Historiography at the End of the Millennium." *Estudios Mexicanos/Mexican Studies* 14, no. 1 (1998): 1–24.

Chávez, John R. *The Lost Land: The Chicano Image of the Southwest.* Albuquerque: University of New Mexico Press, 1984.

Clifford, James. "Diasporas." *Cultural Anthropology* 9, no. 3 (1994): 302–38.

Cockcroft, James. *Intellectual Precursors of the Mexican Revolution, 1900–1913.* Austin: University of Texas Press, 1968.

Conde, Rosina. "Arroz y cadenas." In *Arrieras somos,* 9–16. Culiacán, Sin., 1994.

Cordoba, Arnaldo. *La ideología de la Revolución Mexicana.* México, D.F.: Ediciones Era, S.A., 1973.

Córdova, Teresa. "Roots and Resistance: The Emergent Writings of Twenty Years of Chicana Feminist Stuggle." In *Handbook of Hispanic Cultures in the United States: Sociology,* edited by Félix Padilla, 175–202. Houston: Arte Público Press, 1994.

Córdova, Teresa, et al., eds. *Chicana Voices: Intersections of Class, Race, and Gender.* Albuquerque: University of New Mexico Press, 1993.

Cotera, Marta P. *The Chicana Feminist.* Austin: Information Systems Development, ca. 1977.

———. *Diosa y Hembra: The History and Heritage of Chicanas in the U.S.* Austin: Information Systems Development, 1976.

Cumberland, Charles C. *The Mexican Revolution: The Constitutionalist Years.* Austin: University of Texas Press, 1972.

Cypess, Sandra Messinger. *La Malinche in Mexican Literature: From History to Myth.* Austin: University of Texas Press, 1991.

de Certeau, Michel. *The Writing of History.* Translated by Tom Conley. New York: Columbia University Press, 1988.

de Landa, Diego. *Relación de las cosas de Yucatán.* México, D.F.: Editorial Porrúa, 1959.

de las Casas, Bartolomé. *Historia de las indias.* 3 vols. México, D.F.: Fondo de Cultura Económica, 1951.

de la Torre, Adela. "Hard Choices and Changing Roles among Mexican Migrant *Campesinas.*" In *Building with Our Hands: New Directions in Chicana Studies,* edited by Adela de la Torre and Beatríz M. Pesquera, 168–80. Berkeley: University of California Press, 1993.

de la Torre, Adela, and Beatríz M. Pesquera, eds. *Building with Our Hands: New Directions in Chicana Studies.* Berkeley: University of California Press, 1993.

de Lauretis, Teresa. *Alice Doesn't: Feminism, Semiotics, and Cinema.* Bloomington: Indiana University Press, 1984.

———. *The Practice of Love: Lesbian Sexuality and Perverse Desire.* Bloomington: Indiana University Press, 1994.

———. *Technologies of Gender: Essays on Theory, Film, and Fiction.* Bloomington: Indiana University Press, 1987.

De León, Arnoldo. *Ethnicity in the Sunbelt: A History of Mexican Americans in Houston.* Houston: Mexican American Studies Program, University of Houston, 1989.

———. *The Tejano Community, 1836–1900.* Albuquerque: University of New Mexico Press, 1982.

———. *They Called Them Greasers: Anglo Attitudes toward Mexicans in Texas, 1821–1900.* Austin: University of Texas Press, 1983.

de Sahagún, Bernardino. *Historia general de las cosas de Nueva España.* México, D.F.: Editorial Porrúa, 1982.

Del Castillo, Adelaida R. *Between Borders: Essays on Mexicana/Chicana History.* Encino, Calif.: Floricanto Press, 1990.

———. "Malintzin Tenepal: A Preliminary Look into a New Perspective." In *Essays on La Mujer,* edited by Rosaura Sánchez and Rosa Martínez Cruz, 129–49. Los Angeles: Chicano Studies Research Center Publications, University of California, 1977.

Del Castillo, Adelaida R., and Magdalena Mora, eds. *Mexican Women in the United*

States. Los Angeles: Chicano Studies Research Center, University of California, 1980.

Deleuze, Gilles, and Félix Guattari. *Anti-Oedipus: Capitalism and Schizophrenia.* Minneapolis: University of Minnesota Press, 1983.

———. *A Thousand Plateaus: Capitalism and Schizophrenia.* Vol. 2. Translated by Brian Massumi. Minneapolis: University of Minnesota Press, 1987.

Derrida, Jacques. *Of Grammatology.* Translated by Gayatri Spivak. Baltimore: Johns Hopkins University Press, 1976.

———. *Positions.* Translated by Alan Bass. Chicago: University of Chicago Press, 1981.

Deutsch, Sandra McGee. "The Right under Radicalism, 1916–1930." In *The Argentine Right: Its History and Intellectual Origins, 1910 to Present,* edited by Sandra McGee Deutsch and Ronald H. Dolkhart, 34–63. Wilmington, Del.: Scholarly Resources, 1993.

Deutsch, Sarah. *No Separate Refuge: Culture, Class, and Gender on an Anglo-Hispanic Frontier in the American Southwest, 1880–1940.* New York: Oxford University Press, 1987.

Díaz, Bernal. *The Conquest of New Spain.* New York: Penguin, 1963.

Dreyfus, Hubert L., and Paul Rabinow. *Michel Foucault: Beyond Structuralism and Hermeneutics.* Chicago: University of Chicago Press, 1982.

Dysart, Jane. "Mexican Women in San Antonio, 1830–1860: The Assimilation Process." *Western Historical Quarterly* 7 (October 1976): 365–75.

Ewen, Elizabeth. *Immigrant Women in the Land of Dollars: Life and Culture on the Lower East Side, 1890–1925.* New York: Monthly Review Press, 1985.

Fernández de Castillejo, Federico. *El amor de la conquista: Malintzin.* Buenos Aires, 1943.

Flores, Guillermo V. "Race and Culture in the Internal Colony: Keeping the Chicano in His Place." In *Structures of Dependency,* edited by Frank Bonilla and Robert Girling. Stanford, 1973.

Flynn, Elizabeth Gurley. *I Speak My Own Piece: Autobiography of "The Rebel Girl."* New York: International Publishers, 1955.

Foley, Neil. *The White Scourge: Mexicans, Blacks, and Poor Whites in Texas Cotton Culture.* Berkeley: University of California Press, 1998.

Foucault, Michel. Preface to *Anti-Oedipus: Capitalism and Schizophrenia,* by Gilles Deleuze and Félix Guattari. Minneapolis: University of Minnesota, 1983.

———. *The Archaeology of Knowledge.* New York: Pantheon Books, 1972.

———. *Discipline and Punish: The Birth of the Prison.* New York: Vintage Books, 1977.

———. *History of Sexuality, Volume One: An Introduction.* Translated by R. Hurley. New York: Vintage Books, 1980.

———. *The Order of Things: An Archaeology of the Human Sciences.* New York: Vintage Books, 1970.

———. *Power/Knowledge: Selected Interviews and Other Writings, 1972- 1977.* Edited by Colin Gordon. New York: Pantheon Books, 1980.

———. "Technologies of the Self." In *Technologies of the Self: A Seminar with Michel Foucault,* edited by Luther H. Martin, Huck Gutman, and Patrick H. Hutton, 16–49. Amherst: University of Massachusetts Press, 1988.

Fregoso, Rosalinda. *The Bronze Screen: Chicana and Chicano Film Culture.* Minneapolis: University of Minnesota Press, 1993.

Frye, Northrop. *Anatomy of Criticism: Four Essays*. Princeton: Princeton University Press, 1957.

Fuery, Patrick. *Theories of Desire*. Carlton, Victoria: Melbourne University Press, 1995.

Galarza, Ernesto. *Merchants of Labor: The Mexican Bracero Story—An Account of the Managed Migration of Mexican Farm Workers in California, 1942–1960*. Charlotte and Santa Barbara: McNally and Loftin, 1964.

Gamio, Manuel. *The Mexican Immigrant: His Life Story*. Chicago: University of Chicago Press, 1930.

García, Alma M. *Chicana Feminist Thought: The Basic Historical Writings*. New York: Routledge, 1997.

———. "The Development of Chicana Feminist Discourse, 1970–1980." *Gender and Society* 3, no. 2 (1989): 217–38.

———. "Studying Chicanas: Bringing Women into the Frame of Chicano Studies." In *Chicana Voices: Intersections of Class, Race, and Gender*, edited by Teresa Córdova et al., 19–29. Albuquerque: University of New Mexico Press, 1990.

García, Mario T. "Americanization and the Mexican Immigrant, 1880–1930." *Journal of Ethnic Studies* 6 (1978): 19–34.

———. "Americans All: The Mexican American Generation and the Politics of Wartime Los Angeles, 1941–45." In *The Mexican American Experience: An Interdisciplinary Anthology*, edited by Rodolfo O. de la Garza et al., 201–12. Austin: University of Texas Press, 1985.

———. *Desert Immigrants: The Mexicans of El Paso, 1880–1920*. New Haven: Yale University Press, 1981.

———. *Mexican Americans: Leadership, Ideology and Identity, 1930–1960*. New Haven: Yale University Press, 1989.

Garro, Elena. "La culpa es de los tlaxcaltecos." In *La semana de colores*, 11–29. México, 1987.

Gaspar de Alba, Alicia. "Malinchista, a Myth Revised." In *Three Times a Woman*, 16. Tempe, Ariz.: Bilingual Review Press, 1989.

———. "Selena Bio: Pura Homegirl." *San Antonio Express-News*. 24 March 1996, 4–5.

———. "Tortillerismo: Work by Chicana Lesbians." *Signs: Journal of Women in Culture and Society* 18, no. 4 (1993): 956–63.

Gilroy, Paul. *"There Ain't No Black in the Union Jack": The Cultural Politics of Race and Nation*. Chicago: University of Chicago Press, 1987.

Glenn, Evelyn Nakano. *Issei, Nisei, War Bride: Three Generations of Japanese American Women in Domestic Service*. Philadelphia: Temple University Press, 1986.

Gómez-Quiñones, Juan. "On Culture." *Revista Chicano-Riqueña* 5, no. 2 (1977): 29–47.

———. *Roots of Chicano Politics, 1600–1940*. Albuquerque: University of New Mexico Press, 1994.

———. *Sembradores: Ricardo Flores Magón y el Partido Liberal Mexicano*. Los Angeles: Chicano Studies Research Center Publications, 1973.

———. "Toward a Perspective on Chicano History." *Aztlán* 2, no. 1 (1971): 1–49.

Gómez-Quiñones, Juan, and Luis Arroyo. "On the State of Chicano History: Observations on Its Development, Interpretations, and Theory, 1970–1974." *Western Historical Quarterly* 7, no. 2 (1976): 155–85.

González, Deena. "Chicana Identity Matters." In *Culture and Difference: Critical*

Perspectives on the Bicultural Experience in the United States, edited by Antonia Darder, 41–53. Westport, Conn.: Bergin and Garvey, 1995.

———. "La Tules of Image and Reality: Euro-american Attitudes and Legend Formation on a Spanish-Mexican Frontier." In *Building with Our Hands: New Directions in Chicana Studies*, edited by Adela de la Torre and Beatríz M. Pesquera, 75–90. Berkeley: University of California Press, 1993.

———. "Malinche as Lesbian: A Reconfiguration of 500 Years of Resistance." *California Sociologist*, Special Issue, 14 (Winter/Summer 1991), 90–97.

———. *Refusing the Favor: The Spanish-Mexican Women of Santa Fe, 1820–1880*. New York: Oxford University Press, in press.

———. "Speaking Secrets: Living Chicana Theory." In *Living Chicana Theory*, edited by Carla Trujillo, 46–77. Berkeley: Third Woman Press, 1998.

González, Jovita. "Tales and Songs of the Texas Mexicans." *Publications of the Texas Folklore Society* 8 (1930): 86–116.

González, Rosalinda M. "Chicanos and Mexican Immigrant Families, 1920–1940: Women's Subordination and Family Exploitation." In *Decades of Discontent: The Women's Movement, 1920–1940*, edited by Lois Scharf and Joan Jensen, 59–83. Westport, Conn.: Greenwood Press, 1983.

Gordon, Milton M. *Assimilation in American Life: The Role of Race, Religion, and National Origins*. Oxford: Oxford University Press, 1964.

Griswold del Castillo, Richard. *La Familia: Chicano Families in the Urban Southwest, 1848 to the Present*. Notre Dame: University of Notre Dame Press, 1984.

———. *The Los Angeles Barrio*. Berkeley: University of California Press, 1980.

Grosz, Elizabeth. "Refiguring Lesbian Desire." In *The Lesbian Postmodern*, edited by Laura Doan, 67–84. New York: Columbia University Press, 1994.

Guerin-González, Camille. *Mexican Workers and American Dreams: Immigration, Repatriation, and California Farm Labor, 1900–1939*. New Brunswick, N.J.: Rutgers University Press, 1994.

Guerin-González, Camille, and Carl Strikwerda, eds. *The Politics of Immigrant Workers: Labor Activism and Migration in the World Economy since 1830*. New York: Holmes and Meier, 1993.

Guha, Ranajit. "Dominance without Hegemony and Its Historiography." *Subaltern Studies* 6 (1987): 210–309.

Gutiérrez, David G. "Significant to Whom? Mexican Americans and the History of the West." *Western Historical Quarterly* 24, no. 4 (1993): 519–39.

———. *Walls and Mirrors: Mexican Americans, Mexican Immigrants, and the Politics of Ethnicity*. Berkeley: University of California Press, 1995.

———, ed. *Between Two Worlds: Mexican Immigrants in the United States*. Wilmington, Del.: Scholarly Resources, 1996.

Gutiérrez, Ramon. *When Jesus Came, the Corn Mothers Went Away: Marriage, Sexuality, and Power in New Mexico, 1500–1846*. Stanford: Stanford University Press, 1991.

Gutiérrez-Jones, Carl. *Rethinking the Borderlands: Between Chicano Culture and Legal Discourse*. Berkeley: University of California Press, 1995.

Haas, Lisbeth. *Conquests and Historical Identities in California, 1769–1936*. Berkeley: University of California Press, 1995.

Hall, Stuart. "Cultural Identity and Diaspora." In *Colonial Discourse and Post-Colonial Theory*, edited by Patrick Williams and Laura Chrisman. New York: Columbia University Press, 1994.

Haraway, Donna J. "Situated Knowledges: The Science Question and the Privilege of Partial Perspective." In *Simians, Cyborgs, and Women: The Reinvention of Nature*, 183–202. New York: Routledge, 1991.

Hart, John. *Anarchism and the Mexican Working Class, 1860–1913*. Austin: University of Texas Press, 1978.

Hutcheon, Linda. *The Poetics of Postmodernism: History, Theory, Fiction*. New York: Routledge, 1988.

Jensen, Joan M., and Darlis A. Millar. "The Gentle Tamers Revisited: New Approaches to the History of Women in the American West." *Pacific Historical Review* 40 (1980): 173–214.

John, Elizabeth A. H. *Storms Brewed in Other Men's Worlds: The Confrontation of Indians, Spanish and French in the Southwest, 1540–1795*. College Station: Texas A&M University Press, 1975.

Joseph, Gilbert M. *Revolution from Without: Yucatán, Mexico, and the United States, 1880–1924*. New York: Cambridge University Press, 1982.

Kansteiner, Wulf. "Hayden White's Critique of the Writing of History." *History and Theory* 32 (1993): 273–95.

Kelly Gadol, Joan. "Did Women Have a Renaissance?" In *Becoming Visible: Women in European History*, 2nd ed., edited by Renate Bridenthal, Claudia Koonz, and Susan Mosher Stuard. Boston: Houghton Mifflin, 1987.

Kessler-Harris, Alice. *Out to Work: A History of Wage-Earning Women in the United States*. New York: Oxford University Press, 1982.

Kreneck, Thomas H. "The Letter from Chapultepec." *The Houston Review* 3, no. 2 (1981).

———. *A Pictorial History of Houston's Hispanic Community*. Houston: Houston International University, 1989.

Lacan, Jacques. *Ecrits: A Selection*. New York: W. W. Norton and Co., 1977.

LaCapra, Dominick. *History and Criticism*. Ithaca, N.Y.: Cornell University Press, 1985.

Langum, David. "California Women and the Image of Virtue." *Southern California Quarterly* 59 (Fall 1977): 245–50.

Laplanche, Jean, and Jean-Bertrand Pontalis. *The Language of Psycho-Analysis*. Translated by Donald Nicholson-Smith. New York: W. W. Norton, 1973.

Lemert, Charles C., and Garth Gillan. *Michel Foucault: Social Theory and Transgression*. New York: Columbia University Press, 1982.

Le Roy Ladurie, Emmanuel. *Carnival in Romans*. Translated by Mary Feeney. New York: Braziller, 1979.

Limerick, Patricia Nelson. *The Legacy of Conquest: The Unbroken Past of the American West*. New York: W. W. Norton, 1987.

Limón, José L. "Selena: Sexuality, Greater Mexico and the Song-and-Dance with Hegemony." *ETNOFOOR* 10 (1997): 90–111.

Macías, Anna. *Against All Odds: The Feminist Movement in Mexico to 1940*. Westport, Conn.: Greenwood Press, 1982.

———. "Felipe Carrillo Puerto and Women's Liberation in Mexico." In *Latin American Women: Historical Perspectives*, edited by Asunción Lavrin, 286–301. Westport, Conn.: Greenwood Press, 1978.

———. "The Mexican Revolution Was No Revolution for Women." In *Is the Mexican Revolution Dead?*, edited by Stanley R. Ross. 2nd ed. Philadelphia: Temple University Press, 1975.

Marsh, Margaret S. *Anarchist Women, 1870–1920*. Philadelphia: Temple University Press, 1981.

Martinez, Oscar J. "On the Size of the Chicano Population: New Estimates, 1850–1900." *Aztlán* 6 (Spring 1975): 43–68.

May, Todd. *Between Genealogy and Epistemology: Psychology, Politics and Knowledge in the Thought of Michel Foucault*. University Park: Pennsylvania State University Press, 1993.

Mazón, Mauricio. *The Zoot Suit Riots: The Psychology of Symbolic Annihilation*. Austin: University of Texas Press, 1984.

McComb, David G. *Houston: A History*. Austin: University of Texas Press, 1969.

McWilliams, Carey. *North from Mexico: The Spanish-Speaking People of the United States*. Boston: J. B. Lippincott Co., 1949.

Memmi, Albert. *The Colonizer and the Colonized*. Boston: Beacon Press, 1967.

Mendieta Alatorre, Angeles. *La mujer en la revolución mexicana*. México: Talleres Gráficos de la Nación, 1961.

Milkman, Ruth. *Gender at Work: The Dynamics of Job Segregation by Sex during World War II*. Urbana: University of Illinois Press, 1987.

Mirandé, Alfredo, and Evangelina Enríquez. *La Chicana: The Mexican-American Woman*. Chicago: University of Chicago Press, 1979.

Montejano, David. *Anglos and Mexicans in the Making of Texas, 1836–1986*. Austin: University of Texas Press, 1987.

Nandy, Ashis. *The Intimate Enemy: Loss and Recovery of Self under Colonialism*. New Delhi: Oxford University Press, 1983.

Nieto-Gómez, Anna. "Chicanas in the Labor Force." *Encuentro Femenil* 1, no. 2 (1974): 28–33.

———. "La Feminista." *Encuentro Femenil* 1, no. 2 (1974): 34–37.

Nietzsche, Friedrich. *The Use and Abuse of History*. Translated by Adrian Collins. Indianapolis and New York: Liberal Arts Press and Bobbs-Merrill, 1957.

Novick, Peter. *That Noble Dream: The "Objectivity Question" and the American Historical Profession*. Cambridge: Cambridge University Press, 1988.

Ocaña, Lucila, et al. *La Herencia de Foucault*. México, D.F.: Ediciones El Caballito, 1987.

Orozco, Cynthia. "Chicana Labor History: A Critique of Male Consciousness in Historical Writing." *La Red/The Net* 77 (January 1984): 2–5.

Padilla, Genaro. *My History, Not Yours: The Formation of Mexican American Autobiography*. Madison: University of Wisconsin Press, 1993.

Paredes, Américo. *With His Pistol in His Hand: A Border Ballad and Its Hero*. Austin: University of Texas Press, 1971.

Pascoe, Peggy. *Relations of Rescue: The Search for Female Moral Authority in the American West, 1874–1939*. New York: Oxford University Press, 1990.

Patoski, Joe Nick. *Selena: Como la Flor*. New York: Little, Brown and Co., 1996.

Payo, Gerald E., and Gilberto M. Hinojosa. "Spanish Texas and the Borderlands Historiography in Transition: Implications in United States History." *Journal of American History* 75 (September 1988).

Paz, Octavio. *The Labyrinth of Solitude*. Translated by Lysander Kemp. New York: Grove Press, 1961.

Pérez, Emma. "A La Mujer: A Critique of the Partido Liberal Mexicano's Gender Ideology on Women." In *Between Borders: Essays on Mexicana/Chicana History*, edited by Adelaida del Castillo, 459–82. Los Angeles: Floricanto Press, 1990.

———. "Oral Narratives as Chicana (His)story Text." Working Paper No. 32, Southwest Institute for Research on Women. Tucson: University of Arizona, 1994.

———. "Selena's Sisters." *Lesbian Review of Books* 2 (Autumn 1995): 4.

———. "Sexuality and Discourse: Notes from a Chicana Survivor." In *Chicana Lesbians: The Girls Our Mothers Warned Us About*, edited by Carla Trujillo, 159–84. Berkeley: Third Woman Press, 1991.

———. "'She Has Served Others in More Intimate Ways': The Domestic Servant Reform in Yucatán, 1915–18." In *Las Obreras: The Politics of Work and Family*, edited by Vicki L. Ruiz. *Aztlán* 20, nos. 1–2 (1993): 11–33.

Pérez-Torres, Rafael. *Movements in Chicano Poetry: Against Myths, Against Margins.* New York: Cambridge University Press, 1995.

Pescatello, Ann, ed. *Female and Male in Latin America: Essays.* Pittsburgh: University of Pittsburgh Press, 1973.

Pesquera, Beatríz M. "'In the Beginning He Wouldn't Even Lift a Spoon': The Division of Household Labor." In *Building with Our Hands: New Directions in Chicana Studies*, edited by Adela de la Torre and Beatríz M. Pesquera, 181–95. Berkeley: University of California Press, 1993.

Pichardo, José Antonio. *Pichardo's Treatise on the Limits of Louisiana and Texas.* 2 vols. Translated by Charles Wilson Hackett. Austin: University of Texas Press, 1931–32.

Poole, David. *Land and Liberty: Anarchist Influences in the Mexican Revolution—Ricardo Flores Magón.* Sanday, U.K.: Cienfuegos Press, 1977.

Pratt, Mary Louise. *Imperial Eyes: Travel Writing and Transculturation.* London: Routledge, 1992.

Quintal Martín, Fedelio. *Yucatán, un período de Historia contemporanea, 1910–24.* México: Ediciones de la Universidad de Yucatán, 1974.

Raat, W. Dirk. *Revoltosos: Mexico's Rebels in the United States, 1903–1923.* College Station: Texas A&M University Press, 1981.

Radhakrishnan, R. "Nationalism, Gender, and the Narrative of Identity." In *Nationalisms and Sexualities*, edited by Andrew Parker, Mary Russo, Doris Sommer, and Patricia Yeager, 77–95. New York: Routledge, 1992.

Reisler, Mark. *By the Sweat of Their Brow: Mexican Immigrant Labor in the U.S., 1900–1940.* Westport, Conn.: Greenwood Press, 1976.

Ricoeur, Paul. *Time and Narrative: Volume I.* Translated by Kathleen McLaughlin and David Pellauer. Chicago: University of Chicago Press, 1984.

Rodriquez, Gustavo A. *Doña Marina.* México, 1935.

Romano, Octavio Ignacio V. "The Anthropology and Sociology of the Mexican Americans: The Distortion of Mexican American History." *El Grito* 2 (Fall 1968): 13–26.

Romo, Ricardo. *East Los Angeles: History of a Barrio.* Austin: University of Texas Press, 1983.

———. "Responses to Mexican Immigration, 1910–1930." *Aztlán* 6, no. 2 (1975): 173–94.

Rosaldo, Renato. *Culture and Truth: The Remaking of Social Analysis.* Boston: Beacon Press, 1989.

Rosales, F. Arturo. "Mexicans in Houston: The Struggle to Survive, 1908–1975." *The Houston Review: History and Culture of the Gulf Coast* 3, no. 2 (1981): 224–48.

Rouse, Roger. "Mexican Migration and the Social Space of Postmodernism." *Diaspora* 1, no. 1 (1991): 8–23.

Ruiz, Vicki L. *Cannery Women, Cannery Lives: Mexican Women, Unionization, and the California Food Processing Industry, 1930–1950.* Albuquerque: University of New Mexico Press, 1987.

———. *From Out of the Shadows: Mexican Women in Twentieth Century America.* New York: Oxford University Press, 1998.

———. "'Star Struck': Acculturation, Adolescence, and the Mexican American Woman, 1920–1950." In *Building with Our Hands: New Directions in Chicana Studies,* edited by Adela de La Torre and Beatríz M. Pesquera, 109–29. Berkeley: University of California Press, 1993.

———. "Texture, Text, and Context: New Approaches in Chicano Historiography." *Mexican Studies/Estudios Mexicanos* 2 (Winter 1986): 145–52.

Saénz Royo, Artemisa. *Historia política-social-cultural del movimiento femenino en México, 1914–1950.* México: M. León Sánchez, 1954.

Safran, William. "Diasporas in Modern Societies: Myths of Homeland and Return." *Diaspora* 1, no. 1 (1991): 83–99.

Said, Edward. *Orientalism.* New York: Vintage Books, 1978.

Salas, Elizabeth. *Soldaderas in the Mexican Military: Myth and History.* Austin: University of Texas Press, 1990.

Saldívar, José David. *Border Matters: Remapping American Cultural Studies.* Berkeley: University of California Press, 1997.

Saldívar-Hull, Sonia. "Feminism on the Border: From Gender Politics to Geopolitics." In *Criticism in the Borderlands: Studies in Chicano Literature, Culture, and Ideology,* edited by Hector Calderón and José David Saldívar, 203–20. Durham, N.C.: Duke University Press, 1991.

Samora, Julian, et al. *Gunpowder Justice: A Reassessment of the Texas Rangers.* Notre Dame: University of Notre Dame, 1979.

Sánchez, George I. *The Development of Higher Education in Mexico.* New York: Columbia University Press, 1944.

———. *Forgotten People: A Study of New Mexicans.* Albuquerque: University of New Mexico Press, 1940.

———. *Mexico: A Revolution by Education.* New York: Viking, 1936.

Sánchez, George J. *Becoming Mexican American: Ethnicity, Culture and Identity in Chicano Los Angeles, 1900–1945.* New York: Oxford University Press, 1993.

Sánchez, Rosaura. "The Chicana Labor Force." In *Essays on La Mujer,* edited by Rosaura Sánchez and Rosa Martínez Cruz. Los Angeles: Chicano Studies Research Center Publications, University of California, 1977.

———. *Telling Identities: The California Testimonios.* Minneapolis: University of Minnesota Press, 1995.

Sandos, James A. *Rebellion in the Borderlands: Anarchism and the Plan of San Diego, 1904–1923.* Norman: University of Oklahoma Press, 1992.

Sandoval, Chéla. "Re-entering Cyberspace: Sciences and Resistance." *Dispositio/n* 19, no. 46 (1994): 75–93.

———. "U.S. Third World Feminism: The Theory and Method of Oppositional Consciousness in the Postmodern World." *Genders* 10 (Spring 1991): 2–24.

Saragoza, Alex M. "The Significance of Recent Chicano-Related Historical Writings: An Appraisal." *Ethnic Affairs* 1 (Fall 1987): 24–62.

Schlissel, Lillian; Vicki Ruiz; and Janice Monk, eds. *Western Women: Their Land, Their Lives.* Albuquerque: University of New Mexico Press, 1988.

Schofield, Ann. "Rebel Girls and Union Maids: The Woman Question in Journals of the AFL and IWW, 1905–1920." *Feminist Studies* 9 (Summer 1983): 335–55.

Scott, Joan Wallach. *Gender and the Politics of History.* New York: Columbia University Press, 1988.

Segura, Denise. "Labor Market Stratification: The Chicana Experience." *Berkeley Journal of Sociology* 29 (1984): 57–91.

Segura, Denise A., and Beatríz M. Pesquera. "Beyond Indifference and Antipathy: The Chicana Movement and Chicana Feminist Discourse." *Aztlán* 19, no. 2 (1989–90): 69–92.

Sheridan, Thomas. *Los Tucsonenses.* Tucson: University of Arizona, 1988.

Smith, Justin H. *The War with Mexico.* Gloucester, Mass.: Peter Smith, 1963.

Soja, Edward W. *Postmodern Geographies: The Reassertion of Space in Critical Social Theory.* London: Verso, 1989.

Sosa-Riddell, Ada. "Chicanas and El Movimiento." *Aztlán* 5, nos. 1–2 (1974): 155–65.

Soto, Shirlene. *The Mexican Woman: A Study of Her Participation in the Revolution, 1910–1940.* Palo Alto, Calif.: R & E Research Associates, 1979.

Spivak, Gayatri Chakravorty. "Can the Subaltern Speak?" In *Marxism and the Interpretation of Culture,* edited by Cary Nelson and Lawrence Grossberg, 271–313. Chicago: University of Chicago Press, 1988.

———. "A Literary Representation of the Subaltern: A Woman's Text from the Third World." In *In Other Worlds: Essays in Cultural Politics.* New York: Routledge, 1988.

———. "Subaltern Studies: Deconstructing Historiography." In *Selected Subaltern Studies,* edited by Ranajit Guha and Gayatri Chakravorty Spivak, 3–32. New York: Oxford University Press, 1988.

Stevens, Evelyn. "Marianismo: The Other Face of Machismo in Latin America." In *Female and Male in Latin America: Essays,* edited by Ann Pescatello, 89–101. Pittsburgh: University of Pittsburgh Press, 1973.

Stimson, Grace. *Rise of the Labor Movement in Los Angeles.* Los Angeles: University of California Press, 1955.

Stoler, Ann Laura. *Race and the Education of Desire: Foucault's History of Sexuality and the Colonial Order of Things.* Durham, N.C.: Duke University Press, 1995.

Taylor, Paul S. *An American-Mexican Frontier: Nueces County, Texas.* Chapel Hill: The University of North Carolina Press, 1934.

Tentler, Leslie Woodcock. *Wage-Earning Women: Industrial Work and Family Life in the United States, 1900–1930.* New York: Oxford University Press, 1979.

Thernstrom, Stephan. *The Other Bostonians: Poverty and Progress in the American Metropolis, 1880–1970.* Cambridge: Harvard University Press, 1973.

Thompson, Edward P. *The Making of the English Working Class.* New York: Vintage Books, 1966.

Tilly, Louise A., and Joan W. Scott. *Women, Work, and Family.* New York: Routledge, 1978.

Todorov, Tzvetan. *The Conquest of America: The Question of the Other.* Translated by Richard Howard. New York: Harper and Row, 1984.

Trinh T. Minh-ha. *Woman, Native, Other: Writing Postcoloniality and Feminism.* Bloomington: Indiana University Press, 1989.

Trujillo, Carla. "Chicana Lesbians: Fear and Loathing in the Chicano Community." In *Chicana Lesbians: The Girls Our Mothers Warned Us About*, edited by Carla Trujillo, 186–94. Berkeley: Third Woman Press, 1991.

Turner, Ethel Duffy. *Revolution in Baja California: Ricardo Flores Magón's High Noon.* Detroit: Blaine Etheridge Books, 1981.

Vasconcelos, José. *La raza cósmica: Misión de la raza Ibero-Americana.* México, D.F.: Aguilar S.A. de Ediciones, 1961.

Webb, Walter Prescott. *The Texas Rangers: A Century of Frontier Defense.* Cambridge: Houghton-Mifflin Co., 1935.

Weiner, Lynn Y. *From Working Girl to Working Mother: The Female Labor Force in the United States, 1820–1980.* Chapel Hill: University of North Carolina Press, 1985.

Welter, Barbara. "The Cult of True Womanhood, 1820–1860." *American Quarterly* 18 (Summer 1966): 151–74.

White, Hayden. *The Content of the Form: Narrative Discourse and Historical Representation.* Baltimore: Johns Hopkins University Press, 1987.

———. "'Figuring the Nature of the Times Deceased': Literary Theory and Historical Writing." In *The Future of Literary Theory*, edited by Ralph Cohen, 19–43. New York: Routledge, 1989.

———. *Metahistory: The Historical Imagination in Nineteenth-Century Europe.* Baltimore: Johns Hopkins University Press, 1973.

———. "Writing in the Middle Voice." *Stanford Literature Review* 9, no. 2 (1992): 179–87.

Wolff, Janet. "On the Road Again: Metaphors of Travel in Cultural Criticism." *Cultural Studies* 7, no. 2 (1993): 224–39.

Yans-McLaughlin, Virginia. *Family and Community: Italian Immigrants in Buffalo, 1880–1930.* Ithaca: Cornell University Press, 1971.

Yarbro-Bejarano, Yvonne. "The Lesbian Body in Latina Cultural Production." In *¿Entiendes? Queer Readings, Hispanic Writings*, edited by Emilie L. Bergman and Paul Julian Smith, 181–97. Durham: Duke University Press, 1995.

Zamora, Emilio. "Sara Estela Ramírez: Una Rosa Roja en el Movimiento." In *Mexican Women in the United States*, edited by Adelaida Del Castillo and Magdalena Mora, 163–69. Los Angeles: Chicano Studies Research Center, University of California, 1980.

———. *The World of the Mexican Worker in Texas.* College Station: Texas A&M University Press, 1993.

Zamora, Emilio, and Roberto Calderón. "Manuela Solis Sager and Emma Tenayuca: A Tribute." In *Chicana Voices: Intersections of Class, Race, and Gender*, edited by Teresa Córdova et al., 30–41. Albuquerque: University of New Mexico Press, 1993.

Zavella, Patricia. *Women's Work and Chicano Families: Cannery Workers of the Santa Clara Valley.* Ithaca: Cornell University Press, 1987.

Zunz, Olivier. "American History and the Changing Meaning of Assimilation." *Journal of American Ethnic History* 4 (Spring 1985).

Dissertations, Theses, and Unpublished Papers

Blackwell, Maylei. "Contested Histories and Retrofitted Memory: Chicana Feminist Subjectivities between and beyond Nationalist Imaginaries—An Oral

History of the Hijas de Cuauhtémoc." Qualifying Essay, History of Consciousness, University of California at Santa Cruz, May 1997.

Castañeda, Antonia I. "Presidarias y Pobladoras: Spanish-Mexican Women in Frontier Monterey, Alta California, 1770–1821." Ph.D. dissertation, Stanford University, 1990.

Chacón, Ramón D. "Yucatán and the Mexican Revolution: The Pre-constitutional Years, 1910–1918." Ph.D. dissertation, Stanford University, Stanford, California, 1983.

Chávez, Ernesto. "Creating Aztlán: The Chicano Movement in Los Angeles, 1966–1978." Ph.D. dissertation, University of California, Los Angeles, 1993.

Gómez-Quiñones, Juan. "Social Change and Intellectual Discontent: The Growth of Mexican Nationalism, 1890–1911." Ph.D. dissertation, University of California, Los Angeles, 1972.

González, Deena. "Lupe's Song: On the Origins of Mexican Woman-Hating in the U.S." American Historical Association, 11 January 1998.

González, Jovita. "Social Life in Cameron, Starr, and Zapata Counties." M.A. thesis, University of Texas at Austin, 1930.

Hernandez Tovar, Ines. "Sara Estela Ramirez: The Early Twentieth Century Texas-Mexican Poet." Ph.D. dissertation, University of Houston, 1984.

Orozco, Cynthia E. "The Origins of the League of United Latin American Citizens (LULAC) and the Mexican American Civil Rights Movement in Texas with an Analysis of Women's Political Participation in a Gendered Context, 1910–1929." Ph.D. dissertation, University of California, Los Angeles, 1993.

Soto, Shirlene. "The Mexican Woman: A Study of Her Participation in the Revolution, 1910–40." Ph.D. dissertation, University of New Mexico, 1977.

Topp, Michael Miller. "Immigrant Culture and the Politics of Identity: Italian-American Syndicalists in the U.S., 1911–1927." Ph.D dissertation, Brown University, 1993.

Vargas, Deborah. "Cruzando Fronteras: Selena, Tejano Public Culture and the Politics of Cross-Over." American Studies Association, Washington, D.C., 31 October 1997.

Zamora, Emilio. "Mexican Labor Activity in South Texas, 1900–1920." Ph.D. dissertation, University of Texas at Austin, 1983.

INDEX